GULF STREAM CHRONICLES

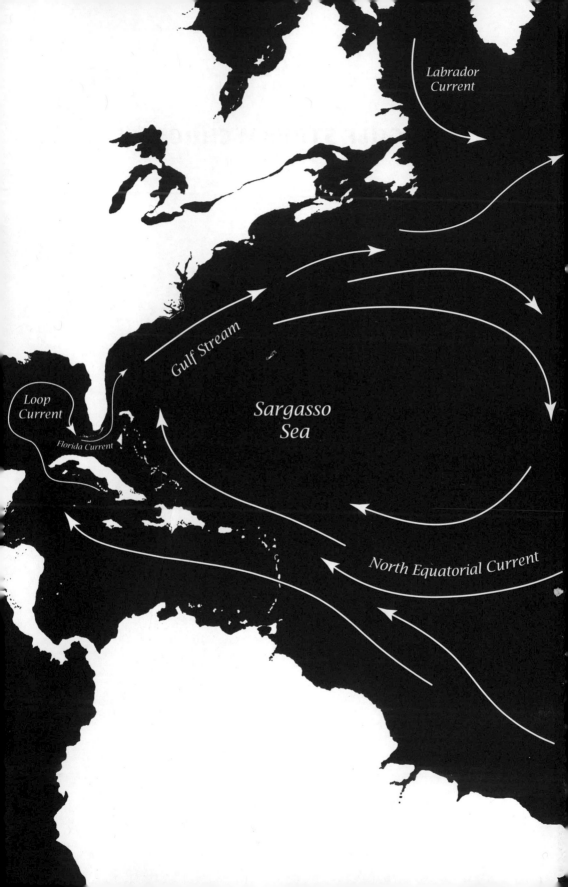

DAVID S. LEE

With a foreword by J. Christopher Haney

and line drawings by Leo Schleicher

GULF STREAM
CHRONICLES

A Naturalist Explores Life in an Ocean River

The University of North Carolina Press CHAPEL HILL

With appreciation for Frank and Elizabeth Skidmore
and their generous support of The University of North Carolina Press

© 2015 The University of North Carolina Press
All rights reserved

Designed and set in Quadraat Pro by Rebecca Evans
Manufactured in the United States of America

The paper in this book meets the guidelines for permanence and
durability of the Committee on Production Guidelines for Book
Longevity of the Council on Library Resources. The University of
North Carolina Press has been a member of the Green Press Initiative
since 2003.

Jacket illustration: Atlantic flyingfish (Cheilopogon melanurus),
Red Circle Images RM © Unlisted Images / Fotosearch.com

Library of Congress Cataloging-in-Publication Data
Lee, David S. (David Stephen), 1943– author.
Gulf Stream chronicles : a naturalist explores life in an ocean river /
David S. Lee ; with a foreword by J. Christopher Haney and line
drawings by Leo Schleicher.
pages cm
Includes bibliographical references and index.
ISBN 978-1-4696-2393-1 (cloth : alk. paper)
ISBN 978-1-4696-2394-8 (ebook)
1. Marine biology—North Carolina—Hatteras, Cape.
2. Gulf Stream. 3. Florida Current. I. Schleicher, Leo, illustrator.
II. Haney, J. Christopher, writer of foreword. III. Title.
QH92.5.H38L44 2015
578.7709756′175—dc23
2015018764

DEDICATION My husband David S. Lee died before his book was published. A couple of years ago as he and I were working on different things in the same room I said to him, "You know you're my favorite person ever." Without stopping or looking up from his work he responded, "My favorite person is Archie Carr." I was neither hurt nor surprised by his response. When it was my turn for a book-club selection, Dave always had one suggestion: So Excellent a Fishe, by Archie F. Carr. The late Dr. Carr was a pioneering conservationist, best known for his efforts to protect sea turtles and their habitats, and he was all things Dave valued—a highly regarded teacher, an engaging speaker, a prolific writer, an avid conservationist, and an all-around nice guy.

Dave believed in the power of the individual to make significant change— Dr. Carr was his role model. His modern-day hero (and good friend), Dr. David Wingate, has made a lifelong effort to bring back the Bermuda petrel, or cahow, from near extinction by the holistic restoration of an entire island, among many other efforts. This book is dedicated to David Wingate, and to all those like him, who follow through with their commitments to conservation with consistent on-site action.

And this is for Dave's mother, June Weatherbe Lee Bash, who from the beginning indulged her son's interests in all things wild and wonderful and encouraged his writing and offbeat humor (often at her expense).

MARY KAY CLARK
December 21, 2014

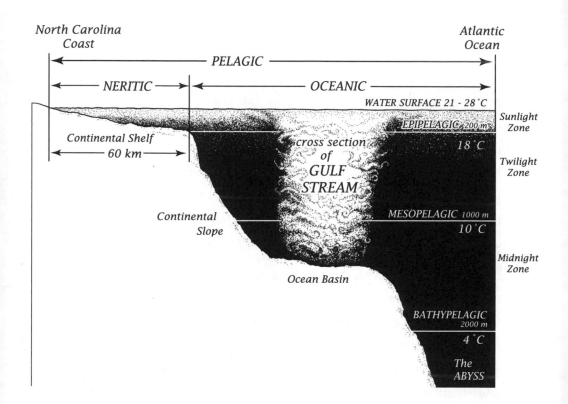

North Carolina
Coast

Atlantic
Ocean

PELAGIC

NERITIC

OCEANIC

WATER SURFACE 21 - 28 ˚C

EPIPELAGIC 200 m

Sunlight
Zone

Continental Shelf
60 km

18 ˚C

Twilight
Zone

cross section
of
GULF
STREAM

Continental
Slope

MESOPELAGIC 1000 m

10 ˚C

Midnight
Zone

Ocean Basin

BATHYPELAGIC
2000 m

4 ˚C

The
ABYSS

CONTENTS

A gallery of photographs appears on pp. 126–133.

ILLUSTRATIONS

FOREWORD

Despite dabbling in the marine sciences for over 30 years now, even launching my career in the cobalt waters of the Gulf Stream, I didn't realize how much there was that I still didn't know about this vast ocean realm. That is, not until after I had devoured David S. Lee's sweeping saga *Gulf Stream Chronicles: A Naturalist Explores Life in an Ocean River*. Like my friendship with Dave, *Gulf Stream Chronicles* furnishes a steady unveiling of new delights and surprises, not to mention a sublime delivery in the hands of one extraordinary storyteller.

Reading this book, you might not even notice at first a subtle tutoring going on (Dave started his career as a high-school science teacher). Instead, you get hooked entirely from the outset on the easy read, it becomes too late to set the story down, and you can't wait to see what comes up next. Dave has an eerie knack for finding nuggets of insight that make one come to a full stop, re-evaluate cherished assumptions, then go off chasing a new idea in some other direction. *Gulf Stream Chronicles* serves also as a showcase for Dave's persuasive enthusiasm for revealing to us North Carolina's maritime history, the long strand of the Outer Banks, and the globally important environmental hotspot known locally as "The Point," one of the Gulf Stream's hottest offshore fishing destinations.

If not for his dogged persistence, Dave and I easily could have become competitors instead of lifelong colleagues. In the early 1980s, I struggled as a new graduate student to find some project that would convince my skeptical professors to grant me a doctorate. After a fortuitous run-in with a plankton ecologist and accidentally discovering that primitive satellite images might be used to map seabird habitats in the Gulf Stream, I at last found my ticket to that unlikely degree. Not long thereafter, I got even luckier. Non-stop invitations to collaborate began to arrive from a David Lee stationed up at the North Carolina State Museum of Natural History in Raleigh. Dave's constant badgering was usually aimed at us writing up together some new finding about seabirds in the southeastern United States. He and I circled a bit warily around each other at first, testing each other's intentions, but with his many enthusiasms so impossible to resist, that tentativeness didn't last long.

Our fellowship quickly mushroomed into galvanizing collaboration. From then on, he would synthesize various anecdotes from his vast repertoire in life histories and such, then generate a compelling hypothesis that absolutely nobody else had thought of. Or had thought of deeply enough. Or was brave enough to try to find a confirmation. After I recovered from my initial astonishment at his creativity, I'd try to find an appropriate methodology for testing the idea, often resorting to what Dave called somewhat derisively, but always good-naturedly, "higher math." Hop-flavored beverages often infused a bit of inspirational lubrication to our collegial conspiracies.

It was not until a scorching day down in the Dry Tortugas, Florida, however, that I would first see him in genuine action. On these remote carbonate islands, I came to comprehend just how wide-ranging were Dave's interests and abilities. I was ostensibly leading a birding tour on a vastly overcrowded boat leaving from Key West. When we were not all struck down by heaving seasickness, my charge was to point out to visiting birders eager to add to their life list a vagrant species like black noddy or white-tailed tropicbird. Yet, while listening to Dave nonchalantly point out the identity and habits of every living thing within sight (and many that were hidden, except to him), from bright tropical fish to obscure island plants, I realized he would have been a far better guide that day. From then on, he never failed to dazzle me with his field skills. Just like going into the field with Dave, *Gulf Stream Chronicles* always presents some novel adventure for the attentive reader.

Dave's mastery of all things natural history is a major reason why *Gulf Stream Chronicles* is so successful in its synthetic presentation. The stories woven together here put on display his abilities as a prodigious naturalist. Book chapters are organized sensibly into four over-arching themes, each distinguished by whether the subject matter occurs mainly over, on, or deep beneath the constantly in-motion Gulf Stream. The third section links all of this dynamic water to adjacent dry land, thereby serving us several "Unexpected Connections" that bring other Gulf Stream secrets right into our daily living rooms.

Of the 20 chapters that make up *Gulf Stream Chronicles*, my personal favorite is "The Loon Craze." Rather than some dry incantation about these ungainly aquatic birds, we are treated to the cultural fondness of Harker Islanders for stewing the greasy, fishy-tasting fowl, known locally as a Harker Island turkey. In addition to this quaint historical narrative, one that celebrates a coastal North Carolina tradition that no longer is, we also hear of loon legends passed down from the Micmac tribe of eastern Canada. Eventually we come to realize that loons are facing a number of daunting conservation threats year-round, but this sobering message is virtually incidental to the captivating read. In just a few pages, then, we are both taught and entertained. This is typical of *Gulf Stream Chronicles*, and sturdy confirmation for the very apt subtitle that describes Dave's book.

Chapters are also tagged enticingly so that the reader cannot help but be intrigued by the content lurking within. Is "A Community of Castaways" about some gang of unlucky mariners stranded on a remote desert isle? No, it isn't, but the real story is even more bizarre. Giving away more here would just spoil a reader's fun. In "Chickens, Sailor Gulls, Witches, and Devils," the book's narrative stiches together effortlessly such diverse themes as the Doldrums, feather mites, the Divine Virgin, an 18th-century priest in Guadeloupe named Père Labat, avian necropsies, and the authentic origin of the true James Bond. Seriously, now, where can you get this from a mere natural history book? Well, you can't. But you can find such tales embedded all over the place in *Gulf Stream Chronicles*, and so much more.

After at last I finished and reluctantly put down my copy of *Gulf Stream Chronicles*, it dawned that Dave's lively writing had brought me all the way back to a forgotten home. Dave's talent for reconstructing the varied colors, tones, and moods of the crystal-blue Gulf Stream reminded me vividly of that first-sight love 30 years ago when I was blessed to go spend hundreds of days exploring and researching that riveting current system. *Gulf Stream Chronicles* is a book that only David S. Lee could write. Only he could make the mysteries of North Carolina's Gulf Stream come so alive to enlighten the rest of us. We are the better off for this book, and even more so for having had him in our midst.

J. CHRISTOPHER HANEY
Chief scientist, Defenders of Wildlife
Washington, D.C.
December 5, 2014

PREFACE

It was a gray October day. Even the clouds lacked character. The previous weekend North Carolina's Outer Banks had barely been spared the fury of yet another hurricane. While the storm was adjusting its path, Ocracoke and Hatteras Islands were completing evacuation. During the night the storm turned farther out to sea, its name already forgotten by the time the residents returned. Thursday's cold front was accompanied by rain, and by Friday the winds were blowing strong from the northeast. I was expecting to go offshore, but all of the captains in the fishing fleet at the local marinas had canceled their charters. So that Friday I walked to the beach.

The wind, the cool air, and the previous week's hurricane threat had all combined to rid the beach communities of tourists. The rain and wind even removed footprints and tire tracks. I had the beach to myself. The tourist season was all but over, and for the next five months the barrier islands that make up the Outer Banks would once again look like the wild remote places that they are. The surf pounded the sand. Due to the high winds the herring and laughing gulls' flight labored against the winds, and the ring-billed gulls chose to waddle out of my path rather than take off into the near gale-like winds. Sanderlings rushed at angles over the wet beach, probing only for seconds at the lowest exposed sand before they scurried back ahead of incoming waves. The willets were less hurried, with longer legs they were not obligated to be as precisely in tune with the rhythm of the breaking surf. But still their movements were a dance with the sea; the scurrying sanderlings simply looked like rush-hour commuters. Yet, compared to the oceanic birds I had hoped to be surveying today, these shorebirds seemed awkward and mechanical, so unlike the shearwaters and storm-petrels that take command of the open sea with fluid flight.

Just offshore bottlenose dolphins could be seen heading south. Their dorsal fins broke the churned surface with a regular and rolling cadence. Today they were hard to follow because of the heightened waves. From other visits I knew that they were moving southward in modest-sized groups of up to 25 individuals. Family pods that summered along the Atlantic coast were working southward for a winter of warmer waters. These dolphins were about a third smaller than the resident pods that lived year-round along the edge of the continental shelf. Biologists who study these dolphins suspect that the inshore migratory groups and the resident offshore ones are different species. The situation is complex when viewed at a global scale, and while there are lots of beached specimens to work with, of the inshore dolphins, there is little research material available from the populations of the deeper waters, as most of the specimens available for study come from the inshore animals that die and wash ashore or strand on our beaches.

Higher on the beach, but now and then lapped by the waves of the incoming tide, was a long band of *Sargassum*, marine algae that had been washed ashore some days before by the passing storm. This plant matter was mostly dark brown, some of it black, with other pieces a sun-bleached yellow. For the most part it was shriveled and lifeless. This beached *Sargassum* was decorated with pieces of plastic and Styrofoam and an occasional board covered with gooseneck barnacles. Much of it was partly buried in the sand by seaward runs of previous tides. From what I could see I suspect it stretched for miles. On the summer beaches of south Florida, where the Gulf Stream is often in sight of shore, the deposits of *Sargassum* are a phenomenon of almost daily occurrence. Beachfront tourist communities usually bury it beneath the sand as if it is some foreign unsightly debris. People familiar with the algae only from sun-shriveled beach-stranded samples can't appreciate the camouflage backdrop, or the three-dimensional world it provides for all sorts of associated creatures when drifting in the open sea. For beach-stranded *Sargassum*, not only the color but much of the character is lost as the scores of species that inhabit it have shriveled in the sun and been picked over by the gulls. Even the most detailed study of the *Sargassum*, dead and blackening on the sand, would give little indication as to the vast marine community it supports, or even that there are many kinds of animals totally dependent on it for existence. Here on the Outer Banks, mass strandings such as this are an unusual occurrence. People who see only the occasional beached pieces of *Sargassum* have no idea how common it can be just 30 miles offshore. Mostly it rides the currents of the Gulf Stream as it is swept northward.

⌒

The previous evening, I had given a talk to the captains and mates of the Oregon Inlet fishing fleet, discussing the potential effects of offshore oil and gas exploration on the fauna of the area. It seemed like a fair thing to do. For the previous 15 years I had been chartering their boats in order to conduct my studies on the pelagic birds occurring off the Outer Banks. And for 15 years I had pounded them with endless volleys of questions as they ran their boats to and from the Gulf Stream.

While projecting contrasting slides, I drilled home the point that if we confined our knowledge to that gleaned only from the birds, marine mammals, or fish that are washed up, we would have just a few random clues as to the complexity of the offshore marine community. Covering the table in front of me were study skins of various seabirds that could be affected by a proposed offshore drilling operation. Most of the specimens on the table were of species seldom, if ever, seen from land, but all were common inhabitants of the Gulf Stream. These were the types of birds that were known by the charter-boat captains. I explained that mostly what is found on the beach are the diseased, sick, dying, and dead animals that by their very condition are not necessarily typical of what lives offshore. The complex current systems that occur along the Outer Banks and flow past the edge of the continental shelf are capable of transporting floating corpses from almost anywhere in the eastern North Atlantic.

One cannot learn much from a single beached shearwater, the single lifeless body has little to teach us about the overall season of occurrence or its abundance off North Carolina. We cannot learn from it the age structure of the population that is living off our coast, the sex and age ratios of the fall population, or even much about their abundance. The captains had no idea that most of the Cory's shearwaters that they saw every day, sometimes by the thousands during the summer months, hatched on islands in the Mediterranean Sea. And the large skuas found offshore in August were from Antarctica, birds that had fattened themselves during their summer by feeding on penguin chicks. The seabirds off the Carolina coast are not some accidental assemblage of feathered objects; each has a particular life history, a specific place of origin, and a distinct way of making a living in the open sea. Seasonally these species gather off our coast for specific reasons.

Many of the bird study skins on the table were of species that migrate farther in a single year than most of the 80 or so people in the room will travel in their lifetimes. I described the various breeding areas, ones distributed throughout the Atlantic basin and beyond, and why they came to the deep waters off the North Carolina coast. The specific area being discussed is known locally as "The Point," a place where the bottom contours range from 30 to 100 fathoms (180–600 feet) and pinch together to form a steep drop along the edge of the continental shelf. Because of the complexity of the surface and the deep ocean currents in the region, some influenced by the underwater topography of The Point itself, the site is unusually rich in life. In contrast, surrounding areas only a few miles distant are virtual biological deserts. Thus, it was not by chance that the captains of the Oregon Inlet fishing fleet found this site a major place to focus their activities, or that I had chosen it as my primary study area. Why this exact location had been chosen as one for exploratory oil and gas drilling was not clear to us. Naturally, the compatibility of sport fishery and an oil operation was a concern. The audience was in attendance not to learn about the fish resources, but to learn about the other biologically significant aspects of the area. Why had this site been identified as one of global importance? Knowledge was essential to help fight the foolishness of making the Outer Banks into another refinery-dominated landscape. My audience already knew about their world-class fishing area, they wanted information on the significance of the whales, sea turtles, and seabirds. The fishermen had some good questions and made a number of good points. I left the meeting feeling that I had probably learned more than the audience.

———

I thought about this meeting as I walked the beach that morning. Staring toward the rising, cloud-covered sun, I could see wave crests stretching from the beach out three miles or so, the distance that one should be able to see when looking seaward. There was no clue as to how rough it must be out at The Point, or the types and numbers of birds that were there gliding stiff-winged in the wave troughs. Offshore, the wind blowing across the northbound current of the Stream was creating sea conditions I was happy not to be experiencing. I enjoyed my morning of solitude on the beach, and when I returned to my car was surprised how far I had walked that morning. During the five-hour drive back to Raleigh I recalled forgotten anecdotes and experiences I had at The Point, ones I'd intended to share with my audience. The everyday occurrences that captains and mates encounter remain unknown to most. People who spend entire summers at the beach mistakenly think they are familiar with the sea. Thirty miles offshore it's a totally different world, or at least the edge of one. What goes on there is the subject of this book.

GULF STREAM CHRONICLES

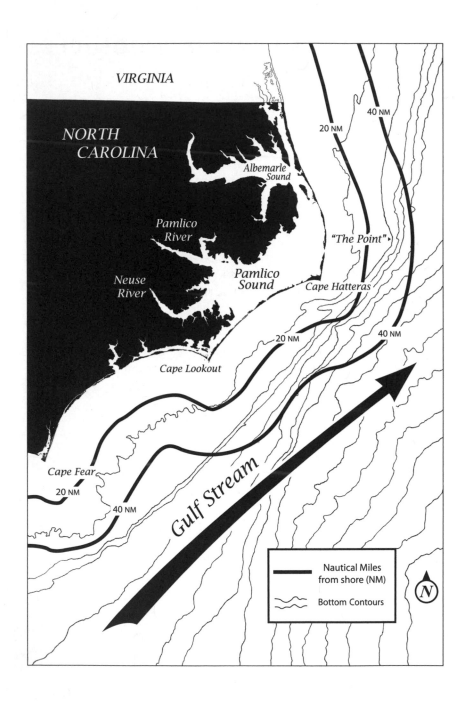

INTRODUCTION
The Gulf's Blue Waters

In June 1975 I changed jobs, transferring from working at the Florida Museum of Natural History to a job as the bird curator at the North Carolina State Museum of Natural Sciences. The newly created position was part of a major restructuring of the museum. The nearly 100-year-old institution had lost its accreditation, and the state, determined to get the museum back into good standing, recruited a number of new staff members. The collection I was hired to oversee was historically important but small. Except for containing the state's first specimen records of this and that, the collection itself had little scientific merit. Even on a local scale the collection I was going to be overseeing held little research potential. Over the years, educators had constantly raided the collection cases for teaching props—the specimens were in disarray and many were missing. And while the museum had an interesting and proud history, its bird collection had not been properly cared for since the late 1940s; as the museum's first curator of birds I had my work cut out for me.

In addition to overseeing the collection, my duties included a variety of research projects relating to the state's avifauna. In narrowing down what would be most rewarding, it did not take much time for me to discover that the marine birds occurring off the coast were virtually unstudied. After a year or so of poking about and going on a number of offshore excursions, I came to appreciate the area east of Cape Hatteras where the Gulf Stream ran across the outer continental shelf. Of all the places one might observe and collect seabird specimens, this section of coastal water was clearly going to be the most promising. For the next three decades I focused my research activities here. It turned out that this was a good choice. Perhaps too good: now over a decade into retirement, I am still spending much of my time working on getting various aspects of my findings ready to submit to appropriate academic journals. But I am getting ahead of myself. Let me first introduce you to the place at the core of my work and at the heart of this book.

Technically, some insist, the Gulf Stream starts somewhere offshore of Cape Hatteras; south of there it's properly referred to as the Florida Current. These are just terms, like the semantic difference between nightclubs and cocktail lounges. They are listed separately as such in the yellow pages, but the patrons of each freely move from one to the other and are unlikely to be aware that there are any real differences. Most people, the charter-boat captains that took me offshore included, consider the Gulf Stream as a single oceanic river running from the passage between Florida and Cuba all the way to the European coast. Like most rivers the Stream is confined by banks, and while sea level is essentially, well . . . level, throughout the world there are minor differences in the water levels in various areas of the ocean. The Sargasso Sea, an area as large as the United States, forms the east bank of the Stream. Winds over the Sargasso Sea drive the warm waters to its center and the waters pile up, forming a bulge along the western boundary of the sea. The pressure in the center of the Sargasso Sea is greater than at the edges, thereby forcing water near the center outward, creating a bank of water that is perhaps six feet higher than the adjacent Gulf Stream. The west side of the Stream is bound by the continental shelf and bordered by the cooler southward flowing waters of the Labrador Current and the coastal, fresher waters along our Atlantic coast. In wording at its simplest—our ocean has a river in it.

The Gulf Stream exists not to move excess rainwater off continents, but instead to move heat out of the tropics; in the Gulf Stream, "downstream" is up—actually north. It's sort of the aquatic version of hot air rising. In summer and fall this heat transfer is assisted by hurricanes. The Stream itself is the major part of a North Atlantic gyre that moves in a clockwise fashion up the west side of the Atlantic and down the east, crossing back toward the Americas. The current starts back up again through the pass between the Bahamas and Florida. Overheated water building up in the Gulf of Mexico also escapes into the Atlantic via the Loop Current, a fickle current that sometimes connects with the Atlantic somewhere south of Key West. The Loop Current, when connected, sends Gulf water into the Florida Current, which in turn becomes the Gulf Stream, and the whole circular process continues.

For people who are not that familiar with boats, the Atlantic, or the various charts that attempt to map it, there are other factors that can be confusing to landlubbers trying to understand the Gulf Stream. While most people tend to think in terms of feet and miles, nautical charts plot depth in fathoms, scientific literature records it in meters, and Jules Verne measured it in leagues. Distance is discussed in nautical miles, direction in degrees, and ship and wind speed is given in knots. Air and sea temperatures are presented in Celsius on government research ships, but charter boats and the Coast Guard use Fahrenheit. Port is not just where you dock, it's also the left side of the vessel when you are facing the bow (front). But it's still the port side even if you are facing the stern (rear) and it's on your right.

The tools used to record things at sea can also seem complicated. Navigation has progressed over time, from watching stars and the direction of the flights of seabirds, to sextants, loran A and B, satellite-delivered latitude and longitude coordinates, and now GPS to decimal digits telling you within several meters where you are. The sea conditions are expressed on something called the Beaufort scale, and if you are on the bridge of a ship (where the ship is commanded) there are all sorts of digital gauges with blinking numbers that reveal everything you need to know except the afternoon's baseball scores. For us land-based folks, at-sea orientation requires a lot of adjustment and some re-education.

Speaking of re-education: as every schoolchild knows, the Gulf Stream is characterized by its deep blue waters. It's fun to think that the blue waters of the Gulf Stream come directly from the Gulf of Mexico. And to some extent they do. It's the blue part that is misleading. Like all water, that of the Gulf Stream is essentially as colorless as what is piped into your bathroom toilet. If you lift a glass filled with its water and examine it, the water is clear and there is no trace of blue. The blue is merely reflected light, not from the sky, but from the nature of light itself when it penetrates the sea. On overcast days the Gulf Stream still runs blue.

Blue water—like that of blue alpine lakes and turquoise seas—tends to be relatively devoid of life, especially in contrast to murky rivers and the gray-green waters of estuaries that teem with nutrients and phytoplankton supporting food chains of fast-growing, hungry, rapidly reproducing life forms of all tropic levels. In the estuaries, the light coming from the sun feeds the photosynthetic process, and, at the same time, most of the light waves are reflected back in some form of murky green, with the darker waters for the most part being the most fertile. Unproductive waters absorb most of the wavelengths of natural light. Without the silt, and the microscopic green phytoplankton, light passes through the perfectly clear water. The light is absorbed bit by bit as its energy is dispersed into the water as heat. Different wavelengths of the spectrum penetrate the water differentially so the various

Most of the white-footed mice living in our storage sheds will all live their lives, as did the generation before them, within perhaps a hundred yards of their place of birth. They know every corner of the shed and what's to be found on each shelf. Each mouse has its own self-made nest, carefully concealed and tucked into a secret place. Likewise, the migrating birds in our woodlot, even ones that wintered in tropical South American forests, return season after season to re-stake their claim on the same real estate they occupied the previous year. Bluegills in farm ponds, wolf spiders under logs, otters in a salt marsh, and neon gobies on a mound of brain coral all have general, or often very specific, places they recognize and defend as their own.

For the creatures of the open sea—pelagic creatures—perceptions of home are very different. The term *pelagic*, from the Latin and Greek words for "sea," is not hard to understand: it refers to the creatures that live in open oceans and seas rather than waters near land. But how pelagic organisms actually go about making a living certainly is difficult for us land-based creatures to comprehend. In the open water, the reference points that might anchor an organism to its habitat are few, and those that exist—like the angle of the sun or the surface of the sea—are constantly changing. For many of these creatures, life is an opportunistic ride on currents, countercurrents, and eddies. Spending part of May drifting off the Carolinas, early June somewhere east of New Jersey, and August near the Azores would, for pelagic sea creatures, all seem rather much the same. North Atlantic pelagic species have done this not for days or seasons but for lifetimes, generations, and over the eons. The marine mammals, seabirds, and larger fishes that make a living in the high seas have a choice as to where they are going, but they too are somewhat dependent on the whims of storms and currents to direct them to the patchy and ever-shifting resources of the open sea. Many spend their lives on the move, not like a lost family dog looking for home, but searching for new areas where, for the moment, the conditions are right. For those pre-adapted to this pelagic existence, it's a successful lifestyle.

But don't misunderstand, a pelagic lifestyle does not equate to aimless wandering. Each species has time-honored contracts with the winds and currents, assuring that they will be transported at the proper season to an area of the North Atlantic where they can make a successful go of it. Over eons these populations of pelagic creatures have continued to fine-tune the timing of their reproduction or the seasonal growth rates of larvae to maximize their chance for success.

That said, the world of the open ocean is not generally well understood—it's best known only by a few ardent scientists and by the tuned-in sailors who have somehow come to understand the complexities and curious simplicity of this ocean habitat. How can the pelagic world be complex and simple at the same time? As the following chapters suggest, pelagic lifestyles show extreme variation, which means the particular organisms, their adaptations, and their interactions with the winds and waters can seem very challenging to understand. Yet there is an elegant simplicity evident in the lives of these creatures once you understand the basic outlines of their existence. The pages that follow will give you an opportunity to appreciate both.

Just a simple list of the species that live in the open sea would rival in length the yellow page listings of a major city's telephone directory. And like the businesses listed in the phone book, all are there for reasons—different reasons, each performing a specific task. Some, like the marlin, are just individual fish, while others, like the multitude of *Sargassum* associates, are contributing members of major ecological communities. And as in our communities, all of these species interact on some level, often with important regularity.

⌐

The pelagic fauna occurring off the southeastern coast of the United States includes not only numerous marine invertebrates and larval fishes that are for the most part distributed by predictable currents, but also small shorebirds that during the summer months live on the northern Canadian tundra. Phalaropes, unlike other shorebirds, have webbed toes for swimming and two species of them live far at sea during migration and throughout the winter. At these times they feed on small pelagic invertebrates. The red phalarope that winters off North Carolina specializes in feeding in mats of floating *Sargassum* as it drifts northward in the Gulf Stream. Here it feeds primarily on a small snail that lives solely in the floating algae. There are also three species of jaegers, highly predatory gull-like birds that also occur at sea. The three jaegers, all of which also nest each summer on the Arctic tundra, feed primarily on lemmings and voles. Like the phalaropes, they are unable to make a living on the tundra once it is frozen over, and in migration and throughout the winter they totally change their way of life and take on a pelagic existence. Their food shifts to modest-sized fish, and they make a good portion of their livelihood aggressively robbing prey from other seabirds before they have a chance to swallow it. As they swoop down on a tern or a gull, they can tell by the other bird's cries of alarm whether or not the bird they are after has a fish in its throat. Those that do are harassed unmercifully until they forfeit their catch.

Many pelagic creatures devote only portions of their lives to the open sea. Some larval marine invertebrates and fish transform into bottom-dwellers once they become adults. The young of marine turtles drift with floating gulfweed during their early life, but later many take up residence in sounds and bays and over shallower shelf waters. A large number of the pelagic seabirds, even though they are tied to land during their nesting periods, make their entire living off of the surface of the sea, some commuting on a weekly basis thousands of miles between reliable foraging areas and their cliffside nests. Sooty terns spend the first seven years of their life at sea; many never see land again until they become full adults, when they are genetically obligated to return to their nesting colonies. Now here is the interesting part: sooty terns lack significant oiling in their feathers to allow them to land on water. If they do, they sink and drown. One would think they would have learned to rest on floating boards and the backs of sea turtles as bridled terns do, but instead they fly. Day and night the young terns are in flight for years on end, and they actually sleep on the wing. These various creatures all have one thing in common. They are forever on the move as their local supermarkets keep going out of business or changing their address. Prime foraging areas shift either because of specific species' changing age-related needs or simply because the sites of high productivity disappear and re-franchise elsewhere.

And we are just seeing what is on the surface. Perhaps we should think of pelagic plants and animals as honored veterans, not of wars, but as genetic survivors struggling with the elements, whose time-tested instincts have allowed them to master living in the open sea. It's an interesting way of life, free of many of the constraints land-based life forms endure on a daily basis. It might be tempting to regard these open-ocean nomads as creatures lacking a nationality; I prefer to think of them as citizens of the world.

CHAPTER 1 A COMMUNITY OF CASTAWAYS

As much as textbooks can tell us today about the minutest details of life, it's hard to put ourselves in the minds of those earliest observers whose records of the natural world served as a foundation for our current scientific knowledge. Back in the days when dragons were believed to be real, life certainly was simpler, or at least easier to explain. In those times, the odd parts of strange animals provided "evidence" for the existence of the mythical, and the origins of really weird-looking animals were often attributed to plants. Take the katydid: it looked like a leaf, so surely it must have been. The naturalists of the day would have comfortably explained that it simply broke free of its parent plant to live on its own. Similarities of the shapes, textures, and colors of animals to those of particular plants were proof enough of their botanical origins.

I like to imagine how much the scholars of long ago would have enjoyed poking about in *Sargassum*: a blotchy brown seaweed that teems with blotchy brown-colored animals. These creatures so resemble the appearance of the algal stalks that indeed they seem to be part of it.

As a kind of algae there is nothing particularly impressive about *Sargassum*. Its name is nothing more than Portuguese for seaweed. While many people use the generic name *Sargassum*, or sargassum weed, it is also often referred to as gulfweed, and occasionally sea holly. The eight or so species that the genus comprises are but a few of the many types of brown algae that thrive in marine environments. Rigid supportive structures do not work in a world of pounding waves and rushing currents. Unlike some of the bottom-dwelling rockweeds and kelp that have developed floats to keep their long flexible branches upright in the water, thus assuring a good distribution of light to the surface of their leaves and stems, pelagic *Sargassum* has floats to keep the entire plant floating near the surface.

For the longest time, it was assumed that the gulfweed seen drifting at sea was simply an accumulation of *Sargassum* that had broken free from inshore algal beds. In a survey of the Sargasso Sea conducted in the 1940s it was estimated that there was a standing crop of about seven million tons of *Sargas-*

While drifting with the current, Sargassum provides a home on the open ocean surface for a host of cryptic castaways, including shrimp, crabs, young sea turtles, and pipefish, all specially adapted to life among its floating branches and air bladders.

sum, an amount that exceeded all possible production from coastal rockweed beds. After sorting through about 5,000 pounds of *Sargassum* hulled from the ocean, biologists found that two species, *Sargassum natans* and *S. fluitans,* made up over 90 percent of the pelagic algae community. These are not inshore species; they lack the "holdfast" their coastal relatives use to grasp the bottom. They also lack any means of sexual reproduction and simply grow vegetatively; the growing tips randomly break off, starting new clumps. *Sargassum* is one of the few brown algae that can live in warm waters, and satellite imagery recently allowed scientists to determine that most of the pelagic *Sargassum* originate in the northwestern Gulf of Mexico, finding their way into the North Atlantic in early summer via the Loop Current that passes between the Florida Keys and Cuba.

Satellite imagery shows that some *Sargassum* slicks are up to 3,000 feet wide and can exceed 100 miles in length, but strong winds, over time, cause these large patches to disintegrate and, later, to reform. The long rows parallel the wind direction and drift northward in the stream. The same downwellings that form the windrows also concentrate plankton, providing a food source for the sundry inhabitants of the algal mats. Additionally, these same oceanic features bring nitrogen and phosphorus to the gulfweed, enhancing photosynthetic capacity and productivity.

Were it not for the circular currents of the North Atlantic, the algae would be caught up in ocean currents that would transport them into areas too cold and with too few hours of daylight to support their growth. Instead, the drifting *Sargassum* moves in a clockwise gyre, the center of which is the Sargasso Sea. In this area (roughly the size of the United States) the water is comparatively motionless, and large concentrations of these plants grow and accumulate.

The warm Sargasso Sea is not a solid tangle of algae. The plants live and grow only in a very thin layer near the surface. They drift in small patches; here a patch an acre in size is unusual. Nonetheless, even now serious authors describe the Sargasso Sea as so thickly matted with seaweed that vessels have trouble passing through it. This idea originated from the journals of Columbus's third voyage. He writes, "And I also found all the sea full of vegetation of a kind which resembles pine branches full of fruit like that of a mastic tree. And it is so dense that, on the first voyage, I thought that it was a shallow and that the ships would run aground." That it thrives here at all is a biological curiosity. The Sargasso Sea has limited productivity and the clear nutrient-poor waters have often been referred to as a biological desert. At peak abundance this seaweed accumulates at densities of two to five and a half metric tons per square nautical mile, more than 1,000 times less dense than crops of related algae growing along the rocky Maine coast.

⤝

Pelagic *Sargassum* forms its own biological community. Hiding in the algae, clinging to its leaf-like brown growths, crawling among them and swimming beneath, is a wonderful variety of marine organisms—an entire ecosystem of castaways. Compared to our terrestrial communities—deciduous forest, tall-grass prairies, and cactus-filled deserts—*Sargassum* ecosystems are communities in motion. The colonists of this community come from nearly all the major evolutionary lines of the animal kingdom, and most have taken on the sober hues of the yellow and brown algae. Their splotchy, mottled patterns so match the *Sargassum* that casual observers may miss the teeming life altogether. The animals found here were pre-adapted for life in the floating *Sargassum*. The fauna is composed mostly of species, or close relatives of species, that are bottom-dwellers, living among coastal *Sargassum* beds and similar inshore habitats. The number of individual animals living in the *Sargassum* is impressive. Biologists from the Virginia Institute of Marine Science, collecting just 34 dip-net samples off Cape Hatteras and in the adjacent Sargasso Sea, found 11,234 free-living invertebrates and fishes, representing a total of 67 species. Additionally, several kinds of flying fish lay their eggs in *Sargassum*, and over 100 species of larval fishes are known to use the floating algal mats as a nursery.

The most common animals are the least obvious, and because they are attached to the *Sargassum* they were not counted in the dip-netted tallies. They are encrusting species, invertebrates with planktonic larvae and immobile adult forms, and many are designed for specific sites of attachment on the *Sargassum*. Some types only attach to the new algal growth, while larger and erect species of hydroids only occur on the older stems and blades. They live in self-oozed lime-encrusted housing projects that adhere profusely to the algae. Hydrozoans, bryozoans, barnacles, and polychaete worms are present in such numbers that the alga feels hard and rough to the touch. Most of these inhabitants are filter feeders, capturing minute prey in pulsing nets and tentacle-like arms. On the older stalks, the growth of these encrusting species often weighs down the alga, pulling it away from the surface. In the decreasing light of deeper waters, it eventually dies and sinks.

Most conspicuous are the larger free-living invertebrates. Marine snails, several species of brown-blotched swimming crabs (*Portunus*), and two genera of tan-colored shrimp (*Leander* and *Latreutes*) are all present in astonishing numbers. Whenever I take others to the Gulf Stream I feel obligated to show them the secrets of *Sargassum*. A few handfuls of the seaweed shaken over a water-filled bucket will always reveal hundreds of individuals representing numerous species in various sizes, the largest often no more than an inch in length. Upon encountering the vast concentrations of *Sargassum* in the Sargasso Sea, Columbus's crew was in near mutiny, having been at sea for weeks in unchartered waters. Columbus took advantage of the teeming life around them and hauled up several buckets of the strange brown seaweed, showing the small swimming crabs to his men as evidence that they were nearing land, a ploy that averted all-out revolt.

While the shrimp and crabs are the most abundant of the hitchhikers, probably the most interesting components of the *Sargassum* community are the fishes. Many species spend their entire lives in the algae, while others find it a convenient shelter during the early parts of their lives; still others congregate there as adults to prey on the other inhabitants. Ichthyologists, those who study fish, have found that no fewer than 23 families and 54 species of fish represented in the *Sargassum* of the Gulf Stream off our southeastern coast. The actual fish biomass is usually slightly less than 1 percent of the algae. Still, this represents incredible numbers of fish: In 1966 and 1977, researchers collected and sorted through 3.5 tons of *Sargassum* pulled from the sea off Florida, an analysis yielded approximately 8,400 individual fish. The vastness of the Sargasso Sea, the ability of many fishes to avoid nets, and the unidentified larval forms that are present in the algae suggest the actual number of species using the gulfweed as a refuge is certainly much greater that what's on record.

Nearly all of the fishes recovered from *Sargassum* have been found in other habitats and many are not primarily pelagic species. Two species, however, are restricted to the pelagic *Sargassum* and are obligated to it for their existence: the sargassum fish and the sargassum pipefish. The appropriately named sargassum fish is just 1 of 41 members of the frogfish family—squatting, normally bottom-dwelling creatures that prey by deceit on other fishes. Frogfish can swallow fish up to their own size and even ones that are somewhat larger. Sargassum fish are pelagic frogfish that lurk among the *Sargassum* stalks waiting to ambush whatever hapless fish come by, including other sargassum fish. They also possess a modified dorsal fin ray that is positioned far forward of the other fin rays. Wiggled as a lure, it has a fleshy "bait" at the end that attracts other fish to within gulping range.

As a teenager I was fascinated by these odd little fish—although they get larger, for me a big specimen was no more than an inch and a half in length. On lazy summer days I would look for them by sorting through *Sargassum* mats that had drifted close to the beach. On the rare occasions that I found more than one, often only one was left by the time I got home. In aquariums, I discovered, sargassum fish had to be kept by themselves, or within a week or two they would have eaten everything else in the tank, including each other. Their cannibalistic nature is well known to anyone who has tried to keep them.

To aid this fish in snatching prey, it has developed one of the best examples of camouflage to be found in the sea. Small white spots and lines are superimposed on the yellow-and-brown-mottled pattern. The coloration does not simply imitate the algae, it also imitates the broken color patterns caused by the epiphytic growth on its blades and stems. The eye is masked by pigmentation that extends to the margin of the pupil and three dark bands that radiate outward from the eye. Even a portion of the inside of the mouth is mottled to simulate the algae. Furthermore, these fish can change color rapidly from light to dark. These changes can be produced by stimulation or by major changes in the color of the surroundings. Their fins are modified into hand-like appendages and the pectoral fins have arms that allow the fish to grasp the alga and literally crawl through it. Even the fin lopes match the growth habits of the gulfweed. Most assume that the mimicry of its habitat is for protective resemblance, allowing the fish to remain nearly invisible to passing potential predators. While this is true, the camouflage also serves as a passive feeding strategy, assisting in their ability to ambush unsuspecting prey.

Sargassum fish have a reduced gill structure, but this apparently poses no problem in the wave-washed, oxygen-saturated surface environment in which they live. By forcing water through the small gill openings, these fish can even jet propel themselves for short distances to escape predators. They are weak swimmers, but the males do sometimes swim from one algal patch to another during the mating period. More often, however, even this is unnecessary as patches of gulfweed are constantly breaking apart and reforming with adjacent ones, transporting the fish from clump to clump. Because adult sargassum fish consider any fish their size, or smaller, prey, it is unusual to find more than one per clump of gulfweed. Courtship lasts for up to one day and fertilization occurs in a brief second encounter. The male then moves on or is eaten.

The eggs emerge as a buoyant raft. Thousands of eggs are produced per raft by the four-to-five-inch female, and well-fed females produce egg rafts at intervals of three to nine days for a period of two to four months. The larvae hatch quickly—two to four and a half days, depending on water temperatures. The development is so rapid that the yolk of the egg is still large at hatching and the young fish floats belly-up until the yolk is absorbed. After normal buoyancy is stabilized the larvae drift and develop in depths of 150–1800 feet. At lengths of about two-tenths of an inch they migrate back toward the surface with the hope of finding *Sargassum* patches. Surviving larvae grow to two inches in four to five months and take on the adult coloration at about half this size, feeding mostly on sargassum shrimp until they reach an inch in length.

The reproductive output of sargassum fish is enormous, making the inefficient method of larval dispersal work. A mean egg production of 2,000 eggs per raft, six days between raft production, three months of active egg laying, and a stable population would indicate a chance of just 1 in 15,000 eggs resulting in a reproductive-sized adult. This ratio could easily be two or three times lower. Whatever the survival rate, the system works. The same species of sargassum fish is found in the *Sargassum* communities of the Pacific and Indian Oceans.

The sargassum pipefish is four to six inches, and, except for its pelagic lifestyle, it is similar to other pipefish. It too is found in the Pacific and Indian Oceans. It is brown, but otherwise its coloration does not closely mimic the alga. Compared to the sargassum fish its reproductive methods are much less wasteful, but its dispersal ability does not seem as effective. Like seahorses, male pipefish have brood pouches on the undersurface near the tail into which the female deposits eggs. The eggs are laid in modest numbers and develop in the male's pouch. Researchers have shown that despite the large amount of yolk present in pipefish eggs, the embryos receive additional nourishment directly from the male. The pouch fluid, extracted from the bony rings of the male parent's tail, is a source of calcium for the dozens of growing egg-bound young. Furthermore, on some pipefish the pouch is so tightly sealed that biologists suspect gases and nitrogenous waste products are conducted out through the pouch lining.

The larval stage is largely completed within the egg, causing a rather long incubation period. When the young finally hatch they look like miniature adults. While some are transported passively by currents, all start out their lives in the same *Sargassum* patches in which they hatched. As they grow into adults, however, they have the opportunity to disperse as different patches of algae drift together only to be separated by storms and currents.

While both extremes of reproductive strategies work, neither evolved for a pelagic existence. Both types of fish come from evolutionary lines in which their manner of reproduction was firmly established prior to a time when their ancestors took up a pelagic life. That both systems work on the high seas is intriguing.

The difference in the dispersal ability of the fishes and other animals living among the floating island-like *Sargassum* beds is pronounced, and it becomes apparent in the variation between faunal composition of *Sargassum* patches in different seasons and regions. Biologists studying fishes in these communities in the Gulf of Mexico were able to find only 15 families representing 40 species of fishes compared to the higher (23 and 54) totals in the Gulf Stream. In the Gulf of Mexico, a single species of filefish represents 84.5 percent of the total species assemblage. While the species diversity was lower in the Gulf of Mexico, the density of fishes per unit of *Sargassum* was considerably higher. This reverse relationship is predictable in many natural communities. Whenever a community is simplified by a limited diversity, this limitation is often overcompensated by the increase in abundance of just a few species. In this case, juvenile plane-headed filefish took advantage of the void left by the absence of other types of fish. When these filefish grow older, they leave the alga community and become sedentary bottom-dwelling adults.

～

Off our coast, gulfweed is transported northward by the Gulf Stream, moving 100 miles or more a day. A given clump may be off the coast of the Carolinas for a few days in May, somewhere off New Jersey in early June, and near the Azores by July. Where the Stream takes a sharp turn at Cape Hatteras and heads out into the international waters of the Atlantic, so too do the buoyant beds of the marine algae and all the sundry creatures that regard this patchy, current-swept world as theirs. As *Sargassum* moves northward in the Stream, the number of fish associates decreases and by the time the *Sargassum* reaches the Azores only six species are still present. In some cases this is clearly a result of different fishes completing segments of their life cycle and moving out of the community, in others it is probably an indication of the low survival rates of individual tropical species transported into more northern latitudes. Of course, predation also comes into play; the frogfish need something to eat. Nonetheless, some Caribbean species complete the trip, moving northwest with the Gulf Stream and then past the Azores, Portugal, Madeira, and northern Africa. The northern and eastern part of the journey is completed on the North Atlantic drift and the Canary Current. A similar pattern exists in the Pacific.

～

An approximation of 2,400 individual fishes per ton of *Sargassum* has been suggested to exist in the Gulf Stream. If this also represents a figure similar to the average annual density found in the Sargasso Sea, and preliminary samples suggest it is, and if the algal standing crop of the 1930s is still correct (and it was in the 1980s; the amount was recalculated then and found to be the same), then there are about 17 billion fish living in the *Sargassum* of the North Atlantic. This estimate does not include all those transported in the North Atlantic gyre or all the filefish in the Gulf of Mexico. Estimating the invertebrate associates would require calculations comparable to the national debt. While the various species achieve peak abundance at different seasons, average diversity and density figures remain about the same throughout the year.

With such a dependable prey base some predatory oceanic fishes find *Sargassum* beds ideal foraging grounds. Peering down into the blue waters of the Gulf Stream, one can make out the forms of larger fishes as they cruise beneath the drifting seaweed. Exactly what fish are there cannot even be guessed. Conventional surface sampling does not capture the fast-swimming predatory species. Nevertheless, the fish are there, often stacked in layers. Sport fishing off the Outer Banks shows that dolphins and wahoos at least are frequently associated with *Sargassum*. I recall sorting through the stomachs of a number of two-year-old dolphins I was cleaning—each was packed with freshly consumed three-to-five-inch seahorses that had clearly been snatched from the *Sargassum* beds the dolphins were caught under. Surprisingly, I had failed to find a single seahorse when dip netting the *Sargassum* earlier that day.

A number of years back I was involved in a research project where we suspended video monitors under the *Sargassum* beds off Cape Hatteras. The number of jacks and other large fishes that regularly visited the beds we were watching was surprising. So was the turnover—school after school came and went. I should add that watching the underwater sloshing of gulfweed on a small TV monitor in the cabin of a rolling research vessel was the closest I have ever come to understanding the phenomenon called seasickness.

In addition to the banquet provided by the community's inhabitants, the undersea shadows produced by the *Sargassum* also attract fish, particularly dolphins. There seems to be no end to the number of scholarly studies that attempt to explain why predatory fishes lurk in shadows. I think the same logic that causes villains to seek out dark alleys applies. In most studies it has been concluded that in shadows fish are more efficient predators. Not only do the shadows and scattered light beams conceal the predator and break up its outline, but the fish sees better. With eyes shaded, searching for prey out in the open sea, the fish receives a benefit similar to the one obtained when our eyes are shaded by the visor of a baseball cap.

━

Some of the members of the *Sargassum* community not only face the problems resulting from a drifting planktonic lifestyle, they also need to have a fixed reference on land to which they return. They must effectively cope with both worlds. Marine turtles and seabirds have particular places where they return to nest, but they live out their early years or the non-breeding season far at sea. Some obligated to a pelagic lifestyle follow the drifting *Sargassum*. Several decades of studying the ways of pelagic seabirds refocused earlier interest I had in the algae. Seabirds observed off North Carolina freely range over extensive areas along the edge of the outer continental shelf, seeking patchy food sources along current lines and upwellings where drifting *Sargassum* concentrates. I found that many seabirds forage in and around *Sargassum* and several appear to be *Sargassum* feeding specialists.

Most notable of these are bridled terns and Audubon's shearwaters, tropical pelagic birds that are nearly always associated with *Sargassum*. Stomach-content analysis shows they feed largely on fishes that live in the gulfweed, with filefish being the most common food item. Red-necked phalaropes, royal terns, and tropicbirds spend a great portion of their time at sea feeding among *Sargassum* although all are not as closely tied to it as the bridled terns and shearwaters. These birds lead a nomadic existence once their nesting season is over, some following drifting gulfweed beds northward from their nesting cays in the Caribbean. The summer food resources off Cape Hatteras are more dependable than those in the tropical portions of the Atlantic, so the birds disperse from nesting areas quickly. Young bridled terns, for example, are sometimes seen riding on drifting boards as the parents fly in to feed their begging, recently fledged young. Bringing the young along cuts down on commuting time between the food-rich Gulf Stream and their Caribbean nesting sites. As egg-laying season nears, the adults, at least, return to specific home nesting islands. The young take several years to mature and simply remain at sea near dependable food sources.

How dependent are these seabirds on the *Sargassum*? Five species of our seabirds are *Sargassum* specialists. My observations of birds at sea, along with the examination of their stomach contents, showed that 59 percent of Audubon's shearwaters' diet was composed of animals living in the algae. For several other species it was also quite high: royal terns get 40 percent of their food from the *Sargassum*, bridled terns 58 percent, red-necked phalaropes 62 percent, and masked boobies 100 percent. While other birds relied on the *Sargassum* feeding stations less frequently, they remain important to many species (9 of 10 petrels, storm-petrels, and shearwaters, and 12 of 25 gulls and terns). The prey items selected were mostly ½ to 2-inch fishes, but each bird used the resource in specific ways—some only seasonally. The birds were mostly feeding on *Sargassum*-associated fishes, but the phalaropes were the exception. They focused on a small marine snail, one that lives exclusively in the gulfweed.

Marine turtles are also dependent on the pelagic *Sargassum* community. The hatchlings swim to sea and then use the algae as a place to both hide and feed. Young loggerheads, Kemp's ridleys, hawksbills, and green sea turtles give up their pelagic existence when they are older, but for years it was unclear where neonate sea turtles went after they left their nests. Most researchers assumed that they drifted passively for the first year, since their size prevented extensive swimming and diving. The first records of turtles in the *Sargassum* were of one young green sea turtle and eight young loggerheads removed from the stomach of a dolphin caught under drifting *Sargassum*. Off North Carolina it is not uncommon to find young loggerheads in the gulfweed. Ones hatched on beaches in the Greater Antilles, the Bahamas, or south Florida, based on the northward speed of the Gulf Stream, could only be several weeks old by the time they drift past the Outer Banks, yet all of those I have seen had already increased from the size of hatchlings by 20–30 percent. These speedy growth rates attest to the rich and predictable food resources in the *Sargassum*.

Thus, the faunal obligates and dependents are not ones that magically shifted from a plant to an animal and broke loose of the algae to take up a life of their own. The community is made up of organisms converging from diverse marine origins. The majority, like the gulfweed itself, was originally derived from fixed shallow-water bottom communities, a strange contrast to their adopted open-ocean lifestyle. The gulfweed community teaches us what we all eventually come to learn—life is an opportunistic ride.

CHAPTER 2 *PHYSALIA*
Iridescent Bubbles with a Zap

Popularly known as the Portuguese man-of-war, *Physalia pelagica* is a simple life form that makes a living in what appears to be an equally simple two-dimensional world, the surface of the open sea. I love seeing *Physalia*, which appear as delicate neon purple bubbles, seemingly out of place so far out in the ocean. As the angle of the sunlight shifts, their color seems to play out in shades of pink and lavender. If you're in the midst of a long day counting sea-birds, it's easy to watch *Physalia* and to let your mind drift along with them.

But the innocent happiness suggested by their bubble-like appearance hides the danger that lives beneath. Fiery tentacles, sometimes trolling ten fathoms beneath the translucent bubbles, are often masked by reflections of light on the water's surface. The tentacles hitch rides on currents while gas-filled floats serve as sails to catch the wind. This simple yet highly specialized life form is a strong indication that when it comes to *Physalia*, there's much more than meets the eye.

A detailed description of *Physalia* is difficult because they lack named parts that we can relate to. They are coelenterates, water bags whose cells are never more than two layers thick. A between-cell soup transports food and adds a third layer that confuses students responding to invertebrate zoology exams. Relatives include other vaguely familiar animals: sea nettles, anemones, and hydras, as well as corals, sea fans, and other colonial invertebrates. *Physalia* resemble jellyfish, but taxonomically they are in a class by themselves. They are similar to the other major types of coelenterates only in cell structure and arrangement, not in outward appearance.

Many coelenterates are colonial—corals, for example, form elaborate structures that are organized by the independent growth of thousands of individual animals, sometimes forming structures that take generations to build. The man-of-war is also a colonial animal, but it differs from other colonial creatures in that it is free living and the colony is formed by many hundreds of different styles of cells. Technically, each cell grouping is a separate individual animal. Instinctively self-arranged and self-programmed, yet

Predators of the Portuguese man-of-war may appear harmless, but the fish swimming within the tentacles and the floating violet snail are specialized to munch away at tentacles and the creature's bubble without feeling the adverse effects of its stinging, toxic cells.

totally without the capacity for even a rudiment of thought, the different parts are specialized for catching and ingesting food, defense, flotation, and reproduction. Unlike a single coral polyp, which could theoretically live on its own, *Physalia* live only collectively, in complex colonies. The various colonists function as tissues, and the dividing line between a colony of different cell types and an individual animal composed of a variety of tissue types is very thin. Not risking the detail and terminology of a college zoology text, I will skip over the finer points of this aspect of *Physalia*. If you have any questions, just remember that it is a specialized hydrozoa and as such is easy to look up. Or, if you wish, remember that the colony's modified polypoid parts are for feeding and the various medusoid individuals do the rest.

This primal organization of life usually confused students. I always made *Physalia* the focus of these discussions. Yes, it looks like an animal, and it behaves like an individual, but it is actually a colony. My explanation resulted in students' questions: "When they die and go to heaven, do the different colonies get in separately or does St. Peter accept them as a group?"

The most distinctive feature of a man-of-war is its pink, blue, and lavender balloon-like float. If you like words that you don't get to use often, this balloon is called a pneumatophore. On very large individuals the float may be more than a foot long. John White, an artist-naturalist on Sir Walter Raleigh's 1585 expedition to the New World, illustrated flying fish, seabirds, loggerheads, and the man-of-war. He was clearly fascinated by the marine life he encountered during the voyage. White prepared two plates of *Physalia*. In both, the bubble is shaped like the hull of a two-bowed ship. One plate bares the caption, "This is a lyuing fish, and flote vpon the Sea, Some call them Carvels."

The crest of the float of the man-of-war carries a deflatable sail-like ridge. The sail can be extended or furled quickly. And when tipped by waves, the long tentacles act as a counterbalance, righting the sail almost instantly. The sail is controlled by gas, mostly nitrogen, with some oxygen and a trace of argon, a rare inert gas produced in the main float. The float's wall is strongly muscular, allowing control of the overall shape. The colony can apparently dictate the angle of the float to the wind, and a gas gland controls the size of the balloon and thereby its speed. The float constantly rolls and dips and then rights itself, preventing it from drying out in the tropical sun. While dependent on currents and winds, these creatures have surprising control over their angle of drift and speed. From the sail-like pneumatophore hang the feeding polyps, thin transparent lips that capture and engulf prey paralyzed by the long trailing tentacles. Digestive fluids are pumped into larger prey, disintegrating the tissues so that they can be sucked up by the feeding polyps and later pumped into the soupy intermediate layer and shared with other members of the colony.

⤙

The creature's name, man-of-war, would at first seem a humorous spoof on Portuguese frigates, but the stinging tentacles pack quite a wallop and I suspect whoever came up with the name did so out of respect for both the animal and the warships. In Portugal they are called *caravella*, a name also derived from its supposed likeness to the Portuguese fighting ships. The scientific name was at one time *Caravella carvella*. Several seabirds were also named for the fast frigate ships of the 16th and 17th centuries—frigate birds (also known as man-of-war birds) and frigate petrels—suggesting such comparisons were common and confirming that our early sailors were good observers. All share the wind as their primary means of transport, in fact the frigate birds, which can neither walk nor swim, are completely dependent on sea winds. Accordingly, all these various creatures have recently become friends on Facebook.

The man-of-war's reputation for giving a nasty sting is as widespread as the beast itself. *Physalia* are found throughout all tropical and subtropical seas, and currents like the Gulf Stream often transport them far to the north. Some marine biologists consider the Pacific form to be a separate species; unlike the one in the Atlantic, they have only one fishing tentacle. A cross section of a tentacle reveals a gastrovascular cavity used for digestion, while a microscopic view of the tentacles shows a near solid field of tube-stuffed capsules. These are the nematocysts—explosive poison darts. All hydrozoans have them, but in the case of most corals and anemones they are not powerful enough to penetrate human skin. Each one has a trigger-like bristle projecting from its surface. Within the nematocyst is a long, neatly coiled, spring-like tube. Some merely entangle prey like snares, while others are equipped with hypodermic darts. The armed tubes fire when the trigger is disturbed, and they become embedded in whatever they touch, injecting minute but painful amounts of poison upon contact. The man-of-war uses the poison both to paralyze prey and as a defense. The relatively large size of the capsules and the length of the threads (several hundred times longer than the capsule) are what make *Physalia* so potent. Unsuspecting medical researchers discovered that a discharged nematocyst can even penetrate surgical gloves. As painful as the stings are, human fatalities from these creatures have not been verified. Nevertheless, there are numerous unconfirmed reports of human deaths from *Physalia* poison. Recurrent stings from some coelenterates may produce a sensitivity to the toxin with fatal results. The presence of *Physalia* in recreational areas deserves attention; in south Florida, beaches occasionally have to be closed during periods of man-of-war invasions.

The hidden danger of *Physalia* comes from the length of their tentacles. When fully extended they are nearly invisible and may trail as much as 90 feet below the float. Swimmers seeing the distinctive floats may cautiously stay well away only to discover the longshore currents have carried the tentacles into their arms and legs. The tentacles are in continuous rhythmic movement, alternately contracting and relaxing, constantly sampling the water for prey. Small prey may face a discharge of only 20–50 of the nematocysts, while a larger creature might experience a discharge of several hundred thousand. Vigorous resistance on the part of the prey results in the coiling of the tentacles and the firing of additional nematocysts. Contact causes the tentacles to contract, but different sections do so at different rates, causing the nematocysts within the slower sections to be thrown into loops and folds that form stinging batteries. These can be quite formidable. It has been estimated that as many as 750,000 nematocysts are present on every tentacle. The fiery pain and elongated welts left by a man-of-war encounter are distinctive and unforgettable. The sting is as painful as any received from swarms of wasps or hornets.

The venom (5-hydroxytryptamine) comes from the capsular fluid within the nematocysts. It is a histamine-like substance that causes welts, redness, and painful burning sensations. The intensity of the stings is dependent on the length of time of contact with the skin. The exact composition of the venom is little known. There is evidence that at least three separate toxins are involved. One paralyzes the nervous system, one retards respiration, and one causes the pain. The welts last one to four hours, the pain usually persists from 30 minutes to several hours. The symptoms can also include headache, weakness, malaise, primary shock, collapse, muscular cramps, abdominal rigidity, nausea, vomiting, chills and fever, and, not unexpectedly, hysteria.

I have been zapped on more than a few occasions and while the stings were fierce, like most poisonous things, the man-of-war does not live up to its dreaded reputation. In fact, as long as one is aware of the direction and potential length of the drifting tentacles it is not too difficult to swim among them without getting nailed. I remember that when I was a youngster, we would pop the balloon-like floats of specimens that had washed up on the shore. And when we felt really daring, we'd play catch with them until someone got stung. The only really scary situation with a stinging coelenterate that I can recall was not with *Physalia* at all but with the short-tentacled, relatively mild-stinging moon jellyfish, *Aurelia aurita*. A friend and I were snorkeling a quarter of a mile or so off the Ft. Lauderdale beach when my friend surfaced under one. I looked up just as he emerged with the large jellyfish covering his head and one shoulder. I failed to warn him in time not to inhale through his snorkel. When he did, it was instant panic. It took a little doing to remove the partly inhaled and still stinging jellyfish and to calm my companion enough to get him back to shore. He sputtered and spit the whole way. For humans, I think the real danger of coelenterate stings is panic; from what I witnessed, the sting won't kill you, but drowning surely could.

Except for reports in local papers, when large numbers drift up on summer beaches alarming south Florida tourists, college textbooks and related academic works are the primary source for information on the Portuguese man-of-war, but the cold facts do not do justice to the animal. In *The Old Man and the Sea*, Hemingway relays basic information in a style that captures well the spirit of *Physalia* and its place in the scheme of things:

> And nothing showed on the surface of the water but some patches of yellow, sun-bleached Sargasso weed and the purple, formalized, iridescent, gelatinous bladder of a Portuguese man-of-war floating close beside the boat. It floated cheerfully as a bubble with its long deadly purple filaments trailing a yard behind in the water.
>
> "Agua mala." The man said. "You whore."
>
> From where he swung lightly against his oars he looked down into the water and saw the tiny fish that were colored like the trailing filaments and swam between them and under the small shade the bubble made as it drifted. They were immune to its poison. But men were not and when some of the filaments would catch on a line and rest there slimy and purple while the old man was working a fish, he would have welts and sores on his arms and hands of the sort that poison ivy or poison oak can give. But these poisonings from the agua mala came quickly and struck like a whiplash.
>
> The iridescent bubbles were beautiful. But they were the falsest thing in the sea and the old man loved to see the big seaturtles eating them. The turtles saw them, approached from the front, then shut their eyes so they were completely carapaced and ate them filaments and all. The old man loved to see the turtles eat them and he loved to walk on them on the beach after a storm and hear them pop when he stepped on them with the horny soles of his feet.
>
> He loved the green turtles and the hawks-bills with their elegance and speed and their great value and he had a friendly contempt for the huge, stupid loggerheads, yellow in their armour-plating, strange in their love-making, and happily eating the Portuguese man-of-war with their eyes shut.

It's difficult to believe that a marine organism this seemingly unappetizing and lacking in nutrition and equipped with an armament of explosive stinging cells would be prey for anything. It was once believed that loggerhead sea turtles had immunity to the stings from antibodies in their blood, but this is not the case and it is still not clear how the turtles can stand to eat them. They are clearly affected by the nematocysts' toxins as their eyes and facial tissues swell after eating *Physalia*. The scales and shell partly protect the exterior, but what of the turtle's tongue and esophagus?

Animal predation is not always the result of stalking, high-speed chases, or other visually captivating activities captured by the cameramen on TV nature specials. Researchers studying the epiphytic hydrozoans of *Sargassum* communities found that the gut contents of these sessile forms contained large numbers of the unfired nematocysts of *Physalia*. I assume, from what I have witnessed at sea, that the trailing tentacles become entangled and break off in the *Sargassum* and their cells are eventually consumed. *Physalia* are commonly seen within *Sargassum* rafts; the same winds and currents that concentrate the algae also capture the man-of-war. At times hundreds of *Physalia* of various sizes can be seen in patches of *Sargassum* that are only several square yards in size.

A lack of action-packed predation is often made up for by the bizarre nature of the predators themselves. Remarkably, there is a predatory marine snail that specializes in the man-of-war. The violet snails, *Janthina*, like their prey, are pelagic. Their delicate lavender-colored shells are lightweight—they have even shed their door-like operculums to further lighten the load. Graceful mollusks that evolved from bottom-dwelling predators of sea fans and corals, they ride the sea winds fastened to a bubble float of their own making. In addition to transportation, the float also serves as a nest into which eggs, or, in the case of one species, live young, are deposited. Their self-made floats are critical, not just for transport, but for survival. If the snails are dislodged from their float, they sink, and, unable to return to the surface, they die. The largest species is one-and-a-half inches across its rounded, whorled shell, and the smallest is about half that size. When disturbed, all five species of this genus discharge a purple fluid. Many people have seen the purple stains on wave-washed beaches without understanding the source—violet snails displaced by storms.

These snails are hunters that passively "stalk" their prey on the same winds and currents that transport *Physalia*. It is inevitable that they meet. The snail simply crawls from the bubble float onto the man-of-war and, with its numerous elongated teeth, begins to dine. The attack is quite unceremonious and not particularly different than a snail or slug consuming a prized house plant. When finished (they eat nematocyst and all), the violet snail repairs its float and sails onward. It is not clear why the nematocysts don't discharge, but researchers suspect that the snail's purple dye acts as a narcotic and deadens the sensitivity of the cysts.

I have watched for violet snails in the Gulf Stream off the coast of North Carolina without success but suspect they are difficult to spot hanging upside down from their bubbles. Nevertheless, they are probably rather common; a large percentage of the pomarine jaeger stomachs I have examined contained pieces of *Janthina* shells. In fact, flotillas of violet snails covering over 200 nautical miles have been reported. Collectively they must have quite an impact on regulating *Physalia* populations.

For years my encounters with violet snails had been limited to occasionally seeing their empty homes in coastal shell shops. One winter I had the opportunity to spend several months in the open waters of the Gulf of Mexico doing surveys to help determine the impacts of the April 2010 BP oil spill on the pelagic community. Net sampling for surface plankton would often catch a man-of-war along with a few of the snails. My cabin mate was overseeing the night plankton sampling and, knowing my interest in the snails, he sent someone to fetch me one night when a few showed up in the survey nets. The snails clung to their bubble life jackets through it all and, even when handled and poked, the bubbles failed to pop. These weren't small, soft, soap-like bubbles but relatively large ones, few in number, firm, and round, the texture of the plastic in bubble wrap. The net had also collected a number of *Physalia*, and portions of their tentacles had broken free and became intermixed with the *Sargassum*. I pretended not to notice the red welts on the arms of everyone who had been sorting through this late-night sample.

Janthina are hermaphroditic (both sexes occur in the same individual), a common phenomenon in lower invertebrates. However, sex changes can take place in the life cycle—perhaps more than once, and it is not clear if the snail can be both sexes simultaneously or if self-fertilization occurs. Dissection shows that some species of violet snails at least start off as males and as they get larger change to females. However, other researchers found distinct males and females of similar size. But they also found sterile individuals, hermaphroditic specimens, and very large males. How fertilization actually takes place is unknown. There is no copulatory organ and females have no special organs for receiving or storing sperm. It gets stranger yet. Two types of sperm are produced. The typical spermatozoa are used to fertilize eggs, but large flat-headed sperm, covered by a membrane, are produced in smaller numbers. This second type has an undulating movement and a long slender tail. They have only part of a chromosome set and are not capable of fertilization. This larger sperm acts as a transport carrier for the normal sperm that attach to it in large numbers. Exactly how this odd arrangement benefits fertilization is not apparent, but somehow these swimming busloads of sperm find adult snails that, for some period at least, are acting as females, and somehow they enter her body.

And while I am discussing the peculiarities associated with this particular snail I should mention its parasites. Like many mollusks, violet snails have parasites, but one parasitic copepod is particularly abundant, found in 92 percent of the *Janthina* examined. Two stages of the parasite were present— intermediate stages were attached to the gills, and adults were found swimming freely in the mantle cavity. While the alternate host of the younger stage is not known, they probably live in lanternfish, in that this is where all other species of this parasitic genus reside. How strange, a parasite that completes one part of its life cycle 3,000–6,000 feet below the surface and the remainder within a snail that rides about the surface on a bubble.

A second remarkable man-of-war predator is *Nomeus gronovii*, more appropriately named the man-of-war fish. These fish sport patches and bands of blue, distinguishing them from all other species. Hemingway knew of them, as does almost anyone who has spent any time in tropical seas. Nearly every man-of-war of reasonable size has half a dozen or more small *Nomeus* swimming among its tentacles. Furthermore, the man-of-war's tentacles are the exclusive home of the young of these fish. *Nomeus* are members of a small family called butterfishes. Most are pelagic and several are common associates of drifting *Sargassum* beds. Thus, their lifestyle was pre-established, but how they cope with the stinging cells of *Physalia* is surprising.

It was long assumed that *Nomeus* were immune to the stinging tentacles, as most invertebrates and other fish caught in the tentacles are paralyzed and consumed. Close study revealed, however, that this fish is simply agile enough to avoid the tentacles. On reasonably calm days man-of-war fish are easily seen from above, usually swimming just three or four feet below the float and darting out to grab passing food. The diet of *Nomeus*, like most other fish, shifts with age. When the fish are young they use the man-of-war for shelter, feeding on plankton that are more numerous in the shade of the coelenterate than in open water. As they increase in size, the fish begin to feed on food captured by their host, often eating the tentacles and other parts of the host as well. The nematocysts are harmlessly discharged in a special pouch in the rear of the *Nomeus*'s mouth before they are swallowed. As adults, the fish are free-living and eat *Physalia*. If this seems like a rather one-sided relationship, it is, although it is also likely that very young man-of-war fish represent tempting bait that may attract larger fish into *Physalia*'s tentacles. While people attempting to really oversimplify ecological principles often cite *Physalia* and the man-of-war fish as a good example of commensalism, this is clearly not the case. What's involved here are natural examples of economics where the balance of use of assets cannot be allowed to run amuck in that it would crash community stability. Wall Street investors take note: you can destroy any number of your hosts, just don't try to eat them all simultaneously.

Amazingly, the man-of-war does not have a monopoly on its own nematocyst defense. A dainty pelagic sea slug, *Glaucus atlanticus*, eats whole sections of *Physalia*. When *Glaucus* makes its meal, the *Physalia*'s stinging cells pass undischarged through the slug's digestive tract; they are stored, undischarged, in several sacks at its back end. These sacks appear as a waving fringe that also serves as substitute gills. The recycled *Physalia* nematocysts in the slug's gills protect it from nibbling fishes. Occasionally this sea slug is responsible for stings reported by bathers, and since they carry the same nematocysts as their prey they should be treated with equal respect. Like its prey, *Glaucus* floats passively on the surface. And like the violet snail, it is derived from bottom-dwelling relatives. The slugs achieve their buoyancy by swallowing air and storing it in their digestive tracts.

Given this bizarre description, it won't surprise you when I say that *Glaucus* is an odd-shaped creature, looking like a miniature version of some evil alien spacecraft left over from a *Star Trek* episode. Of course as science-fiction fans know, producers of that show frequently modified obscure oddities from the natural world to make their visual designs seem realistic and lifelike.

One researcher reported that the young of certain octopi pick up fragments of *Physalia* tentacles and use them as offensive and defensive weapons against other marine animals. This behavior was observed only in captive animals—it is not clear how a bottom-dwelling octopus would have access to *Physalia* at sea. Furthermore, it is strange that an animal that should never come in contact with a surface-dwelling pelagic creature would even know how to do this.

～

Although they are not common in winter, I have seen *Physalia* at all seasons in the Gulf Stream off Cape Hatteras. On rare days when the current and wind agree on the same direction, the seas are flat and *Physalia* race northward. On days of conflict, the colonies bob like corks without much direction. At times, thousands of them accumulate in the current fronts. It's enjoyable to watch the bobbing, sailing, purple bubbles leaning with the wind, trailing long elastic tentacles and sheltering schools of young man-of-war fish—predators that will one day betray their host. Floating among them are other unseen predators that are examples of ecological economics, as well as nature's original recyclers. To the unknowing, *Physalia* seems to represent simply a sleek, primitive, and straightforward lifestyle—neon bladders just drifting about, yet actually traveling many thousands of miles with little expenditure of energy. However you look at it, this is the ultimate pelagic lifestyle.

CHAPTER 3 FISH THAT FLY

I looked up in time to see a flying fish sailing past at eye level, 15 feet above the water. Turning to Captain Harry Baum, I asked whether any had ever landed in this boat. While he was telling me that in 26 years of fishing in the Gulf Stream, that had never happened, an 11-inch-long flying fish crash-landed on the deck below. I rushed down, secured my prize, and hurried back to the bridge to ask Captain Baum if his boat had ever been struck by lightning. What I thought was the best one-liner of the day was not appreciated. The captain proceeded to recount the times his boat had been struck, how insurance companies refused to insure electrical navigational equipment, and how, when . . . well, you get the idea.

During the warm months, flying fish are commonly seen in the Gulf Stream off North Carolina. So at times when there is not much going on aboard ship, and when other creatures of the open sea are scarce, I watch fish fly. It's sort of a mindless pastime, but always interesting. The movement of the boat, or perhaps the sound of the engine, seems to make them take flight. Usually they take to the air when we are 10 or 20 yards away. Occasionally whole schools of 50 or more launch themselves simultaneously, but normally there is simply one here or two here and there. In the course of an hour it is not uncommon to see several hundred take flight. Sometimes I try to estimate flight distance or duration, the sole scorekeeper in the outer continental shelf fish Olympics. Watching flying fish I was reminded of the lines from Kipling's poem "Mandalay": "Where the flyin'-fishes play, / An' the dawn comes up like thunder . . . ," wishing I could recall more of the verses and wondering about the real order of the ones I remember.

After my earliest excursions to the Gulf Stream, I combed libraries for information on flying fish. Information was scattered, mostly repetitive trivia, but in combination, an interesting dossier was pieced together. Much of the literature contained only summaries of the family Exocoetidae in general, keys to species occurring in various oceans and things like that. Of the 25 species known to live in U.S. waters, 17 occur in the Atlantic, including 2 species shared with the Pacific. As best I could figure, about 15 of these species

Flying fishes burst unexpectedly from the sea, sailing above the waves for several yards with fins outstretched like wings before plunging back into the water.

have been found off North Carolina, but these numbers include flying-fish relatives like ballyhoos, halfbeaks, and flying halfbeaks—fishes that think flight simply involves jumping out of the water. Still, there are at least 12 species of flying fish that I might be seeing in the Gulf Stream. I could recognize five, perhaps six, different types, but really I had no way of knowing what species I was seeing. This predicament was somewhat alleviated by the fact that flying fish come in two basic models, two winged and four winged. The four-winged types have large pectoral and pelvic fins and look a lot like little biplanes.

Steve Ross, a friend who specializes in marine fishes, identified the specimen that crashed onto the deck of Captain Baum's charter boat as *Hirundichthys affinis*, one of the four-winged fishes flying about. Was this the species I was regularly seeing, or were there several types of large, silvery, bluntnosed, four-winged fishes in the area? The solution was to get more specimens. I had read that people in the Caribbean capture flying fish at night by placing a lantern next to a sail. The fish fly into the light, hitting the sail and flopping into the boat. I considered variations on this theme and then went out and purchased several boxes of No. 9 shotgun shells for my 12-gauge. It took almost one box of shells for me to see that I constantly shot well behind the fish, often missing them by several yards. Gad, sometimes I wasn't even that close. There was no speculating about the miss; the shot pattern clearly sprayed the water. My failed attempts provided the captain with great amusement and he delighted in announcing my score over the radio to the rest of the charter-fishing fleet. The fish flew faster than I thought and it took a number of shells from a second box before I learned how to lead them. Altogether I hit six or eight fish using two boxes of shells. We retrieved four specimens, the others sank. All were the same large, silver-colored, four-winged flying fish.

I have seen other types that are quite distinctive in coloration, but to date I have been unable to collect or identify them. Except for *Hirundichthys*, most of these seem to live in *Sargassum*. One is an inch-long species with tan, blotched wings that has a maximum flight distance of several yards as it scoots from one *Sargassum* patch to another. A second, biplane type, with velvet black wings, also lives in the *Sargassum*. It grows to six or eight inches, but also seems limited to short flights. I have not seen flying fish of any type in the winter months. Their seasonality suggests that they are migratory and are not simply being passively transported by the Gulf Stream.

Though flying fish are scattered widely throughout the warm oceans of the world, and I knew there were a number of local species I could watch, I really only had one identified. I limited my note taking to *Hirundichthys affinis*. I estimated the longest flights to be between 100 and 125 yards and they lasted for 10–20 seconds. (One Pacific species has been reported to fly a quarter of a mile.) Usually the fish flew less than a few feet or so above the surface, but in strong winds they were sometimes lifted 6 to 10 feet into the air. Based on the forward trolling speed of the charter boats, I estimated flight speeds to be about 35 mph, partly explaining my difficulty in collecting specimens with a shotgun. (Researchers with high-tech equipment have since documented top speeds of up to 40 mph.) The fish would typically fly out at angles of 20° or so from their presumed predator or charter boats, but if we got too close, the direction of flight would often shift to near 45°. In flight, the fish angle upward, so on takeoff and landing the tail always touches the water last and first. With their sculling tail movement they sometimes made two or three composite flights in succession, at times ricocheting from the top of a wave and continuing their flight. Successive flights tended to be shorter in time and distance—the fish simply ran out of gas. Unlike the two-winged species, four-winged flying fishes exhibit a controlled flight even in strong winds. While the two-winged varieties waffle about erratically in the air, I observed that Hirundichthys flew straight, or even banked and changed direction. On calm days, the ripples of their lopsided, lobed tail fins left trails on the surface runways.

The specimens I collected ranged in size from 10–12 inches long and weighed 97 to 258 grams. Pectoral fin lengths ranged from 5 to 6 inches, making the total wingspan somewhat greater than the length of the fish. By tracing out the wings on a piece of paper and calculating the area, I ascertained that the wing-loading ratio (combined surface area of both pectoral and pelvic fins divided by the weight of the fish) was about the same as that of a Cessna. When the dimensional relationships of various species of flying fishes are compared to each other, and to flying insects, birds, and bats, the ratios of weight-to-wing area and wing length all show logarithmic coordinates producing a line whose slope is three. OK, that's enough math.

These fish were spawning off the Carolina coast in August. Dissecting the specimens showed that about half of the females had recently laid eggs and the others soon would. While not a shocking piece of biological information, documentation of such tidbits eventually adds up to understanding the biology of poorly understood species such as flying fish. I was impressed with the large swim bladders of my specimens. The same device that provided buoyancy for surface-scooting oceanic fish allowed the ones I collected to float long enough for me to scoop them from the sea.

For years, the mechanism by which flying fish were able to fly was the focus of much debate. Did they flap their enlarged pectoral fins as birds and insects flap their wings? Careful observation and high-speed photographic images eventually showed that flying fish swim forward and upward through the water at great speed. If their initial spurt fails to get them airborne, the enlarged lower lobe of the tail, the only part of the fish still submerged, vibrates rapidly from side to side, up to 50 beats per second, oscillating until the fish achieves a taxiing speed fast enough for liftoff. This sculling motion is only slightly modified from how the fish normally moves through the water. On outstretched wings—excuse me, fins—these fish soar above the sea until they lose momentum and drop back into the water. Sometimes they fold their fins and, with a splash, plunge beneath the waves. At other times their tail action again takes over and off they soar once more.

The conclusion from these observations was that flying fish don't actually fly, but rather that they glide. While I don't wish to make a big thing of this, there is some latitude of interpretation here. Dictionaries are not particularly informative in defining flight: "flight: act or mode of flying"; "flying: act of one that flies"; "fly: to move in or pass through the air." This subject demands common sense, not circular logic. But keep in mind if you fly from the Raleigh-Durham Airport to Atlanta you are not flying, you are being flown.

Everyone would agree that hawks, bats, moths, and airplanes fly, and that canned hams, cement building blocks, and box turtles don't. In between are a small number of things that seem, to different degrees, to fend for themselves against the pull of gravity—like red maple and dandelion seeds, parachutes, and Tarzan. Also there are objects designed to minimize wind resistance that can be projected for considerable distances when hurtled into the air—Frisbees, cruise missiles, and footballs for example—but when left on their own, each pretty much stays put. The next sequence of thought brings us to "flying" squirrels and lemurs, and "flying" frogs, geckos, and snakes. It is generally accepted that these animals, using various skin flaps, appendage modifications, and streamlined body designs, simply glide. After launching from a high perch, these creatures succumb to gravity and come down gracefully in a downward swoop to a pre-selected landing site. They are parachutes with self-control and never achieve the kind of lift that would free them from the pull of gravity or create a force great enough to overcome the resistance of the air.

Unlike paper airplanes or creatures that jump from high places, such as "flying" squirrels, flying fish become airborne on their own power by propelling themselves upward and then forward in a relatively straight flight path parallel to the surface of the ocean. They are not thrust into the air by an outside energy force, nor are they simply getting from point A to point B by jumping and gliding from a higher position to a lower one. They appear to exhibit considerable control over both their course and direction. Thus, the only real topic for discussion centers on whether bird-like wing flapping is an essential part of the definition of flight. The Wright brothers didn't think it was, and nobody accuses albatrosses, which can soar for hours on set wings, of not being capable of flight. Like conventional aircraft using a self-contained fuel source, or albatrosses that must run headfirst into the wind for takeoff, flying fish are quite capable of propelling themselves and flying for impressive distances before their forward momentum no longer provides enough lift to sustain flight. Frustrated marine predators who try to snatch them from the air believe they can fly, and so do I.

Because of their small size, flying fish have an ocean of predators, but, from what I could see, the most eager are dolphins. Rushing under them, cutting the water's surface, the dolphins tried to single out individual fish as they zipped off in different directions. While flying fish can move through the air at speeds of 35–40 mph, dolphins have been clocked at 37 mph. The dolphins' speed is only important in the initial charge, as they're only able to swim at high speed for short distances. The flying fish, on the other hand, coast once they are airborne, covering long distances quickly with little expended energy. I never witnessed a capture. On several occasions I watched large male dolphins below and greater shearwaters above, both in hot pursuit of the same fish. The shearwaters were snapping the air and the dolphins followed, but during the 150-yard chases the flying fish always gave their predators the slip.

Both tropicbirds and boobies have learned to fly above or alongside boats, as the flying fish are constantly scooting off at 20–30° angles ahead of the bows of boats. Tropicbirds and boobies, being plunge divers, fold their wings and descend onto their target, timing their dive to intercept the fish as it re-enters the water. Often the bird's momentum will cause it to go several feet below the surface. The birds are about 50 percent successful—you can often see the fish protruding crosswise in their bills when they bob back up to the surface. Although they also eat other types of fish and squid, both boobies and tropicbirds are tropical species that specialize in flying fish. One summer our mate had a flying fish he was saving to use as bait. When a white-tailed tropicbird flew over our boat he took out the bait and showed it to the bird. It was obvious that the bird recognized it as it changed its flight direction so it could eye the fish that was still in the mate's hand. After a minute or two and several false approaches, the bird descended, hovered above the mate, and eventually gently snatched the fish from his open hand. Over the years I have tried several times to duplicate this, but the birds, while they would often show interest, never actually went for the fish.

⌣

The large four-winged flying fish are well designed for flight, and, if the history of aviation were not so well known it would be a logical, though incorrect, assumption that early aircraft were modeled after the fish's basic body plan. The two-winged flying fish can be compared to planes with a single pair of wings. The four-wingers are advanced designs for biplanes with underwings, which seem to function as elevators, staggered far back. In both types, the pectoral fins spread out after the body of the fish has been lifted out of the water by rapid swimming. To open them beforehand would cause too much drag. Drag is further reduced because only the lower lobe of the tail fin is in the water, and power can be effectively added as needed until enough lift is achieved. Just prior to takeoff, the pelvic fins, which remain tightly folded against the body while the fish is on the runway, are suddenly and broadly spread and the fish gracefully rises into the air.

The pelvic fins are constantly, and often independently, repositioned to keep the fish on course and the flight stable. The large forward wings remain fixed. This combination of decreasing resistance in the air and a strong sculling motion in the water is quite effective. Once the lower tail lobe leaves the water, it immediately stops its oscillation. At this point the tail and tail fin are only used in turning, like a rudder on a plane. The drag of the air is reduced because the fish doesn't require landing gear, and friction is slight because of its wet, mucous-covered skin.

Lift is obtained by the pair of anteriorly placed fins. The upper surface of each wing is smooth and flush and the necessary mechanical strength is in the supporting fin rays that are found below, causing the lower surface of the fins to be ribbed. This arrangement reduces air turbulence on the upper surface and is important for lift. In the four-winged species, additional lift is provided by the pelvic fins and the fish's square body. The flat lower surface also assists lift, a design much like the fuselage of large cargo planes. The square-bodied four-wingers have maximized lift and stability; the two-winged types have speed. Stability is gained with some sacrifice to flight, by the angle of both the pectoral and pelvic fins. Thus, all the wings tip forward several degrees, for longitudinal stability and, in a dihedral angle not unlike a soaring turkey vulture, for lateral stability. The flight sacrifice is due to the wing's tipping, which decreases the effective wing area. The dihedral angle reduces the length. Horizontal stability is controlled by distribution of the weight. It can be roughly measured when the fish is viewed from the side. Like airplanes, about 51 to 53 percent of the fish's body lies below a central axis running down its center. This slight shift in distribution of weight keeps the fish flying right side up.

These fish are weighted and balanced much like a weather vane that always points into the wind. The flight is therefore, in large part, self-correcting, heading the fish into the wind, which in turn assures maximum lift. Actual tracking of flight shows it to be a compromise between the original course at takeoff and the direction and speed of the wind. Thus, the fish's nose points more or less into the wind while its flight path veers to the right or left.

All my comparisons to aircraft might be misleading. It should be noted that, unlike airplanes, flying fish often need to get away in a hurry; where they eventually splash down is not critical. Landing accidents that would be disastrous for planes are not even minor incidents for fish. There is nothing to break and the runway approach can be imprecise. They don't need pre-approved flight plans and seat belts are not required.

With flying fish qualifying for frequent-flyer programs, it at first seems curious why they, unlike birds, don't come in a greater variety of sizes. Most are between 6 and 12 inches and the largest, *Cypselurus californicus*, a southern California coastal species, is only 18 inches long. The answer lies in problems associated with initial liftoff, not the function of flight itself. The fish are straddling the life of two worlds, and fins that are highly functional in one element are cumbersome in the other. Hindered by this problem, the fish have difficulties in the transition and the resistance of the water. Seaplanes encounter similar problems in escaping the pull of the water and getting airborne.

And there is one other adjustment. The flying fish's lateral line is not down its side as in most fish, but near the belly. I assume this is a logical place for this sensory device that only works underwater when its owner insists on doing belly flops all over the ocean. It's one in a long list of adjustments necessary for successful fish flight. Understanding the need for these adjustments is important, but I regret that the information learned from them has been used as "evidence" for the school of thought that these fish don't fly. Even if technical reasons trump logic and force them to be regarded as mere self-propelled gliders, they are still fun to watch. Then, too, there are always the flying squid . . .

CHAPTER 4 FISH THAT SUNBATHE

The ocean sunfish, a creature that borders on ugly, looks like something created by a committee and then in disgust tossed into the sea. Even the fish's simple scientific name, *Mola mola*, suggests a committee compromise. Almost anyone would be able to guess it's a fish, but only through the process of elimination. It couldn't be anything else. After all, these "sunfish" have two eyes, fins, live in the ocean, and can, in a manner of speaking, swim.

For people unfamiliar with ocean sunfish, a category that includes almost everybody, the name sunfish is most misleading. Our freshwater bluegills, redbreasts, and other familiar sunfishes are related to bass. *Mola mola* is related only to *Mola lanceolata* and *Ranzania laevis*. These three species comprise the only members of the distinct family Molidae, the ocean sunfish. Molids are pelagic ocean dwellers and, as far as is known, live almost exclusively off a diet of . . . yuck, jellyfish.

Even in the scientific literature one never sees much written about ocean sunfish. They are common enough, but people seldom come in contact with them, and even marine biologists find little opportunity for study. The fish are pelagic, have no commercial value, and, because of their dietary constraints, are not likely to be caught on a hook and line. Indeed the literature on ocean sunfish reads like a gazetteer: "The first record of an ocean sunfish from New Jersey," "Sharp-tailed ocean sunfish from North Carolina," and "*Mola mola* in Monterey Bay." The list goes on, each unexpected appearance from various places making its way into scientific literature. When the records are pieced together they suggest that the round-tailed ocean sunfish, *Mola mola*, is a fish of temperate seas; *M. lanceolata*, the sharp-tailed ocean sunfish, is subtropical; and the slender sunfish, *Ranzania laevis*, is tropical. The currents of the North Atlantic redistribute live, sick, and dead ones with enough impartiality and thoroughness to add a depth of confusion to this simplistic interpretation of their distributions. All three can be found off the North Carolina coast, for example.

In North Carolina waters, *Mola mola* is certainly the most commonly encountered of the three species, and I saw them regularly on offshore seabird

The odd-looking ocean sunfish swims open mouthed through the water at the ready to consume its preferred prey, jellyfish.

surveys. They are not particularly hard to spot. Adults are the size of dining room tables, and larger ones can be as much as 10 feet long and 14 feet high, attaining weights of up to 5,000 pounds. They are the heaviest bony fish known. Most other types of fish are not easily seen, much less properly identified far out at sea. Ocean sunfish, however, are one of the exceptions. Their impressive size, coupled with their propensity to sunbathe, makes ocean sunfish unusually recognizable at sea. They lie on their sides close to the surface, so close in fact that their dorsal fin often sticks upright, bent at an angle that exposes it to the air. The fanning fin waves in a motion that would appear to have something to do with forward swimming if only it were under water. These protruding fins are easily seen on relatively calm days, as is the massive body of the sunfish idling just under the surface. While the sunfish appears dim-witted because it does not seem to realize its fins are out of the water, it seems equally dim-witted to me that biologists have not bothered to explain why ocean sunfish have adopted this behavior. The logical assumption would be that sunning helps to elevate internal body temperatures and speeds up body processes such as digesting jellyfish, but who knows? And how hard can it be to digest a Jell-O-like jellyfish?

Hunting down information on ocean sunfish only reveals how little is known about this odd family of fish. Nothing is known, for example, about the location or season of spawning, egg development, age, growth, or even the size at which they reach maturity. Because of their large size and cumbersome weight, few specimens have been preserved for study. Most studies of this fish are conducted entirely by reanalyzing literature descriptions rather than actual specimens. The ocean sunfish's unique anatomy makes it challenging for fish biologists to describe even with their ichthyological terms. Its fin arrangement is so different from most species that biologists cannot even agree on how they should be measured. Minor discrepancies in fish measurements may seem trivial to the public, but such measurements are important to biologists when comparing body proportions. Written descriptions of the fish are perplexing, and, while the North Atlantic species are fairly well known, it is not clear if only three species exist worldwide. Some of the described species are simply the opposite sex of fish previously classified. Others are the same species renamed several times. Sorting all this out is an ichthyologist's nightmare, and, with the lack of preserved specimens for reference and comparison, it's probably also an impossible task. It seems most unlikely that fishermen on the island of Yap, where stones are still used for currency, would be persuaded to invest in multi-thousand-gallon vats of formaldehyde on the off chance that one of the poorly described South Pacific sunfish might wash ashore.

Somewhat annoyed at the lack of available information on ocean sunfish, I began keeping records of their activities, even during the early phase of my seabird studies. There was not much to record. I noted the date sighted, what they were doing, the direction they were headed in, where they were, and the surrounding water temperature. Twenty-five-plus years of record keeping, including additional information from charter-boat captains, has added only a few minor insights into our knowledge of the behavior of these sunbathing fish.

The only species I have personally encountered at sea is *Mola mola*, but the other two species are also known to live in the Gulf Stream. The small *Ranzania* has been reported from the Gulf Stream where I spent most of my survey time. The sharp-tailed ocean sunfish has a distinctive silvery appearance, so I am sure I have not mistaken one for the round-tailed type. In most cases, I have been able to see the tail shape, further confirming my identification.

In fact it is not clear why the sharp-tailed sunfish is found in local waters. Records are all of beached individuals, mostly found in winter. This seems contradictory to the expected habits of a subtropical pelagic fish. I suspect that these isolated individuals might have been numbed by the cool sea and transported northward in Gulf Stream eddies from as yet undetermined wintering areas. It is also possible that the two unobserved species do not "sun" as frequently and are therefore not as likely to be encountered as round-tails.

⤳

My sightings indicate that Mola mola is basically solitary and largely found in waters less than 100 fathoms deep (a fathom is about 6 feet). They do not actually live in the open sea, but in water associated with the continental shelf. Most of my observations are from water between 10 and 40 fathoms. In over 250 sightings of ocean sunfish, I only ever observed one within sight of land. Nearly all were seen in areas where the surface water temperatures were between 50° and 65° F, and sunning behavior was noted as early as 7:30 in the morning and continued throughout the day.

Surprisingly, my years of observation indicate that this sunfish is migratory. The species was absent during the winter and rare during the summer. In the spring, however, large numbers were seen moving northward through the shallow waters over the inner continental shelf. The bulk of the spring movement occurred between mid-April and mid-May. The passing fall migration was primarily in October and November, with scattered individuals moving south as early as late August, or as late as December. Previous records of beached sunfish were so few and scattered up and down the Atlantic coast that no hint of a migratory pattern had emerged. Furthermore, many dead specimens may have been transported long distances by currents, masking their actual seasonal and geographic distributions.

There is no way to know what percentage of the total migration can be seen from the deck of a boat. Ocean sunfish are not obligated to live at the surface—in fact, there are records of these fish at depths of over two miles—and fish even a few yards below the surface would be difficult to spot.

⤳

Biologists separate the molids from other fishes because they are the only ones lacking a caudal peduncle. In the time it takes to look up what a caudal peduncle is (the narrow part of the body to which the tail attaches), you can learn to simply recognize an adult molid because they are the only fish shaped like a 3-foot-thick, 500-plus-pound pancake. They are also lacking in other parts that make fish look like fish. Indeed, you might think you're looking at the severed head of a large fish with a healed-over scar along the trailing end (early authors, in fact, referred to them as head fish). Here and there are a few fins, mostly in the wrong places. The fin rays, which ichthyologists use to compare families of fish and justify evolutionary lines, do not correspond to the fin rays of other bony fishes. Also, the pelvic fins simply don't exist, and the fin on the tail end of the fish is a fused conglomerate of several fins. *Mola* seem to use the tail as a rudder, so it is at least flexible. In addition, these fish lack scales.

The swim bladder, the device most fishes use to adjust buoyancy, has also been omitted, and the skeleton is made of cartilaginous fibers. Ocean sunfish have round mouths and teeth fused into a beak. People who have been around captive sunfish report an audible grinding of the jaws, a sound like "a hog eating corn." The hide is thick and very tough but elastic. The males possess bright red spots and a pointed nose that protrudes out over the mouth. Presumably the female is impressed by this.

What kind of a fish has our committee created? I'm not sure, personally, but some people who classify such things have placed molids between porcupine fish and toadfishes. Others have them at the end of the fish classification system, and regard them as the most advanced of all fishes.

How creatures as large as this can support themselves on a diet of jellyfish defies logic. Actually, it is hard to get a good fix on how it was determined that ocean sunfish eat jellyfish. Nevertheless, this fact is widely repeated in every account I have ever read. Ocean sunfish are frequently seen among large assemblages of jellyfish, both sea nettles and comb jellies. Charles Manooch, a biologist at the National Marine Fisheries Service lab in Beaufort, N.C., told me that once when he was scuba diving 20 or 30 miles out to sea, he saw one *Mola* associating with a large number of sea nettles. Only one of the ocean sunfish I have seen was clearly among jellyfish, but in many cases the transparent prey would be hard to see from above the surface.

Because of their open-ocean habits, I suspect the fish's major food source may be salpas—usually called salps. Their overall abundance would make them a perfect food source. Arranged like small rolls of lifesavers, salps are chain-link colonies of transparent creatures. Like jellyfish, their bodies are 95 percent seawater and another 3 percent consists of the salts needed to retain osmotic balance. This leaves the animal colony with less than 2 percent organic matter. The sunfish would need to consume at least 20 times more of this type of food for daily protein requirements than they would need if they ate more conventional food.

Most of the literature concerning *Mola*—except that listing places where dead ones have washed ashore—relates to their larval development. It seems that scientists have been fascinated not just by the strange-looking adults, but also by their strange-looking spiny-plated, globular larvae. Biologists have been describing the young sunfish since at least 1880. The life cycle is complex, with larvae undergoing more than one complete metamorphosis. Yet even though this interest spans more than a century, knowledge of the early development cycle remains incomplete. The few larval sunfish that have been found have usually come from the stomachs of predatory fishes and have thus been difficult to study, describe, and illustrate. Larval fins, and the important fin rays that biologists use to track development, are usually already partly digested. The number of larval and juvenile sunfish in the North Atlantic must at times be astronomical. Ocean sunfish potentially have the highest reproductive output of any vertebrate. A small female *Mola* examined in 1921 was estimated to contain no fewer than 300 million eggs. (I suspect that the graduate student assigned to document this little tidbit of information shifted their studies to medieval English literature the following semester.) Just recently several marine biologists reported on having found a single larval ocean sunfish in the Florida Current. This was after 284 trawl samples. Not only was the location and date of interest, but they noted that since 1869, when the first one was reported, this was just the 17th documented larval individual ever found. Yet, even small females can produce millions of eggs. The ocean continues to hold many secrets.

Other than seeing shark-like protruding dorsal fins, most charter-boat captains have little firsthand experience with ocean sunfish. "They may seem slow, but we never hit them with the props," Captain "Big Al" Allan Foreman said a number of summers ago. To prove his point, he deliberately ran toward a large one sunning off our starboard. The fish, without ceremony, simply sounded, disappearing into the water. They maneuver effortlessly.

The sunning fish always look like they are swimming in slow motion. One day when our charter boat was temporarily broken down I watched several sunfish swim past our boat, and they were out of sight in several minutes. Time, distance, and speed are so relative that the *Mola* may be a much stronger swimmer that it first appears. Captain Harry Baum once told me of gaffing a small sunfish. He was impressed with the strength of the fish, and only after considerable effort was he able to get it into the boat. He said the fish produced such a stench that everyone on board was in favor of throwing it back. The fish quickly swam off.

~

One of the most remarkable feats involving man and ocean sunfish hangs in the North Carolina Museum of Natural Sciences. Prior to retirement I passed it several times each day going to and from my office. I suspect this specimen is what first piqued my interest in the species. It is a mounted *Mola mola* prepared in the late 1920s by the legendary H. H. Brimley, the first curator and director of the museum. The fish was discovered partly stranded in Currituck Sound on May 30, 1926, undoubtedly a lost migrant. To retrieve the fish, an anchor was hooked into one of its gill openings and the fish was towed to a dock. It was improperly released from its hoist and unexpectedly smashed through the planks of the dock. Its weight was estimated at 1,000–1,200 pounds. Brimley measured the specimen and found it to be 85 inches long. The greatest thickness was 49 inches, and from fin tip to fin tip it was 99½ inches in height. The open mouth was only 3 inches by 5½ inches. The pointed nose indicated it was a male. The skin was slimy and it adhered very closely to the underlying muscular tissue. The actual skinning of such a specimen seemed to Brimley to be a rather hopeless undertaking. Instead, he made a plaster cast of both sides of the fish, saving the fins and a few other parts.

Back in Raleigh, Brimley reconstructed the fish from the mold. Thirty years back I chanced upon Brimley's original sketch of how he proposed to support the hollow cast of the huge fish. There are many building plans that have less construction details than the inside of that fish model. The finished specimen is a masterpiece. Not only is it an excellent example of early-1900s create-as-you-go taxidermy, but it also compares well to fish prepared with modern techniques and synthetic lightweight materials. It is a true museum piece in every sense of the word. To persuade our museum's exhibit committee to put the giant *Mola* back on display took some doing. The specimen was so large that it was too tall to fit into a newly designated exhibit area—a hall devoted to the achievements of the Brimley brothers. In order to display it we had to allow its dorsal fin to extend through the ceiling of the exhibit hall.

Committee creature or not, the specimen is not only a tribute to the self-taught taxidermy skills of Brimley, but it's also a lifelike example of a very strange fish.

CHAPTER 5 MARY'S TUNA

I was on the bridge writing down Loran numbers and water temperatures while simultaneously scanning the horizon for seabirds as Big Al told me story after story. Allan Foreman's boat, the *Country Girl*, was the primary one I chartered during my 30 years or so of seabird surveys. As I was being lulled by the calm of the sea and by Big Al's fish tales, one of the out-rigger lines snapped, and Al's mate Johnny yelled up from below, "TUNA!!"

My wife Mary was on board that day to document any marine mammal encounters. Johnny moved her into one of the stern chairs, set the rod, and adjusted the drag. Allan altered the boat's heading and speed. It was Mary's first tuna; the fight was on. The fish ran with the line and went deep. This is not about fishing with a cane pole and some worms; the fish was going to take some time to bring in. Johnny quickly reeled in the other five lines so they would not get crossed; this was obviously a sizeable fish. Over the years I had hauled in my share of tuna. It's tiring work and uses muscles that for normal people never come into play.

∾

It had taken some time for me to work out an agreeable fishing strategy with the various captains and mates. My offshore excursions were for studying seabirds, not for fishing, but many of the seabirds I was studying focused their foraging over schools of tuna and other pelagic fishes. The tunas drove the small baitfish to the surface, and the birds capitalized on the chaos. The captain would run the boat over to the flocks of foraging birds so I could get better counts, and the tunas would hit the lines, sometimes four or six at a time. By the time we dealt with the fish, the birds had dispersed and the process would start all over again. Additionally, yellowfin tunas often swim below schools of porpoises, and when we would try to move in to get better estimates of the size of various groups of marine mammals, the tunas would go for our baits. We soon became the only charter boat out there pulling in our lines before we approached the schools of feeding tunas. Dolphins were not as bad in that they could be reeled in rather quickly, but marlin were a real

Yellowfin tuna are built for speed and endurance, reaching speeds as high as 50 mph. Desired by sport fishermen and commercial fisheries alike, tunas are overfished and now face conservation challenges.

issue—we would regularly lose an hour or more bringing in even a modest-sized white marlin, only to release it. So my standing order was that we were not going to be fishing for marlin. The mate always tried to slip in a hook baited up for marlin, thinking that I did not know the difference. Finally I just gave up and said, "OK, if you hook a marlin I am going to shoot the line with my 12-gauge." One day, I did just that and the word quickly spread through the fleet. We never ran any marlin rigs out after that. What I did not understand at the time was that the captains and mates had a standing bet each year to see which charter boat would catch and release the most marlin, so my seabird studies became a handicap to Al and to the other captains I frequently chartered for my seabird work.

A limited amount of fishing was good for my work, as the activity actually attracted some types of seabirds to the boat, and the captain and mate could sell the fish back at the dock, which, on a good day, represented a considerable "tip." So the standard exercise was to get the fish reeled in as quickly as possible. This led to some interesting exchanges between the captains and mates: The less experienced mates, in their eagerness to gaff the fish from the stern of the boat, would often wrap the leader around their hand to prevent the fish from running out with more line. The captains, many of whom had once been mates themselves, were always scolding them. If a big fish were to get a second wind, or a shark were to grab a fish and make a run, the leader would cut through fingers and hands—with a big fish, the steel leader can even cut through gloves. One summer a mate from the Oregon Inlet fishing fleet had his hand wrapped in the leader while he was trying to release a blue marlin with the other. The marlin still had quite a bit of fight in it and pulled the mate overboard and under the surface. Neither the fish nor the mate was seen again. OK, yeah, yeah—another Al story, but this one also made the papers. I had already read about it at home in Raleigh several weeks earlier, but it was still interesting to hear Al's perspective. The Atlantic continues to host some really big fish, and big fish spawn some rather big tales.

～

Mary, Johnny, and Al focused on the tuna while I continued to write down seabird sightings and simultaneously watched my wife struggle with her fish. The fish never let up, but occasionally it would make a run that paralleled the direction of the boat, allowing Mary to reel in a few more feet of line; most of the time it was a dead heat with neither the tuna nor Mary gaining on the line. It was like an extended arm wrestling event, with both contestants giving their all and both tiring over time. Every so often the fish would make a run taking out a little more line. Eventually, though, the fish was worked to the surface, and in its frantic attempt to get free allowed some slack that was quickly taken up by the reel. Now it was just a matter of time before the exhausted fish was landed by the exhausted angler. Of course the fish's main battle was with the boat, and unless the line snaps, it's a battle the fish will eventually lose. The captain keeps the fish off the stern of the boat, while the angler keeps the line taut, reeling in line whenever the fish swims in any direction other than away. The captain moves the boat forward and the fish of course fights and tries to swim in the opposite direction or down. The angler's job is trying to keep the fish from running with the line; the fish fights the boat's pull and eventually tires. The pole is just flexible enough to give and keep the line from snapping but strong enough to provide continual resistance. Don't get me wrong, reeling in 50 or 75 yards of line a few feet at a time is a workout for one's back and arms, but I would hate to battle a sizable tuna from a stationary boat.

Somewhere I have a photograph of Mary with the fish. It's impressive, clearly showing that the fish, balanced on the dock by its nose, with Mary holding it in position by the tail, is considerably the larger of the two. On the opposite side of the fish was Big Al, he was smaller than the fish too. The "big" in Big Al is a by-product of Outer Banks sophomoric humor, a high school label that made fun of his small size—one that has stuck in the small fishing community. I forget the exact weight of the fish; it was well over 200 pounds, but nothing even close to record size. The record-sized ones reported by the International Game Fish Association for 1982, the year Mary landed her fish, were in the range of 330 to 380 pounds, and at the time the all-time world sport fishing record was for a yellowfin tuna caught off Mexico in 1977 that weighed 388 pounds, 12 ounces. This one was large enough; we continued to discover packages of tuna buried in our chest freezer for three or four years.

In contrast, there are fly fishermen who go into the Gulf Stream to catch tuna. The first tuna to exceed 100 pounds ever caught on a fly rod was landed by Mike Reed, a former student of mine. There are all types of regulations that need to be met regarding the strength of the line and all sorts of trivia that are important in record keeping. But the basic issue is the boat needs to be neutral when the fish is hooked, and, while it needs to be in gear in order keep the line in position once the fish is on, the boat itself is not actually allowed to put any strain on the fish. It took Mike 2 hours and 15 minutes to land the fish. Its weight was 129 pounds. Talk about sport fishing, Mike well remembers the day—January 26, 1996—the first time ever that a tuna exceeding 100 pounds was taken on a fly rod.

～

Mary's yellowfin was a tuna often encountered in the Gulf Stream off the Outer Banks. It is a tropical-to-temperate species found in the western Atlantic from Massachusetts to Brazil and throughout the Gulf of Mexico and the Caribbean basin. Except for the Mediterranean, they also occur in all of the other warm oceans of the world. These tuna feed at and near the surface, often on jacks and other fishes and invertebrates associated with *Sargassum*. Researchers studying the diets of yellowfins caught off the Carolina coast found 26 percent of them had fragments of *Sargassum* in their stomachs, which suggests that many were feeding directly off fish living in the algae. Yellowfins grow fast, reaching lengths of four and a half feet and achieving sexual maturity in just three years. By their seventh year—about the average lifespan of a yellowfin—they approach six feet in length. Yellowfins are relatively short lived, with seven years being close to their maximum age. Like many marine fish, the largest individuals have the greatest reproductive output. While a two-foot female can produce over three hundred thousand eggs, a five-foot female is capable of laying eight million eggs. This is an extremely important commercial species and hundreds of thousands of tons are taken worldwide by purse seines and longlines.

To appreciate my wife's one-on-one battle with the fish, one needs to know something about tunas. Fish are designed to swim, but tunas have brought swimming to a new level. They are built for speed and endurance, cruising at speeds of about 10 body lengths per second. At top speeds these yellowfin tunas can hit 40–50 mph. So let's compare Mary's hooked tuna to a trout; there is no doubt about it, a sizeable trout on a line can put up a good fight, and their top swimming speed is about 5.3 mph, a bass is about 12 mph. In general, the muscle power of fishes is about 0.002 horsepower per pound of body weight, so a 500-pound bluefin tuna would have the power of one horse. But even a modest-sized fish on a line, and one obviously under stress, can have thrust that requires energy bursts of up to 2.6 horsepower. Only sailfish and swordfish have higher swimming speeds than tuna, reaching top speeds of around 60 mph. But there is more to tuna than size that accounts for their speed.

Many fishes use their fins and tails not just for swimming but also for hovering in place, and their fins often add considerable drag when moving through water. Think of a goldfish in a bowl slowly hovering in place for years on end, then think of a goldfish trying to survive in a raging mountain river. Tunas don't worry about such nonsense as hovering; they are full-throttle, straight-ahead swimmers. Their swimming speed is built on a number of factors in both their external modifications and internal design. This is a fish on the go; there is no idle gear! Tunas are characterized by their streamlined bodies, stiff fins, and rigid tails, traits that enable them to constantly swim at high speeds. The respiratory pump of tunas' gills is designed so that they must remain in constant motion in order to get oxygen into their blood. Tunas can maintain body temperatures up to 10° above the water temperature, creating high metabolic rates that support their energy needs.

Let's examine some aspects of tunas that individually are each features shared with various other species but in combination make tunas the fast, efficiently predatory, hard-fighting fishes that they are. The overall body shape of a tuna is one designed for speed, one evolved to reduce the energy required for swimming. Resistance is decreased by the smooth contour of the fish, cutting down on friction. In developing torpedoes, the Navy might as well have used a tuna for their design. Ichthyology textbooks use the tuna's fusiform body as an example of the ideal body shape for a fast swimming fish. And then there are the muscles. Tuna are essentially a fish head followed by swimming muscles; it's these muscles that we eat. Between the muscles are sandwiched a few necessary organs. The reddish color of tuna meat results from red fibers in the muscle tissue that allow these fish to swim rapidly for long periods, requiring a constant supply of oxygen to the muscles. (Fish with white meat are typically ones that have more sedentary lives, like groupers, catfish, and flounder.) Most fish have body temperatures similar to the surrounding water, but tunas can have body temperatures much warmer than the water. Warm muscles produce more swimming power than cold ones. We think of fish as cold blooded, so how do they do this?

Tunas have developed a highly efficient, heat countercurrent exchange system that seals in their body heat. The problem for a fish in retaining heat is the property of water itself. In addition to the fish's entire body being consistently submerged in water, which cools more efficiently than air, there are great volumes of water passing over the tuna's gills. But warm tropical and subtropical water holds less oxygen, so enormous amounts of water need to circulate past the tuna's gills, offsetting any advantage of the Gulf Stream's water already being warm. The blood going past the gills becomes nearly the same temperature as the water. The internal metabolic process that generates heat is the chemical process of digesting food burned with oxygen as the fish uses its muscles. Blood traveling through the muscles becomes heated before traveling back to the heart and gills, and the cooler, oxygen-loaded arterial blood flows from the gills. They meet in the closely packed vessels of the working muscles where the hot and cold blood flows in opposite directions. The heat is exchanged to the incoming blood so by the time the arterial blood is in the muscle it is almost as warm as the blood that is leaving. The muscle contractions and the speed of nerve transmission in the fish get a threefold boost as a result of the temperature increase. Fish tend to overheat when hooked, and because of its effective heat exchange system, a tuna will often have a very elevated body temperature by the time it is landed.

And swim they must; one of the reasons tuna stay on the move is that they lack fully developed swim bladders. Swim bladders allow a fish to maintain neutral buoyancy—without one, fish are about 5 percent denser than seawater and will slowly sink. The remedy is to swim, allowing the pectoral fins to constantly adjust the angle of ascent or descent. The cost for fish of the open sea, like tuna, is they can never rest or they will sink to the bottom, an obvious disadvantage for species that feed near the surface and are ill equipped to handle the pressure near the sea's floor. So the real question is not why do tunas swim constantly, but why would they not have more efficient swim bladders? First, the buoyancy organ in a fish increases its volume by about 5 percent, and would thus increase drag and decrease the fish's speed. This by itself sounds like circular logic, but there is one more important point to factor into the equation. The primary predators of tunas and their relatives the mackerels, which also lack standard swim bladders, are porpoises and toothed whales. These cetaceans hunt using echolocation, and swim bladders are good reflectors of underwater sound. The lack of a large functional swim bladder makes tunas harder for hungry whales to detect, as they are nearly invisible to sonar.

~

The yellowfin, the most colorful of all the tunas, is but one of a number of species of tuna occurring or migrating off the North Carolina coast. The best known is the large bluefin tuna, which can reach lengths of 10–11 feet and weights of up to 1,600 pounds. Also present off North Carolina are the smaller blackfin and bigeye tunas and the closely related and similar-looking species of mackerels, albacores, and bonitos. Most are important commercial species and several, like the king mackerel, are regarded as game fish. Many, like the yellowfin, are open-ocean species and most are highly migratory. Often skipjack and bigeye tunas will school with juvenile yellowfins, and they are commonly misidentified by even experienced fishermen.

Electronic scans off the Outer Banks show that older tuna tend to forage down in the water column at depths of 10–12 fathoms. They feed at the surface as well, and, because they are often associated with schools of porpoises, there is a high rate of porpoise by-catch by commercial fishermen using purse seines. The younger age classes of yellowfins are mostly surface feeders and are often associated with floating objects; charter-boat captains make it a point to run baits past *Sargassum* mats, boards, and other debris found floating at sea. Commercial fishermen will deploy various floating objects in prime fishing areas since they act as fish aggregating devices.

One of the yellowfin's primary foods is flying fishes. The tunas are obviously much faster in the water, but if the flying fish can get airborne they can outdistance the tuna. Large flying fish can sometimes glide over 1,000 feet at speeds of 40 mph. However, the tuna are typically in schools and while the flying fish may make several consecutive flights they don't necessarily get away. To add to the chaos, the feeding tuna schools are often accompanied by groups of shearwaters that snatch up prey in their frantic attempts to get out of harm's way. Squid are another important prey—it would be interesting to be able to watch tuna working through a school of darting, ink-squirting squid.

While catching a yellowfin in the Gulf Stream off the Outer Banks is not unusual, it is not an everyday occurrence. They are hooked in about one trip out of five, but the fisheries statistics are a little off because they often include off-season and inshore fishing in zones void of yellowfins. One is much more likely to hook onto a little tunny (four out of five trips) or a blackfin tuna (an average of 1.2 per trip) than a yellowfin. While yellowfins are caught off our coast throughout the year, they are most common when the waters are the warmest (from May through October); peak catches are in September. Like other tunas, yellowfins are highly migratory, moving north in the summer and south for the winter, at times occurring far from land in the Sargasso Sea. Spawning takes place from January through early April in the equatorial zone of the Gulf of Guinea, and the juveniles are mostly found in waters off the African coast. Some spawning also occurs off the Cape Verde islands, in the southern Gulf of Mexico, and the southeastern Caribbean. In the fall, adults are at maximum weight after a summer of foraging along the edge of the outer continental shelf.

⌣

Tuna have a rough time of it. Most stocks have now been severely depleted, but at one time the tuna fishery was a large and valuable resource important to our expanding human population. The bluefin tuna in particular were the basis for a number of important North Atlantic fisheries for thousands of years. In times of antiquity, likenesses of tuna were figured in Greek designs. Catch records have been kept for bluefins only in modern times, but they document rather well our overexploitation of the marine environment. In peak years during the 1950s, over 150,000 bluefin tuna were harvested out of the North Atlantic. In just 20 years the annual catch was reduced to 2,000. Norwegians alone were catching 20,000 tons in the midcentury years, but by 1972 the catch was reduced to just 100 tons, and fish traps that once caught 20,000 tuna, by 1972 caught only two fish. The problems continue; overfishing, illegal take, and lax quotas have resulted in even sharper declines since the 1970s. The Atlantic bluefin stocks dropped an additional 60 percent between 1997 and 2007. The efficiency of commercial fishery operations increased tremendously in the second half of the previous century. Bigger and faster ships, an increased effort by trawlers and long-liners, fishermen using gill nets, and a growing Japanese market have collectively taken their toll. Approximately 80 percent of the world's annual tuna catch is sold to Japanese markets. In late 2012 a 489-pound bluefin tuna sold for a record 155.4 million yen (1.76 million US dollars) in Tokyo, over $3,600 a pound.

It is unlikely that regulations and quotas will do much to control the fishery with the growing market demand. And, of course, it is the large tuna that produce the most eggs and are responsible for the stability of the stocks. These larger fish, especially, continue to be overfished. In 2007, the reported catch for the eastern Atlantic bluefin tuna was 34,514 tons. This exceeded the allowable catch by 5,000 tons, and with unreported landings the catch could easily be twice this amount. Globally, the bluefin's stocks have been reduced by 80 percent as a result of overfishing. And smaller tuna species are not overlooked by the commercial fisheries' operations either, as is indicated by all the cans of tuna on your local grocery store's shelves. Most canned tuna is labeled as "white" or "light"; the white is albacore and the light tuna is skipjack tuna.

While the Pacific stocks of yellowfins are relatively stable, there has been an overall decline in Atlantic. Since the peak catches in 1990, the decline in catch has been 44 percent, and this appears to be accelerating as 34 percent of this decline has occurred since 2001. Despite increased efficiency in high-seas fishing techniques, these efforts are not paying off, and the total number of commercial fishing days in the Atlantic has declined by nearly 50 percent, with the western Atlantic being the hardest hit. The average weight of individual fish caught has decreased by about 50 percent since the early 1970s and the bulk of the fish landed are only a year of age or less. Because of the change in the size class of fish landed, estimates of the maximum sustainable annual harvest have dropped by over 30 percent. The ocean is not a bottomless resource, a fact that we apparently need to be reminded of on a daily basis.

~

Like other fish we had brought in, Mary's large tuna flapped about in the Country Girl's fish box, but its flapping seemed to go on forever. Even up on the bridge it was loud. Several years back I saw some footage at the Miami NOAA lab of tunas that were caught by long-liners and were then clubbed on the deck. It took a surprising number of blows to subdue the large tunas and there was blood flying everywhere. This was one of the most gruesome videos I have ever seen, and I was glad that I had not decided to do my bird studies from commercial fishing vessels. I wondered, of being hooked, gaffed, and left to suffocate out of water, or being clubbed to death, which was most humane? And speaking of being gaffed, as we started back to shore Big Al had one more story for me before I climbed down from the bridge. Earlier that summer one of his clients fell overboard. The mixture of a good fishing day, the sun, a rolling sea, and a number of adult beverages often takes its toll. The mate reeled in the baits as Al swung the *County Girl* into position for the pickup. Leaning over the side the mate extended the gaff for him to grab on to but the client started swimming away from the boat. This went on for several passes before they finally got him back on board. All day the poor guy had watched fish being gaffed and yanked into the boat so he logically, well, I guess illogically, assumed the mate was trying to gaff him to pull him out of the water. Some people have no business going to sea, even if it's just for a day of chartered fun.

PART II MARINE BIRDS AND THE CREATURES WHO WATCH THEM

When I first started my seabird studies, I mooched rides on research vessels and fishing boats, but after only a few excursions out to sea from various coastal ports, it quickly became apparent that the trips from Oregon and Hatteras inlets gave me the best access to the pelagic community. In the offshore waters adjacent to Beaufort and Wilmington, the continental shelf is very wide and the Gulf Stream runs far from shore. On one-day trips leaving from the Outer Banks, I could reach the Gulf Stream and the edge of the continental shelf in a few hours rather than endure the much longer trips from other ports. There was also time to conduct comparative studies of the inshore birds foraging over the shallower shelf waters on the way in and out. About the time I started my research, Paul DuMont, a highly skilled birder from the Washington, D.C., area, had also discovered the rich bird life offshore of the Hatteras area, and we often rode along together as the daily cost of the charter boats was starting to add up.

My primary interest was simply in documenting the species out there, as well as their relative abundance and season of occurrence. I assumed that we already had a good handle on which species were present off the North Carolina coast, so it was just a matter of learning to understand how they used the area. It took only a few trips to discover how complex the situation was, however, and I soon found that I was seeing quite a few seabirds that were not known to be present off North Carolina. Some of them hadn't been previously reported in the southeast region, and a few were totally unknown in North American waters. It was an exciting time; probably not since the early naturalists roamed the southern Appalachians had so many birds been added to our lists of the state's fauna. At the time, most of the pelagic seabirds I was observing and collecting had only been studied on their breeding grounds—remote islands in the West Indies, the tropical Atlantic, off the European coast, or in remote sites in the sub-Antarctic. So while my study was a regional one, it quickly attracted the interest of other seabird biologists working in the Atlantic basin.

There are many ways to study birds without collecting them with the help of shotguns, but the natural history aspects I was most interested in really required specimens. I did not just need individual specimens to serve as vouchers documenting their occurrence, I needed a series of birds from different seasons to explain age structures of populations, molt sequence, seasonal food habits, and parasite loads. I was also able to document pollution-related contaminants that built up in the tissues of these birds. In some cases we compared our specimens to those in museums elsewhere, focusing on birds that had been collected from known breeding sites to determine the exact location of these birds' origins. The North Carolina Museum of Natural Sciences's bird collection grew through this work, and today it represents one of the most significant seabird holdings in the country.

As nonsensical as it may sound to some, the information obtained from birds I collected has been used to help address a number of important marine bird conservation issues. Nevertheless, I hope that one day we will have the technology to extract the necessary information without sacrificing the birds. One of the primary barriers to this goal is, of course, the difficulty of getting your hands on the birds while they are flying about at 40 mph or so, far at sea. However, technology is advancing at unbelievable rates; we can now track from our desktops individual seabirds fitted with geolocators via satellites.

Bird watchers quickly became interested in my published findings. There were birds out there worth seeing. Anyone keeping a life list on either a state or North American level needed to see these birds in order to tick them off. Most of the species were relatively common on a global scale, but due to their pelagic nature they were seldom seen from land. Only after hurricanes drove the odd individual ashore were these birds likely to be encountered away from the sea, always a crapshoot. A day trip out of Hatteras gave dependable results, not only would the local life-listers see all sorts of species for their personal state list, but many of the species were difficult to encounter in any other place in North America. One simply needed to match up the time of year with the names of the birds they needed to see. A trip to the Gulf Stream off North Carolina is a must for people interested in such things, and for those who are passionate it takes quite a few trips to tally up some of the rarer birds.

While I was always excited to find birds that were previously unknown and undocumented, my primary interest—the thing that kept me going back at all seasons year after year—was studying the more common species. Through both observations and collection, I discovered how they actually made a living out on the high seas. I often felt that the rarities were a distraction, of immense interest to bird watchers, but little more than curiosities to ornithological research. Still, I was overseeing the state's bird collection, and the addition of specimens of birds that had previously not been suspected of being in the area was important too. In the course of the study, I documented well over a dozen pelagic species that were previously unknown locally or in North America. This is about 20 percent of the state's total marine bird fauna and well over 30 percent of the pelagic species. An additional surprise were birds like band-rumped storm-petrels, white-tailed tropicbirds and bridled terns, all of which were previously considered rare vagrants to North American waters, typically reported once every decade or so when some tropical storm deposited an exhausted individual on a beach. We found many of these species not simply to be of regular occurrence, but, in fact, in the right season, some were relatively common. In the end, we discovered an amazing diversity of species, and that diversity is most impressive when you combine the common, the unexpected, and the truly rare species that all find their way to the Gulf Stream's waters off the North Carolina coast.

My growing interests in seabirds eventually led me to the nesting sites of several species in the Bahamas and West Indies. As it turned out, some of the more tropical seabirds I was regularly encountering offshore had also not been studied in any detail on their nesting grounds. Several were species that we learned had very small populations and were of considerable conservation concern. What started as a simple inventory of the seabirds of the area soon took me in many new directions. Reflecting on that research journey, I see how a straightforward academic study led me to appreciate just how unique these waters are and the importance of protecting an area that supports such an amazing diversity of seabirds.

CHAPTER 6 FEATHERED NOMADS
OF THE OPEN SEA

The wave crests were awash in white foam, adding a distinctive salt taste to the northeast wind—another rough trip into the Atlantic. The charter boat's temperature gauge digitally blinked "72.3, 72.8, 73," and in less than fifty yards the sea's surface temperature climbed to 78.4° F—we were in an area of sharply changing temperatures. The boat was straddling a place where two strong currents, each running with a different force, collided. A pod of spotted dolphins appeared, swam in front and alongside our bow, and then departed. The blue water, strong current, and sudden jump in the temperature reading told me we had reached the edge of the Gulf Stream. On this morning the wind was from the south and as it blew across the northward flowing Stream the water flattened out a bit, giving us a less bumpy road to travel.

We followed the inner edge of the Stream northward knowing that marine invertebrates and small fishes would be caught up in the current lines and, above them, I hoped, hungry seabirds. Within minutes we started seeing storm-petrels, and in the course of a few miles we passed terns perched on floating boards and small flocks of resting shearwaters. Strong-flying jaegers patrolled the edge. Other shearwaters, feeding on fishes concentrated in the refuges of floating *Sargassum*, swam and dove around the algae. In an hour and a half I logged five times the number of seabird sightings that I had in the previous four hours put together. I recorded 14 species and approximately 250 individuals in a little less than 90 minutes. These observations were similar to the other 300 or so excursions I had made off the North Carolina coast. While the species composition varies seasonally, the patterns of seabird concentration became predictable.

One of the richest assemblages of marine birds in the North Atlantic occurs off the North Carolina coast. All told, researchers have now documented 37 pelagic, 9 offshore, and 18 coastal species of seabirds in the area. By chartering a boat for a spring trip to the edge of the continental shelf, for example, one might see gannets from Nova Scotia; phalaropes and jaegers from the Arctic tundra; storm-petrels, which nested during the austral sum-

The elegant white-tailed tropicbird, an open-ocean species, only travels inland for breeding and nesting on the islands in the Caribbean basin and Bermuda.

mer on Antarctic islands; and various kinds of shearwaters from the Mediterranean Sea, the Caribbean, the Canary Islands, and southern South America. Intermixed would be a few gulls and terns, whose nesting colonies are scattered among the coastal islands of the central Atlantic states.

This incredible diversity of seabirds is no accident. Because of its latitude, the waters off North Carolina's coast receive an interesting representation of tropical and subtropical seabirds during the warmer months and cold-water species during the winter. On a day in mid-April, like this one, both tropical and boreal species are present, as are a number of oceanic migrants heading back to their various nesting areas. The close proximity of the Gulf Stream allows some warm-water-dependent birds to occur throughout much of the year, while the cool waters of the southward-flowing Labrador Current provide winter haunts for those of northern latitudes. The interface of these currents, as well as scattered upwellings of cool waters rich in oxygen and nutrients along the edge of the continental shelf, and the churning waves that characterize the so-called Graveyard of the Atlantic all combine to make this area a meeting ground for migratory fishes, making North Carolina's offshore waters renowned as one of the best deep-sea, sport-fishing areas in North America.

The predictability of prey draws birds from throughout the Atlantic and causes many species, which for all purposes should be rare or absent at this latitude, to occur regularly and often in abundance. For example, greater shearwaters are a Southern Hemisphere species that typically "winters" in the cool waters off Canada, where long summer days produce vast plankton blooms that in turn support extensive food chains. Recent offshore studies, however, have shown that a fair number of subadult greater shearwaters "winter" off the North Carolina coast, staying throughout our summer and not just passing through in migration as was previously believed. At the same time, many tropical and subtropical seabirds find our local waters to be much more productive than the warm, oxygen- and nutrient-deprived seas adjacent to their Caribbean nesting grounds. Thus, impressive assemblages of species such as Audubon's shearwaters, bridled terns, and black-capped petrels also occur along the edge of the Gulf Stream off the North Carolina coast. To the north, they are rare or absent; to the south, oceanic productivity is so limited that these birds seldom linger.

A large percentage of our seabirds are truly pelagic, open-ocean wanderers, seldom coming in sight of land except during their nesting periods. Many of these birds nest on remote, essentially inaccessible oceanic islands, while others nest on the Arctic tundra, or steep seaside cliffs where their eggs and young are not disturbed. The secret to successful seabird breeding colonies is their establishment in predator-limited environments where the young, which have protracted incubation and fledging periods, can survive.

The area off Oregon Inlet and Cape Hatteras is not only the best region in North Carolina for observing seabirds, but it is also the best in North America and arguably among the best in the world for outright diversity. Not only are the waters here attractive to foraging birds, many of which are rarely encountered elsewhere in the western North Atlantic, but the edge of the continental shelf and the inner edge of the Gulf Stream converge just 15–30 miles from shore, making one-day boat trips to see and study the impressive pelagic bird concentrations feasible.

Even though the surface of the open ocean looks monotonously unchanging to the inexperienced eye, that is not the case for charter-boat captains, experienced fishermen, and hungry pelagic birds. Changes in water color and temperature, the appearance of tidelines, and accumulations of floating debris have meaning to astute observers. The different bird species have such specific requirements for feeding that they stratify into rather predictable zones. These zones shift from day to day and season to season with changing winds, current edges, and surface-water temperatures, but the patterns of distribution for particular species groups are generally the same. A study of local terns, for example, shows that least terns are nearly always in sight of the beach, as are common terns once the migration period is over. Locally nesting sandwich terns commonly feed up to 15 miles from shore, while royal terns, which nest at many of the same sites, regularly commute up to 40 miles out to sea to fish. Off North Carolina, tropical terns, which do not nest in our area, also occur. The dark-plumaged bridled and sooty terns are seldom found within 20 miles of land except where the Gulf Stream comes closest to Cape Hatteras. And probably 90 percent of all bridled terns observed are within a mile of the inner edge of the Stream itself. Seabirds are opportunistic, however, and at times when large numbers of prey species concentrate and are driven to the surface by feeding predatory fishes, the zones temporarily break down and the feeding frenzies begin.

There is a striking faunal difference between the inshore waters over the continent shelf compared to those in the offshore truly pelagic environment along the outer continental shelf. It is most unusual to encounter the same species in both zones. On this particular trip I saw common loons, as well as a few wintering northern gannets and a small flock of Bonaparte's gulls, neither of which had yet departed to their respective northern breeding grounds. The remainder of the species I encountered were all common coastal and inshore species that are easily seen from Nags Head Beach or hanging about Oregon Inlet—brown pelicans; double-crested cormorants; laughing, ring-billed, and herring gulls; and common and least terns. Many of these birds nest on local beaches and spoil islands of the nearby sounds, and for some the nesting seasons had already begun. Only about 20 percent of my bird sightings are made in the waters of the shallower areas over the continental shelf where the water is less than 30 fathoms in depth.

In contrast, out in deeper water, both the variety and the numbers of birds are obviously higher. The ones I observed along the Stream's inner edge were for the most part the truly pelagic birds— storm-petrels, shearwaters, and petrels. But there were others as well: wintering phalaropes that were lingering because their tundra nesting habitats were probably still iced-over in mid-April; migrating pomarine jaegers, another tundra nesting species, that were heading north and the other two jaeger species that in a few weeks would be working their way northward along the frontal boundary of the Stream; and the prize for the day, a single arctic tern. Though the arctic tern is a common species, commuting from one hemisphere to the other each spring and fall, they migrate far out at sea and are seldom seen off any of the southeastern states. About 85 percent of all records are from the spring migration period, and this was only the fifth or sixth one I had seen since I first reported them off North Carolina in 1979. This one, like most I have encountered off the Carolina coast, was in subadult plumage. In total, I saw almost 1,000 individual birds representing 25 different species on a single 10-hour trip. The vast majority of the birds I saw were recorded in zones beyond the 500-fathom contour. To put this in perspective, in 2010–11, I spent 90-plus days surveying the shelf edge in the Gulf of Mexico where it is not unusual to go an entire day without seeing a single bird. Even on the best days, a good count down there would be perhaps two to four species represented by a total of 200 individuals.

The arrival of the ocean-dwelling birds is seasonal, and locally occurring species can be placed in calendar categories that describe their basic season of occurrence—summer residents and visitors, winter residents and visitors, and migrants. Additionally, there are accidental species that appear irregularly as well as those that do not exhibit clear seasonal patterns. And, as I was witnessing on this trip at certain times in early spring and late fall, summer and winter residents, migrants, and the accidentals are sometimes all here simultaneously.

⤚

The following sketches are of the seasonal variation in prominent species that live over the outer continental shelf of North Carolina. The birds vary widely in both their geographic origin and their arrival and departure schedules. While some birds are simply passing through, others spend most of their lives here, leaving only temporarily to attend to nesting obligations in distant lands.

The summer residents and visitors (May–November) represent the most diverse and interesting species assemblage. The fauna is composed largely of three distinct groups of birds—those nesting locally along the Outer Banks; tropical and subtropical birds coming from the Bahamas, West Indies, and oceanic islands of the Atlantic; and a number of Southern Hemisphere species that breed in the sub-Antarctic. Most of the species in the summer assemblage are common and can be encountered on a nearly daily basis, but even some of the globally rare ones are present in numbers that make their appearance on a one-day outing very likely. Most of the rarely seen types are sporadic summer visitors: some are seen only once or twice in a season, and for others decades may pass between sightings. The birds are nearly all open-water pelagics typically associated with the Gulf Stream. Storm-petrels and shearwaters are the dominant types but this is also the time of year that tropicbirds, boobies, and tropical terns occur.

Winter residents (November–April) are quite different from those found summering in our offshore waters. The species assemblages are less diverse, but the total number of individuals encountered on a one-day trip is considerably higher. Wintering birds are mostly species that move south from northern breeding sites in the western North Atlantic, and many of these are inshore species—loons, gannets, various gulls, razorbills, murres, dovekies, and puffins. Though confined mostly to the shelf and seldom found in the Gulf Stream itself, all of these species can be found over waters that are relatively deep. There are still other winter species that occur farther offshore over the outer continental shelf and along the edge of the Gulf Stream— fulmars, Manx shearwaters, red phalaropes, great skuas, kittiwakes, and Bonaparte's gulls. These too are seabirds that nest in the northern latitudes of Canada, Greenland, and western Europe. During January and February, four species of common gulls (laughing, herring, ring-billed, and great black-backed) make up over 60 percent of the total offshore fauna, and by March just two gull species (herring and Bonaparte's) constitute 80 percent of the birds encountered. While on winter trips to offshore waters in December through March, I only averaged 16–22 species of marine birds; this was the time of year with the highest densities, and average monthly counts ranged from 1,122 to 6,721 individuals per day. The increase in numbers was mostly a result of large numbers of various species of wintering gulls moving into offshore habitats.

The migration period not only overlaps with the periods of summer and winter residency, it could be argued that it extends throughout the year. Not only are birds coming and going from northern nesting colonies, but tropical and subtropical species disperse northward into the Gulf Stream as their nesting seasons come to an end. Added to this are transequatorial and transatlantic migrants coming to the western North Atlantic. If that is not enough, many species time the dispersal of their various age classes differently, while others follow schools of migrating fishes or depend on seasonal shifts in trade winds to trigger their movements. Even for birds that simply move north to south it is not necessarily a straightforward migration, as many that move northward across the western Atlantic fly south in the fall over mid-ocean or on the western side, totally avoiding the Gulf Stream altogether. Those seabirds that nest at inland locations complete large portions of their migration over land but usually follow marine routes that take them well to the north before making sharp turns inland to their final destinations. It's like a noisy and sometimes crowded highway out there with everyone constantly coming and going on different schedules, but with some peak rush hours.

The bulk of spring migration is predictable and large numbers of species and individuals migrate past the Hatteras region between the second week in May and the first week in June. They are in a rush to be among the first to arrive once their nesting areas have thawed, and they fly along the Gulf Stream's inner boundary like homebound interstate travelers. Other species, like greater and sooty shearwaters have completed their nesting chores in southern seas and are in no particular hurry to get to their primary "wintering" grounds off the Grand Banks as the lengthening days are just beginning to increase the plankton blooms that make this bank such a rich feeding ground.

The fall migration period is more protracted; it is first noticed in early August when the red-necked phalaropes start arriving after finishing their nesting duties and are more than happy to escape the hordes of mosquitoes and other parasitic dipterans in the Arctic tundra. The fall migration continues through December when the thick-billed murres begin to filter this far south from sub-Arctic seas.

The feeding behavior and food choices of seabirds are, of course, the key drivers of their marine distributions and seasonal movements and are therefore behind the seemingly strange international assemblage of species I was finding. Combined with at-sea observations and cataloguing what was present in the stomachs of thousands of individuals collected over several decades and in all seasons, I was able to piece together what was going on out here. There were birds like tropicbirds, boobies, and the larger shearwaters that were top-order predators feeding on flying fish, squid, and modest-sized predatory fishes. Many of the birds focused in on small "bait" fishes driven to the surface in crazed frenzies by tunas and porpoises. Others were specialists, feeding largely on small creatures associated with the floating patches of *Sargassum*, while many gulls were feeding generalists and scavengers making the best of whatever the sea had to offer that day. Often, gulls, terns, and pelicans can be seen following commercial trawlers, as the scrap fish that were thrown back after sorting the catch made for easy dining. The skuas and jaegers were opportunists too, but to varying extents they relied on stealing food from other birds before they had time to swallow, at times even tormenting other birds to the extent that they disgorged any recently swallowed food items. Other birds fed directly on the plankton, making up for the small size of the food items with quantity. Perhaps the strangest diets were those of the Wilson's storm-petrels, who half hover and half hop across the surface of the ocean, scooping up minute prey items with their small, wide bills.

The actual methods of feeding are almost as variable as what the sea offers on its menu. Some of the larger birds catch fish by plunge diving into the water from 30 or more feet in the air. Pelicans, gannets, boobies, and tropicbirds hover in place, just for a moment, positioning themselves before folding their wings and diving head first into the sea. Their momentum can take them to depths of 10 or 20 feet if needed. Most of these birds grab their prey with pinpoint accuracy. The pelicans engulf a big bill full of water and hopefully a fish or two. They return to the surface, let the water drain from their pouches, and then tilt their heads back and swallow the fish. The others use their serrated bills to grasp and hold onto their prey. In total contrast, small storm-petrels patter across the surface with outstretched wings, picking and filtering small items directly from the surface. In between is every imaginable variation, from loons sinking and swimming below the surface, to plunge-diving terns that grab their prey and, in the microsecond between the force of their dive sending them underwater and catching their fish, spread their wings and with a single beat re-launch themselves back into the air. With delicate precision phalaropes use their long thin bills in an almost tweezer-like fashion to carefully pick small snails from floating *Sargassum*. The shearwaters and petrels feed mostly on the wing, as do the gulls, seizing food from the surface while in flight. A number of the birds use more than one feeding mode, shifting their behavior with different wind speeds, sea conditions, and prey availability.

The relative densities of the seabirds over the various oceanic zones I encountered could be calculated from counts along known transects across the zones and actual densities determined by factoring in the distance and width of the visual transects. These calculations showed considerable variation between zones in any given season. From the beachfront out to about 30 fathoms I would see only about 10 individual birds per hour. Over the deeper waters of the shelf (30–100 fathoms), the count picked up to about 50 birds per hour, and past the 100-fathom contour the average jumped to 60–80 birds in the same time period. These are really rather well-defined zones, and on most days I could tell how far along we were, not by looking at my watch or the boat's depth gauge, but by simply recording what species I was seeing and tallying their numbers.

Sometimes when I had others along who were interested in seeing the birds up close or photographing them, we would attract the birds by giving them handouts, a practice that's referred to as "chumming." We used the heads, entrails, and other unwanted fish parts for bait. Within minutes of throwing a bucket of the rather smelly and oily fish stew over the stern, we would be swamped with birds, and not just the types we had been seeing for the last several hours, but sometimes a few of the less common species appeared seemingly out of nowhere. After a few seasons of relying on chumming to lure birds close to the boat, I stopped it all together. Looking over the information we were collecting, it clearly showed that while indeed the chumming attracted birds, it was messing up the transect data; not only did the chum bring in birds from outside the transect zones, but it also continued to attract them long after we left the site where the offal was dumped, pulling birds away from areas that we were to survey over the remainder of the day. When we deposited the fish scraps along current edges, the oily mess became caught up in the tide lines and soon extended northward for a mile or more, making the feeding birds' distributions even more linear than they already were.

Despite the problems associated with the chumming method, these accidental observations led the research in another, slightly different direction. We knew the average relative densities of the various seabirds for different zones and seasons, and we knew that a little amount of chum brought in many additional individuals from well outside a one-square-kilometer survey area, many more, in fact. So, knowing this, we could count or estimate the number of birds attracted to our chum and get a crude estimate as to the distances from which our chum was attracting certain species. While this seems like just an esoteric exercise, or an excuse to dispose of unwanted fish parts far at sea where no one is watching, it actually provides an answer to an important question. How do the mixed feeding flocks of seabirds that we were finding far out in the Gulf Stream actually form? Foraging flocks over schools of feeding tuna and along some current edges formed rapidly, often disappearing within 15 or 20 minutes. How were the birds keying in on these patchy and short-lived foraging opportunities?

Ornithological meetings where graduate students and their professors present papers and posters can be rather dull. Session after session of back-to-back 15-minute talks where people pontificate over the finer details of what, to most, would be inherently obvious, gets old somewhere in the three- or so day course of the average meeting. The saving factor is the bars. Once the last session of the day is over, people loosen up and actually talk to each other. Over the course of a few beers, the exchange of information and ideas becomes increasingly productive. It was at such a meeting where my friend Chris Haney and I came up with an idea of how we could use the results of chumming to actually illustrate the finer points of feeding-flock formation. In Chris's studies off South Carolina and mine off North Carolina we had independently calculated seabird densities. By simply looking at the numbers of birds of each species that made up the flocks that formed around our chumming stations, we would have a crude estimate as to the maximum distances from which the birds were attracted. By the fourth or fifth beer, we had our study methods pretty much set.

What we found when we later checked our notes showed that the birds we were encountering in mixed species feeding flocks were attracted from considerable distances. By putting out chum to attract the birds we could see that the birds used two entirely different methods to locate food. The small storm-petrels that forage close to the sea's surface always arrived from downwind, using their keen sense of smell, tacking back and forth into the wind following the scent of the food. The larger, high-flying species hunt visually and were attracted by the sight not just of birds feeding, but also of birds suddenly changing direction and heading for the newly forming feeding flocks. These behaviors allowed both types of seabirds to effectively exploit the patchy food resources and constantly changing conditions of the ocean's surface. By calculating flight speeds and wind and factoring in the zigzag flight patterns of the petrels and shearwaters and the arrival times of the various birds, we could determine the distances that birds traveled to arrive at our chum stations. Based on the size of the flocks and the relatively quick time that it took for them to form, we were impressed, but not actually surprised, to learn the average recruitment distance was two to three miles, with some birds coming from even greater distances.

꿈

As specimens began to accumulate and I was able to look at series of birds collected from my study site, patterns began to emerge. One of the most unexpected finds was that the sexes and ages of the birds were not random. For nearly every species there were pronounced biases. Every Cory's shearwater specimen was an immature or subadult bird, for example, while 95 percent of the Wilson's storm-petrels I collected off the Outer Banks were of breeding age. For the Cory's shearwater the explanation was simple—the period in which they were present was their breeding season, and the adults were all on the other side of the Atlantic looking after nests and chicks. For the storm-petrels the answer was less clear, as they nest in the Southern Hemisphere during its summer, and the entire population migrates into the Northern Hemisphere for our summer. The ones we were seeing were just the adults. Storm-petrels only produce one chick a year, and it takes a number of years for an individual to reach maturity, so even with a high mortality of young birds, the number of immatures and subadults should be similar to that of the adults. Clearly the younger birds were living somewhere else. But where? For northern gannets the age/sex distribution was even more lopsided. Nearly all of the individuals wintering off our coast are adults. Because gannets, like a number of other seabirds, have different age-related plumages, this could be determined simply by looking at the large flocks that frequently forage off our coast. The adult plumage of the two sexes, however, is identical for most seabirds. The examination of the specimens showed that the adult-plumaged gannets wintering off the Carolinas were mostly adult males.

Information like this is important for conservation and management decisions. For example, based on winter counts I made from the sea and counts others made from the shore in February, when gannet numbers peak in the state's waters, as many as 10,000 gannets have been seen together at one time. The total number wintering here must be phenomenal. The waters off the Outer Banks represent the southernmost area of these high concentrations. Ten thousand adult individuals is approximately 16 percent of the western North Atlantic breeding population and an ecological disaster such as a mid-February oil spill, even a small one at the wrong spot, could be devastating. However, because these flocks are made up almost entirely of adult males, the mortality would effectively take out over 30 percent of the known breeding population. Because gannets lay but a single egg each year and take at least five years to mature, it could take decades for the species to recover to their current numbers from a single short-term event. At other times of the year, when the gannets along our coast are mostly migrating young birds, the recovery from such a disaster would be far less serious in terms of the long-term stability of the population.

Whether through just recording age-related plumages for the birds I was seeing or through dissection of specimens collected where the standard-issue feathering changed little if at all with age, species after species showed marked imbalances in the age groups or the sexes of the birds living off our coast. For the migrant species, these biases are often seasonal as different age groups are on distinct schedules for departing breeding and wintering areas.

～

There is a motel on Interstate 95 just a few hundred yards past the North Carolina–South Carolina state line named, appropriately enough, South of the Border. It was there even before the Eisenhower administration came up with the concept of interstate highways. When I was still of junior high age my parents and I would often stay there. It was more or less a halfway point between where we lived near Baltimore and where we vacationed each summer in south Florida. Back in the days when we traveled US 301 in my mother's pink '57 Olds, it was unremarkable as motels go, but one could hardly miss it, as highway signs announcing that it was coming up began to appear 200 miles out. From either direction drivers were reminded that they were 10 miles closer than they were when they read the previous billboard. The wording of the signs were clever and corny "Pedro ses' You never Saw-such a Place," and there would be a depiction of Pedro next to a huge three-dimensional hotdog. No two signs were the same. Advertising works, and with the completion of I-95 the motel grew into a complex. Today, South of the Border is larger than some of the towns in the immediate vicinity. There are restaurants, fireworks stores, several gift shops, carnival rides, and a reptile zoo. It's the only motel I know of that has its own water tower, and if you want to get a bird's-eye view of I-95 from a four-story tower, you can climb up, stand inside a lighted sombrero, and look down at all the wonder. Based on the number of cars in the parking lots they pull in quite a business.

The success of the complex is a combination of the enterprising efforts of the proprietor, sure, but as the real estate folks say, most of it comes down to location, location, location. It's not just I-95 per se—the east/west interstates I-10, I-20, and I-40 also bring travelers to I-95 and to Pedro's front door. It's not just in the right place, but South of the Border has everything a traveler may need.

As funny as it may sound, the Gulf Stream waters off Cape Hatteras are the avian equivalent of South of the Border. The seabirds are seasoned travelers, and they know a good thing when they find it. Just as it is for sport fishermen, marine biologists, ornithologists, and bird watchers, the Gulf Stream is their I-95 and the edge of the outer continental shelf off Hatteras is for some species their destination, for others their perfectly designed way-station—billboards not required. It's biologically as cosmopolitan as any place on earth and its marine life keeps drawing me back. Even after 300-plus days out there I have yet to see all the birds that have been reported subsequent to my studies. So have I yet to see the new reptile exhibit at South of the Border, but I will.

CHAPTER 7 SEA DEVILS
An Epic Tale of Amazing Survivors

"18 April 1983, off Oregon Inlet, NC—water over 1,000 fathoms in depth. Seas reasonably calm." So started my notes on this momentous day. Despite the modest waves and the roll of the boat, I managed to keep the bird framed in my binoculars for some time, eventually getting a really good look. There was no question in my mind that this was the find of a lifetime.

The odds of coming across a Bermuda petrel were beyond minuscule. There are over 31 million square miles of open ocean in the Atlantic and at the time fewer than 35 pairs of Bermuda petrels were in existence. Accounting for young birds that had not yet reached breeding age, the total population might have been 100 individuals. The petrel in my sights had survived a number of historic and recent events, any one of which should have driven it deep into extinction. Prior to the rediscovery of a small nesting group of these birds in Bermuda, this petrel had been assumed to be extinct since the early 1600s. And yet, incredibly, one was flying off our port bow, the first Bermuda petrel ever seen off North America. In fact, this bird was the first one ever seen away from its nesting grounds. To see such a bird 500 miles from Bermuda was not surprising in itself; many of the seabirds regularly encountered off the Outer Banks come from nesting colonies that are much farther away—Greenland, the sub-Antarctic, the West Indies, and the Mediterranean. What was surprising was that I was seeing one at all.

After it was out of sight, I wrote down the field marks and flight behavior, the boat's position, and the water temperature. I continued to record the other seabirds and marine mammals we observed that afternoon, but my brain kept repeating "damn, that was actually a Bermuda petrel!" I was in about the eighth year of my seabird surveys and had by then logged over 100 days at sea. My studies had added numerous species to the state's known avifauna, a number of which were also previously unknown to North American waters. Yet, by then I was no longer expecting any surprises, and even if I had been, this one was almost beyond belief.

Bermuda petrels need secure burrows to raise their young, as do several other pelagic birds. Conservationists have begun to construct artificial burrows to ensure that Bermuda petrels have enough of this critical resource to sustain and grow populations.

I suppose there are many things that set some species apart in our minds—size, bizarre behaviors, rarity, striking colors, funny names. For this one there was no question. I had just encountered the first New World animal reported as driven to extinction as a result of the arrival of European man. It was nearly equivalent to seeing a live dodo.

~

The history—*legend* might be a more appropriate word—of the species is as interesting as the bird itself. The cluster of islands that make up Bermuda was discovered back when Cortez, Drake, and Raleigh explored the seas, but few mariners set foot on the ground. (Bermudians today refer to the whole archipelago that makes up the country as "The Island," though if one were to count all the little rocks and islets, the number surpasses 300.) At the time of its discovery, Bermuda had little to offer and the concept of tourism had yet to be developed. The place was referred to as the Devil's Islands because of its treacherous reefs and the evil sounds that filled the night air. It was not until 1609, when the British ship *Sea Venture* ran aground on Bermuda that anyone actually settled there. The location of the settlement had more to do with the survival instincts of the marooned Brits than a plan for a colony. It turns out the survivors found the island's forested hills and valleys to be inhabited by feral pigs. Spanish explorers attempting to establish a dependable food source for future exploits had dropped off the pigs sometime in the late 1500s. Bermuda's wild hogs, along with various fish, sea turtles, and seabirds, sustained the survivors, and within three years permanent colonists settled Bermuda.

The colonists soon discovered that the petrels were responsible for the eerie nocturnal sounds. In fact, the colonial name for this petrel, the cahow (pronounced k-how), is an onomatopoeic description of its cry. Evidence from early writings as well as fossil and sub-fossil bones indicates that at the time of human contact these pigeon-sized seabirds were extremely abundant, perhaps numbering in the hundreds of thousands. But the population was quickly devastated. The settlers exploited the birds for food and destroyed their habitat with extensive burning and deforestation. Feral animals did damage as well. In 1614 a plague of rats demolished crops to such an extent that the colonists were forced to take refuge on adjacent Coopers Island, the only large island remote enough to have escaped colonization by the pigs and rats. In the process they eliminated the last refuge of a number of native species. When cats and dogs were released on the main island to control the rats, this led to additional problems for the cahow. The problem did not go unnoticed, and Bermuda became the first colony in the world to develop conservation laws protecting seabirds, marine turtles, and other wildlife. The statutes went into effect within four years of the island's settlement, but it was already too late. Bermuda's beaches were decimated, leaving the green sea turtles with no place left to nest, and by 1621 the cahow was no longer seen.

⌒

The continued existence of Bermuda petrels could have been revealed any number of times—opportunities were missed for one reason or another. The nocturnal behavior of the birds was one impediment; a major problem was that no one knew what the legendary cahow actually looked like. The written descriptions from the early 1600s were far from adequate, and its taxonomic relationship to other seabirds was a mystery. The first Bermuda petrel seen in modern times was found on Bermuda's Castle Island in 1906 and was erroneously determined to be a vagrant mottled petrel, a seabird of the Pacific Ocean nesting in New Zealand. A decade later this specimen was re-examined and used to describe the Bermuda petrel as a distinct species. Why this failed to result in an immediate search for the bird is anyone's guess; perhaps it was because of the events of World War I that the specimen was forgotten. In June 1935, a dead petrel was found at St. David's Lighthouse, but it was not clearly identified. Part of the confusion was that a small population of Audubon's shearwaters nested in Bermuda. Prior to piecing together the fossil evidence, many assumed that this vocal and nocturnal seabird was the source of the early stories of cahows. In 1941 a third specimen was found on St. George's Island, and in 1945 a dead adult cahow washed up on Cooper's Island. World War II resulted in the dredging and filling of the Castle Harbor islands for a military airport, and this, combined with intense submarine warfare in the North Atlantic, further delayed a search for the species. But the specimens eventually found their way to the American Museum of Natural History and the Smithsonian where they were definitively identified as the long lost Bermuda petrel. Where had these birds come from? Did the Bermuda petrel still exist?

Robert Cushman Murphy, the bird curator at the American Museum of Natural History and the world's authority on marine birds, immediately recognized the identity and importance of the petrel specimens from Bermuda when he examined the ones in his collection. He contacted Louis Mowbray, the director of the Bermuda Aquarium, Museum and Zoo, and together they planned an expedition to look for the birds. The early accounts of the cahow all indicated that they nested in the winter months, and the four modern-day specimens were all found in the winter, so Murphy concluded that midwinter would be the best time to search for nesting individuals. Mowbray knew that the small islets of Castle Harbor were the only sites not overrun with feral dogs and cats. Mowbray was aware of the natural-history interests of a local Bermuda schoolboy, David Wingate, and he asked Murphy if it was alright to bring him along. Murphy agreed, thinking the lad would be useful in negotiating the rocky cliffs and ledges of the islets. On January 28, 1951, Murphy, Mowbray, and the fifteen-year-old Wingate began their search. Their mini-expedition to the Castle Harbor islets yielded six pairs of nesting cahows, and a seventh was soon discovered. Follow-up searches by Wingate over the next 10 years revealed 18 pairs nesting on five of the small islets. The existence of the phantom bird had finally been proven. The residents of Bermuda were thrilled with the rediscovery of the bird and continue to take pride in what has become an icon of the country. The cahow's image appears on Bermuda's ten-dollar bill.

Murphy and Mowbray published a paper that informed the academic world that the cahow—long believed to be extinct—had been rediscovered. And the young Wingate discovered something far greater—a lifetime career devoted to bringing the legendary bird back from the brink of extinction. The timing could not have been better; the cahow's rediscovery occurred at the dawn of global environmental awareness and soon captured the world's attention.

—⌣—

Bermuda petrels have continued to face many obstacles to survival even in recent decades. The military airport built by connecting Cooper's Island and St. David's Island during World War II became a hub for commercial airlines bringing vacationers during Bermuda's postwar tourism boom. The bright lights coupled with a rat invasion from a NASA station built nearby during the late 1960s are believed to have caused cahow nest abandonment on one of the nearby islets. In 1987 the U.S. Navy Air Station installed extremely bright security lights within half a mile of the remaining breeding islets. Appeals from the Bermuda government to shut down the lights were ultimately successful in 1989. Soon after, between 1995 and 2003, the U.S. naval air station and the NASA station were closed and Cooper's Island was handed back over to the Bermuda government for restoration as a nature preserve. Soon after the lights were turned out, Wingate documented an immediate surge of pre-breeding activity by the petrels.

But during the 1960s it was also discovered that the cahow eggs were suffering from eggshell thinning caused by the insecticide DDT, despite the fact that Bermuda did not use DDT. The runoff from salt marsh mosquito control efforts and farms in the heartland of North America worked their way into the Mississippi and other major rivers feeding into the Gulf of Mexico and then into the Loop Current connecting the Gulf of Mexico with the Gulf Stream. The chemicals worked their way up through the marine food chain and became concentrated in the very areas where the petrels were feeding. DDT and other chlorinated hydrocarbon compounds were detected in unhatched eggs and dead chicks recovered from the cahow's nesting burrows. One egg contained DDT concentrations of as high as eleven parts per million. This was apparently the cause for the decline in reproductive success during the decade that followed the bird's rediscovery. Wingate testified at congressional hearings in Washington, and the plight of the petrel became an important factor in the eventual ban of the chemical. The use of DDT declined rapidly in the 1960s and by the early 1970s the reproductive success of the cahows approached a 60 percent fledgling rate and was much more in line with that of similar seabirds. Since the 1990s there has once again been an increase in egg failure perhaps corresponding with the increased use of DDT in Central and South America.

And then there was the snowy owl that showed up in the winter of 1987. Snowy owls are known to migrate out of the Arctic tundra when the lemming population crashes, but they seldom venture as far south as Bermuda. One of these owls was first noticed on January 10, in the Castle Harbor area, at the time the only recently recorded occurrence of a snowy owl in Bermuda. Amazing as that was, a large nocturnal predator taking up residence on the very islets on which the Bermuda petrel nested was the worst-case scenario for the slowly recovering petrel population. During February alone, David Wingate documented that the owl had killed and eaten five cahows. In the interest of protecting the endangered petrels, a military sharpshooter was asked to shoot the owl. He missed, but Wingate himself shot the owl on March 5. Local bird watchers were quite upset, but they recognized the importance of the petrel program, as the owl was likely to remain for several more months. The bird had already effectively destroyed a significant percentage of the total stock of Bermuda petrels in just a few weeks.

Owls were not the only avian problem. The white-tailed tropicbird, another seabird nesting in Bermuda, competes with the petrels for nesting burrows. This is mostly a modern-day problem, brought about by the petrel's life in exile. Back when they nested on the larger islands, the petrels constructed their burrows in the soil of the forest floor. On the rocky islets, where there is no soil, the birds are forced to makes homes of the natural erosion crevices in the limestone cliffs. These same crevices serve as optimum nesting sites for white-tailed tropicbirds. When the summer-breeding tropicbirds returned in March to start nesting, they usurped the nest cavities occupied by the petrels. The larger and more aggressive tropicbirds would kill the petrel chicks and take over the burrow. Wingate discovered this early in his observations, and he documented over 60 percent of hatched cahow chicks were being killed by tropicbirds at the time of the bird's rediscovery. His solution was simple and effective. He constructed artificial baffles, ones with openings small enough that the tropicbirds could not squeeze through, but allowed the passage of the slightly smaller petrels. It was only the difference of a quarter inch, but it allowed the cahows to raise their young in peace.

Following Wingate's intervention, the petrel colony stabilized and started to grow. Now there was a housing shortage on the small rocky islets. Again, the solution was simple and straightforward. Wingate began constructing artificial burrows, long tunnels of cement and rock with a nest chamber at the end. He built them on the level tops of the islets where the cliff-nesting tropicbirds were less inclined to colonize. Over the nest chambers a removable lid provided easy access to the nest allowing him to monitor the progress of the chicks' development. Each year while the birds were at sea, he added a few new nesting burrows, keeping ahead of the growing population. Wingate likes to call it his government housing project. The nesting pairs are loyal to their fabricated homes and return to the same nests season after season. The cahow population gradually and slowly increased.

⌣

Agency politics and conservation biology do not always complement each other. As the cahow conservation story unfolded here in the United States, it became an interesting political juggling act. The ornithological community and the conservationists became instant believers that the foraging area of the petrel had at last been discovered. However, the U.S. agencies that had to deal with yet another endangered species issue saw this as the sea devil from hell. The Bermuda petrel had long been considered as an endangered species by the U.S. Fish and Wildlife Service, and as such it was entitled to receive all the protection that the Endangered Species Act afforded. The fact that this bird nested only in Bermuda where it was already fully protected and was unknown from U.S. waters made the original listing almost irrelevant.

In the initial published report of my first sighting in 1983, I chose my words carefully. The identification was something that should be reviewed with caution. After all no one had ever seen one of these birds at sea, and with a growing interest in bird watching off North Carolina, I wanted future observers to be careful with their identifications and reports. It turns out I was too cautious with my wording.

Some years after the report of my first Bermuda petrel sighting off the North Carolina coast was published, Mobile Oil proposed some experimental drilling in areas they had leased from the Bureau of Land Management. This called for environmental impact studies. In the end, the Clinton administration and the state of North Carolina opposed the operation and Mobile's leases were revoked. However, in the intervening years there were countless studies and meetings, and thousands and thousands of pages of environmental reports, draft reports, and position papers. The state's Outer Continental Shelf Office drafted me to oversee the aspects of the reports that had to do with seabirds and marine mammals. While there were several endangered species of marine mammals in the area, there was only one endangered seabird—the Bermuda petrel. There were actually a number of globally rare and endangered seabirds using the area, but only the Bermuda petrel was officially listed by the U.S. government as endangered, and thus it had legal bearing on the proposed project. The endangered marine mammals documented from the proposed drill sites fell under the purview of the National Marine Fisheries Service; it was the petrel that was bothersome for the Fish and Wildlife Service.

So the games began. Here was an endangered bird that could easily be contaminated by spilled oil, oil that would accumulate along the inner edge of the Gulf Stream right where Bermuda petrels and many other seabirds forage. The Bermuda petrel is also a species known to be attracted to lights and is thus vulnerable to collisions with oil platforms and support ships on foggy nights. In the environmental impact statement prepared for the offshore drilling it is interesting to see the spin the Bureau of Land Management used to downplay any potential problems, ultimately discrediting my sighting and a second report because of "no specimen confirmation." The petrel was not only an endangered species but also an extremely rare one, and I was not about to confirm its presence by collecting one!

Publishing the sighting did lead to additional reports. The total was up to eight Bermuda petrels sighted off our coast by the time the impact statement was released in 1990. Because denial was becoming less of an option, the strategy shifted to the likelihood of there not being a problem. The Bureau of Land Management found a published statement suggesting that petrels are "relatively invulnerable to oiling" and that there was no record of Bermuda petrels colliding with ships at night, so the lights on the oil platforms were not likely to be a problem. The statement noted that "the limited numbers of sightings not only reflect the very low numbers of Bermuda petrels found over the deep pelagic waters offshore North Carolina, [they] may also reflect the low probability for this species' potential to contact offshore exploration and delineation activities." In conclusion, they cited one of their own in-house memos that stated, "In our view, Lee's sightings of the Bermuda petrel do not represent significant new information justifying new Biological Opinion." Were we about to potentially undo all of Wingate's work and contaminate the only known foraging area for the Bermuda petrel in our greed for fossil-fuel reserves? I found this to be outrageous.

Totally omitted from the report was the expected effect of the release of sediments into the water column during the drilling operations. These were the same areas of upwelling over which the petrels and other seabirds were foraging. These sediments stored mercury and other heavy metals that would enter the food chain. In my studies of the closely related black-capped petrels we found that these birds were less efficient in regulating ingested mercury than any of the other 27 species we had studied. The concentrations of mercury were 7 to 9 times higher than in most of the other seabirds studied. Many were already carrying sub-lethal doses in the muscle, liver, kidney, and brain tissues. The release of additional mercury into the food chain at the very spot where the birds were concentrating their feeding would be a problem not only for the very rare black-capped petrel, but almost certainly for the Bermuda petrel as well. Despite this information being available as early as 1980 and its inclusion in various reports I had sent to the U.S. agencies, this concern never appeared in any of their formal reports.

Nevertheless, by 1998 there were a number of reports and records of cahows off the North Carolina coast; at least seven of these reports were well documented and two were photographic records. In addition, there were a number of other reports of sightings that almost certainly were of this species. There was no longer any question that the species occurs off our coast. In fact, the compilation of reports documented that it was present here throughout the year. (While in the process of writing this I looked through my files and found a letter dated April 4, 1999, from the same field office of the Fish and Wildlife Service that was overseeing the oil-lease impact report. It was to the Naval Facilities Engineering Command alerting them of the presence of Bermuda petrels in an area where they were requesting permission to do some field testing. The letter warned them that the presence of Bermuda petrels had been confirmed, made reference to section 7 of the Endangered Species Act of 1973, and suggested that they contact me to determine the best area to relocate their test. Finally, it seems, our government officially accepted the Bermuda petrel as occurring in U.S. waters.)

For over three decades the waters off North Carolina were the only place, aside from Bermuda, where this rare and highly endangered seabird had regularly been seen. The sterile surface waters of the Sargasso Sea that are adjacent to Bermuda probably do not support a dependable prey base for the cahows. In recent years, biologists applied data loggers recording dates and locations to a number of cahows. When the petrels were subsequently recaptured at their nests, the data loggers were removed and downloaded into computers. The findings were astonishing. The petrels' travels to the Carolinas were nothing in comparison to some of their other destinations. Individuals traveled 4,500 miles to the edge of the North Atlantic pack ice to obtain krill to feed their young chicks. As the chicks grew, their food shifted to squid. In addition, cahows were recorded off the Azores, Canary Islands, Ireland, western Europe, and Nova Scotia. Under good wind conditions, cahows could fly 450 miles a day, and in the course of a year individuals traveled 36,000 to 81,000 miles.

⌒

After my initial sighting, Wingate and I quickly started up regular correspondence about what we each knew of the bird. He made trips to North Carolina to accompany me on several of my offshore excursions and was thrilled to see his birds at sea. Keep in mind there was a near 100 percent chance that every one of them we encountered was an individual he had personally worked with at their nests 500 miles away. He took delight in seeing my study area, a convergence of currents and upwellings where his petrels foraged for small pelagic squid, shrimp, and small fishes. I was, of course, eager to learn more about their breeding site and one winter visited his nesting birds in Bermuda. During my flight I contemplated how much electronic navigational equipment was needed for a commercial plane to find a group of small oceanic islands totaling 21 square miles and 500 miles at sea, a dramatic contrast to the petrel's efficient use of stellar maps in locating the same island.

Wingate had taken it upon himself to schedule me to give a talk for the Bermuda Audubon Society during my visit. I sent him a title for the presentation—"How to Screw Up a Perfectly Good Island." I assumed he would edit the title a little, Bermuda being a British territory and all, but no, that was the title that appeared in all the various announcements. I was surprised at the large turnout; the room was filled, and I was later told that they seldom had audiences of that size. Those in attendance were probably disappointed, assuming my talk was going to be about their island. It was actually about my experiences with the ecological disasters caused to the Marianna Islands by our government's postwar management of the wildlife there. That said, the underlying point of the presentation did not go unnoticed; there is a predictable pattern to the havoc that civilized man brings to remote oceanic islands, and it matters little which ocean they are in or who screws them up.

I got to stay out on the Castle Islands, where the original research lab used by William Beebe, the renowned author and natural history explorer of the early 20th century, still stood. Wingate used it in the winter and spring when he worked with the petrels. I slept in Beebe's room, and it was one of the few times I wished that there were such things as ghosts, so that Beebe would appear and talk to me. By day we crossed the choppy waters of Castle Harbor in a well-used Boston Whaler, visiting each of the nesting islets and examining all the known nesting burrows and Wingate's "government housing program." It was a thrill to open the lids of the artificial burrows and see and hold cahow chicks. For the most part baby birds are quite ugly, but these guys, covered with fuzzy gray down, were adorable—and that's a word I don't use much. On windy nights we sat on cliffs and watched as the adults came in to feed their chicks. Hearing about the history of the birds from none other than David Wingate while climbing about on the very islets where they were rediscovered half a century before, and where they had remained undetected for 300 years, is one of my favorite memories. I was looking at birds that I might be seeing off North Carolina later that month as they commuted to the Gulf Stream to find food for their growing chicks.

The island where we stayed was named Nonsuch, Britspeak for "like no other such place," but the island itself, an ancient sand dune, was actually named after an English Tudor castle. Ever since Wingate returned from Cornell, where he earned his degree in zoology, he has been working on getting Nonsuch back to its original pre-European-contact appearance. The island received total protection by the Bermuda government in 1961, and Wingate moved his family to the island in 1962 when he began his island restoration program. At just 15 acres, the island is huge by Bermuda standards. They have entire national parks on the main island that are only 3 to 5 acres each. Wingate's primary goal was a holistic one—to re-establish the entire native community where the petrels could again nest in their original context, free of mammalian predators and other man-introduced competitors. With actual soil in which to dig burrows, the birds would be able to establish a self-sustaining colony, with no need to worry about competitive tropicbirds, and because of the island's higher elevation, hurricane wash-over would not be a constant concern. There was so much to be done. Rats, marine toads, and other exotic species needed to be eliminated. The native cedar forest had been wiped out by an introduced scale insect epidemic, so Wingate planted thousands of seedling trees started from a few scale-resistant cedar stocks that had survived on the main island. He had a list of former native plants and made every effort to reestablish them. When visiting me in the late 1980s he found one of them growing on our property—the American beautyberry. It had died out on Bermuda, so he carefully harvested the seeds and took them back to Nonsuch. I tried to get him to take some of our poison ivy, as that too once grew naturally in Bermuda, but for some reason he declined.

Native land crabs were so abundant that they were out of control, eating everything in sight, including many of his plantings. In the 1970s, he successfully introduced the yellow-crowned night heron to Bermuda in order to bring the land crab population under control. Avian paleontologists at the Smithsonian later confirmed that the yellow-crowned night heron was likely the ecological counterpart of an extinct Bermuda endemic heron documented in the fossil record. The introduction was a success and the land crabs were eventually brought under control. As one might imagine, all of this took time and an ecological effort requiring a little more commitment than recycling a few soda cans. When I first visited Nonsuch everything looked to be in harmony, though the forest was still maturing. Today, the island is back to its original primeval state. Nearby Cooper's Island, the site of discovery of several petrels in the early 1900s prior to its transformation into a U.S. air base, has also been proposed for restoration. The restoration methods worked out for Nonsuch will work equally well on the even larger Cooper's Island. After renegotiation of a 99-year wartime lease agreement signed in 1941, the island has been handed back to Bermuda.

⌇

For all the emphasis on the threats humans have posed to cahows over the years, nature presents plenty of challenges as well. Hurricanes have been a particular problem for the birds nesting on the low-lying islets of Castle Harbor. In 1989 Hurricane Hugo was likely responsible for an unusually high mortality rate for the cahows at sea, and flooding from another storm that same year resulted in nest failures for at least two pairs. Since 1995 the increased intensity of hurricanes due to global warming caused four more major flooding events during the non-breeding season, damaging half of the nest sites. The storms' damages resulted in the need for major nest repairs before the petrels returned for the following breeding season. It took five men two months to repair the damage. Then on September 5, 2003, hurricane Felix hit Bermuda with sustained winds of 120 mph and wind gusts of up to 145 mph. The hit was direct and the hurricane-force winds blew for more than five hours, creating 30-foot waves and a 12-foot tidal surge. This was the most powerful hurricane to hit Bermuda in anyone's memory. Lives were lost, and homes and businesses, roads and bridges were devastated. Wingate's government housing program for the cahows was also destroyed. At that time of year, though, fortunately the birds were all at sea. The species co-evolved with hurricanes and their nesting cycle is timed so that the chicks are out of the nest long before the hurricane season. But 60 percent of their burrows were damaged or destroyed—both the natural and artificial ones. A previous hurricane had already destroyed all the nest sites on one of the nesting islets, so the number of viable islets was now down to four. A crew spent a good portion of the fall repairing the nesting sites, in some cases constructing cinderblock walls to close in nest cavities where the wave action had destroyed the limestone cliffs. By November, when the birds returned for their pre-breeding rituals, everything was back in place. But this was a wake-up call.

As climate change continues, storm activity is predicted to increase. Sea levels will rise at least one and a half feet within this century, and the low-lying islets will no longer provide a safe haven for the cahow. As hurricane after hurricane damaged Wingate's nesting sites, he determined that the time had come to realize his ultimate goal of establishing a nesting colony on Nonsuch. His plan was simple: once translocated chicks were imprinted on that island they would return to their adopted nests after they came back from their first five years at sea. In the spring of 2004, 14 two-thirds-grown petrel chicks were moved from the islets to man-made burrows on Nonsuch. The birds were about 20 days from fledging and were hand fed in the new burrows. In the years that followed, additional chicks were moved to the larger and safer island. The program was successful and as the birds have started to return to Nonsuch it appears that the translocation program continues to work. There will be other setbacks of course, but the future of the cahow looks promising, especially considering that it survived on the verge of extinction for well over 300 years. The message is a good one: perhaps a little planning and a lot of dedication can assist some of the world's other basket cases.

The success of the overall program can be measured by the gradual growth of the breeding population and the number of chicks that fledge. By 2010 there were 95 established nesting pairs that fledged 52 young. This was the first year since the bird's rediscovery, and perhaps since the 1600s, that the number of chicks leaving the nests exceeded 50. The Nonsuch relocation program is also well along—to date, 19 of the translocated chicks have returned as adults and have been recaptured on the island. Seven pairs have established nesting burrows, and two chicks that hatched on the island have successfully fledged, one in 2009 and one in 2010. I like to think of future petrels digging their nesting burrows among the roots of the beautyberries—shrubs grown from the seeds Wingate harvested from our North Carolina property in the mid-1980s.

In the United States, endangered species programs often focus on single issues, leaving the species in question vulnerable to threats we choose not to address. Funds are spent on university research and overhead and seldom focus directly on helping the creatures of our concern. Dedicated individuals like David Wingate play key roles in helping form sound conservation programs. He was not bogged down with endless committee meetings or the need for interagency reports; he spent his days working on the problems. His half century of effort to bring the species back from the verge of extinction became a personal, and successful, mission. In the end we will see that it isn't the science or the laws and regulations of agencies that save species, though they are important tools, it's the passion of individuals that understand the reality of situations and actually do the work that turns the tide. The birds' presence in the Gulf Stream resulted in a bond between two seabird conservationists living in different countries. Over time, the numbers of reported sightings off the Carolina coast had continued to increase, in part because of an increasing population and in part because of a growing interest in the Bermuda petrel and other pelagic seabirds. Cahows are feathered legends that defied all odds. They don't understand international boundaries or the confinement of small islands, they are simply citizens of our world. And David Wingate does not understand aging and retirement. In his mid-70s he is still out there working with the cahows, timing the wave surges to jump from his old Boston Whaler onto rocky ledges at night, still compelled to check on his petrels. Our world needs more David Wingates.

CHAPTER 8 THE LOON CRAZE

Up until 1950, the annual spring loon shoot on Shackleford Banks of North Carolina was a celebrated local tradition. Though it represents what was probably one of the last vestiges of organized market gunning in this country, the hunt was also a social gathering, driven by Harkers Islanders' fondness for eating greasy, fishy-tasting loons. Despite the complete protection of loons by the Migratory Bird Treaty Act of 1918, for years the hunt itself remained a blatantly illegal, but deeply ingrained, social family outing.

The hunt was something the community looked forward to each year and was key to the local welcoming of spring as is the return of swallows to San Juan Capistrano in Orange County, California. School was even let out so that daughters could assist their mothers in preparing sandwiches and pies and young children could participate by gathering up the fallen loons and piling them high while fathers and sons dropped migrating loons until the barrels of their 12 gauges were too hot to hold.

Wildlife law-enforcement agents were frustrated. The exact date of the early-May hunt varied from year to year and always remained a well-kept secret. Throughout the hunt, someone was always on watch for law officers approaching by boat from the mainland. In 1950, the U.S. Fish and Wildlife Service placed an undercover agent in the community. Hired as a local schoolteacher, he came to be accepted by the residents in the months that followed. With inside information as to the day of the big hunt, 11 federal and state wildlife agents snuck ashore during the night and waited for dawn. Thirty minutes into the hunt, the wildlife officers emerged from their hiding spots in the dunes. More than 100 unsuspecting residents were rounded up, and though over 200 loons had already been shot, only 50 dead loons were taken as evidence. Seventy-eight of the men were formally charged, convicted in federal court, and fined $25 each.

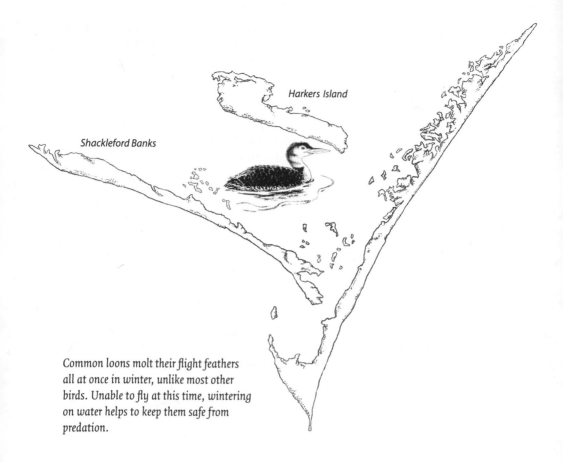

Common loons molt their flight feathers all at once in winter, unlike most other birds. Unable to fly at this time, wintering on water helps to keep them safe from predation.

Cooking the "Harkers Island Turkey" was done outside and took up most of a day. The loon meat was soaked in water with salt or baking soda and then browned with salt pork. The meal was stewed down to a thick gravy with onions, potatoes, rutabagas, and cornmeal dumplings. Old-time residents insist that the bird's fishy taste is barely discernable, and the hardy group of "fisher folk" on the island preferred a "loon-in-the-pot" to a goose or a duck.

The Harkers Island fishermen also historically carved the leg and wing bones of loons into fishing lures. These bone lures were used for trolling for bluefish and Spanish mackerel in the waters in southeastern North Carolina. The part of the leg used was not what protrudes from the bird's body but the longer tibiotarsus (drumstick). Loon bones, much heavier than those of ducks and geese, hold up better to being dragged through the water. Locally, these were the lures of choice up to about World War II, when, over time, they were replaced by metal spoons and other commercially made trolling devices.

Loon hunting was not limited to a single place, nor did it just occur on a single day. The North Carolina tradition dated back to at least the mid-1800s, and the Harkers Island "sport" was reported to have been a part of the region's culture since the earliest days of people living on Shackleford Banks. Once the residents of these Banks moved to Harkers Island following a major hurricane in 1899, the former was used primarily as pasture for horses and cattle. Yet the spring loon hunt continued to take place on the Banks, and the local folks considered it an important ritual. On days of the big shoots the men would go out to the Banks and space themselves along the eight and a half miles of beachfront so that there was no place that a loon could fly without being in range of at least one of the hunters. People recall that the daybreak shooting "was as good of an alarm clock as you could ask for." One morning during World War II, the shooting was so consistent that the residents thought there was an enemy invasion. Each hunter shot up to 18 loons, a limit enforced only by the maximum number of birds a hunter could carry back to his boat.

An editorial in a local paper appeared soon after the wildlife agents' raid suggesting that the overregulation of hunting resulted from the attitudes of "fancy upstate sportsmen." The account went on to defend the hunters and regretted that they were deprived of "the only exciting sport left untouched by the law. Their fathers had done it, their grandfathers before, even before their forefathers had moved from the outer banks. You weren't a man until you had shot a loon." People were addicted to the sport, and in later years it was not the meat but the sport and the tradition that kept people coming back. While these hunts are now a thing of the past, for years after the raid, a number of hunters were further enticed by the additional challenge of shooting loons and not getting caught.

The raid effectively ended this mass exploitation of loons, a species that is recovering slowly, if at all, from indiscriminate slaughter. Loons have a life span of 20 to 30 years or more. Like most long-lived animals, they have a modest reproductive rate—an average of a mere 0.5 young successfully raised annually per mated pair—and a non-reproductive adolescence that typically lasts for four years. Over time, natural mortality in the population is balanced by the longevity of the parents. The problem with this life-history strategy is that it works well only when populations are relatively stable. A higher-than-normal mortality of adults in a single season can take decades to correct. Still, the amount of actual damage done by the annual loon hunts was minor compared to the conservation issues that common loons presently face. It's a double-barreled problem that hits loons both on their northern breeding lakes and in their marine wintering areas.

⤚

The loon's common name does not refer to the moon or "luna," as one might suppose, nor is it based on the bird's lunatic-like vocalizations. The name instead arises from the Old Scandinavian "loom," meaning awkward or clumsy. On land, the birds move very awkwardly because their legs sit far back on the body. Additionally, loons are the only birds whose legs are encased in their bodies down to the ankle joint. Their feet and flattened leg bones stick out behind like twin propellers. While this makes them excellent swimmers, they're blundering clowns on land.

A story passed down by the Micmac Indians of eastern Canada tells of a time when loons lived on land. One was so tame that it had the run of the village. But it clumsily ran in and out of wigwams, knocking over belongings and spilling bowls of food and drink. When the people could stand it no longer, they caught the rascal and threatened to kill him. The loon thought quickly and begged its vindictive captors to throw him into the fire and not into the cold deep lake. They responded by throwing him into the lake and were surprised to hear the loon laughing "just what I wanted, just what I wanted" as it swam away. I wonder if Joel Chandler Harris knew of this legend when he wrote about Br'er Rabbit and the briar patch?

Clear-water lakes and ponds are the summer home of the common loon. It is here that loons raise their young and sing their eerie, drawn-out call note, "ah-ooooooo-aah."

The cry is loud, rising in the middle and falling toward the end. Loons have a number of calls, yodels, laughs, and wails that they use in courtship—vocalizations that fathered the expression "crazy as a loon." But it is the long nocturnal cry of the loon and the ensuing silence that exemplifies the peaceful yet lonely spirit of the North Woods.

The common loon is one of five living species of loons, all members of a closely related, distinct order of diving birds confined to the Northern Hemisphere. They are designed for swimming and diving to depths up to 240 feet. Loons can sink slowly under the water without leaving a ripple by expelling air from their lungs and from under their feathers. Their high specific gravity—an indicator of density and buoyancy—comes in part from solid, heavy bones, which are not hollow like those of chickens and other birds.

Loons also have special blood and body chemistry that makes them resistant to toxic carbon dioxide, allowing them to remain submerged for long periods. Half their day is spent swimming and diving for food—small fish mostly, although in rare instances they feast on fish up to 18 inches long. These larger meals are brought to the surface, but loons suck up smaller fish underwater like swimming pool vacuum cleaners.

Over the last 30 years, I have regularly spotted individuals and small groups of wintering common loons 20 to 35 miles from shore, in waters ranging from 100 to 3,000 feet deep. The birds swim and dive to avoid the path of our boat, sometimes remaining submerged for 3 to 3½ minutes only to reappear 50 yards or more from where they were previously seen. While studies conducted on freshwater lakes show loons' average diving times to be less than a minute, the birds dive for longer periods out at sea, when they are catching fish deep in the water column.

Ocean currents transport loons resting on the surface to oceanic fronts where currents converge. These zones are richer and more productive than the random places that the loons might pick for themselves. At these oceanic frontal boundaries, the loons forage efficiently. A colleague of mine calculated the various densities of loons over the continental shelf of the southeastern United States, finding that approximately 200,000 loons winter in the Atlantic between Cape Hatteras and Georgia. This represents 30 to 40 percent of the species' total population. These large concentrations make the region one of the looniest places on earth.

⌣

Man's altering of habitats no longer allows for a wealth of natural and undisturbed communities. Highly specialized species such as loons are among the first species to be affected because they depend on key seasonal habitats that are degrading simultaneously in different geographic regions of the loon's range.

On their summer lakes and ponds up north, loons face growing pressure from summer recreational activities. People seeking wilderness experiences are drawn to the same remote, clear-water lakes and ponds that are the traditional nesting sites of the common loon. Disturbances at the inland lakes from camping, canoeing, family outings, motorboat traffic, summer cottages, seaplanes, and weekend fishermen all take their toll. To some extent, nesting loons are able to become conditioned to the presence of people, but personal watercraft and nests are usually incompatible. The problem is compounded by a sudden influx of vacationers in late May as the end of the school year, Memorial Day, and, in Canada, the Victoria Day celebration occur almost simultaneously with a particularly critical moment in the life cycle of loons. By late May, adults have just started their nesting cycle and are likely to desert their eggs if disturbed.

Oil spills on lakes, even minor spills, also present a real problem for loons. The birds are constantly in the water, and they react instinctively to any approaching problem—a boat or an oil slick—by diving. Even a small amount of oil on a loon's plumage is usually fatal. The oil-fouled feathers no longer provide adequate insulation, and loons will not climb out of the water to dry out. Attempting to preen the oil from their feathers, they introduce damaging oil and tars into their digestive tracks. Oil spills at sea can be fatal to large numbers of loons. Over the years, I have tried on a number of occasions to clean oil out of a loon's feathers—it's a time-consuming job, and the survival rate is not encouraging. Usually, I've ended up with a really dirty bathtub and a small pile of dead loons. The 2010 BP oil spill in the Gulf was particularly hard on loons, and the dispersants used as part of the cleanup process were probably as detrimental to the loons as the oil itself.

In both their breeding and wintering grounds, loons frequently tangle in monofilament line and get caught in commercial fishing nets and traps. The number of loons accidentally caught and drowned will never be known. When I first came to the North Carolina State Museum in Raleigh, a Chowan River fisherman made me aware of this problem, and I thought that salvaging the drowned loons would be a good way to increase the holdings of our scientific collection. I soon realized the fishermen were reluctant to save the dead birds. They feared that documenting the problem would result in additional regulations, which would have an economic impact on their livelihood. Forty years later the story remains pretty much the same: state fisheries and NOAA continue to have a number of ongoing programs to study the problem, but there is no indication that a fix is in the works.

Shoreline development of northern lakes and ponds causes more problems. Long-term owners of private cabins may be aware of the loon's need for privacy, but visitors to summer camps, resorts, and commercial campgrounds usually are not. In addition to human disturbance, the filling-in of shorelines and the building of retaining walls eliminates prime nesting habitats. Even in relatively undisturbed lakes, studies show that loon reproductive success decreases in areas near summer cottages. Development has the secondary effect of increasing, or at least concentrating, predators of loon eggs and chicks—crows, ravens, gulls, and raccoons, all of which are attracted to human habitation because of the garbage they can scavenge and handouts from well-meaning summer visitors. If that's not enough there's yet another issue—lead weights lost by fishermen. In lakes heavily fished by sportsmen, loons often pick up lost lead sinkers from the bottom and add them to the gizzard stones they collect to aid in milling and digesting food. The sinkers become abraded in the birds' stomachs and lead released into tissues can be lethal.

Acid rain is a problem on northern lakes. Where severe acidification has occurred, the lakes are dead. In those less severely hit, the fish populations crash and the loons feed their young on newts and crayfish. Young fledglings grow well for the first two weeks, but then weaken and die from lack of an adequate diet. On acidified lakes, the dive times of the adults are longer, suggesting a greater time needed to find and capture food. Acid lakes also create chemical changes, increasing the release rate of mercury into the water, which allows an accelerated uptake through the food chain.

‿

Like other long-lived aquatic birds at the top of their food chains, loons accumulate environmental pollutants in their tissues. Winter loon die-offs are now common along the southeastern coast; as many as 7,000 to 8,000 loons died on the Gulf coast of Florida in 1983. The precise causes of these mass deaths are often hard to pinpoint, but symptoms and tissue analysis point to mercury imported in the bird's own tissues from northern lakes. Mercury apparently affects the rods in the loons' eyes and decreases their ability to hunt. As the loons starve, additional industrial contaminants stored in their fat reserves are released into tissues, compounding the problem. The loons eventually become so weakened that they can no longer hold up their heads, and they drown. If this is not bad enough, loons are also likely the victims of the buildup of biotoxins in the food chain. Marine biotoxins are sometimes produced by massive blooms of bacteria and of phytoplankton (including dinoflagellates and diatoms). We mostly hear about these events when mass fish kills are reported or shellfish beds are suddenly closed by "red tides." Biologists studying mass die-offs of loons along the Atlantic and Gulf coasts usually have no precise explanation as to the cause. It is likely that the different die-off events have different causes, and the cumulative effect of a number of unrelated problems cannot be ruled out.

‿

Loons have the least wing surface in proportion to their weight of any flying bird and have trouble getting airborne. On a number of occasions folks have brought me loons that were found in shopping center parking lots and similar places. The birds had landed at night, mistakenly thinking they had found open water. These well-intentioned people logically believed the birds were injured because they could not fly. Even with a complete complement of feathers, loons are incapable of taking off without a running start over open water. They splatter across the surface—half flying, half running. Depending on wind conditions, this requires a runway of 25 yards to a quarter of a mile. The cure for the parking lot loons was simple: I took them to the nearest open body of water and turned 'em loose. The birds would swim from shore for a few yards and get a running start. The little extra lift from their momentum would be just enough to get them airborne.

Each year loons are totally incapable of flight for many weeks. Unlike most birds that molt and replace their flight feathers a few at a time so that they are always able to fly, loons molt their entire primary and secondary wing feathers all at once. This extreme adaptation for feather replacement stems from the loons' poor wing-loading ratios. Loons are heavy birds that are well adapted for their aquatic lifestyles, but they are poor flyers even under the best of circumstances. Because molting loons are incapable of flight, it is advantageous for them to replace all their flight feathers simultaneously and get it over with, getting through the molting business as efficiently as possible. Not only do loons have an atypical style of molting, but they also time it differently than most birds. Because of where they live in the summer, it would be highly likely that a badly timed molt would find them stranded on far-northern lakes, where cold nights would leave them icebound. Because of this, loons renew their flight feathers in their at-sea wintering grounds. To us it seems strange that these birds have evolved to be totally flightless when wintering at sea, sometimes far at sea, but really this is their best survival strategy.

Not that they would actually freeze in the ice, but they would be no more able to take flight from an ice-covered lake than they would from wet shopping center asphalt. Don't think of them as helpless birds bobbing on the surface of the open wintery ocean. Loons are powerful swimmers and quite at home in aquatic environments. Their large bodies, solid bones, and oddly placed, large, webbed feet might get in the way of flight and even walking about, but they have their advantages.

⌣

As the days grow longer, a loon's urge to propagate grows stronger. With feathers renewed and a winter spent fueling up on abundant marine fishes, a loon's spring impulse to migrate northward begins to stir.

The late Harry Davis, a former director of the North Carolina State Museum and a Buxton, N.C., native, studied the pattern of spring loon migration at Cape Lookout. He found that the loons migrated in from the south at night. Coming in over the sea, they became confused by Shackleford Banks jutting out to sea and splashed down. They sat on the ocean through the remainder of the night. But at first light, when the birds could make out land, the loons resumed their flight, with many of them shortcutting above Shackleford Banks. It was at this very point that they were intercepted by the Harkers Island gunners. Harry Davis liked to tell people that you could always tell a loon-eating Harkers Islander by the grease streaks in their underwear.

The Great Loon Shooters Roundup of the 1950s was a clear victory for wildlife enforcement, though certainly an event of more than minor benefit to loons, but it also enacted the loss of a longstanding coastal tradition. The islanders felt betrayed and were furious, but the counterfeit schoolteacher had packed his belongings and was long gone before the raid. There are many people still alive who recall the event, and many who participated in it as children still live on Harkers Island. Are they bitter and resentful of the laws forced on Down Easters by outsiders? Do they feel betrayed by an agent pretending to be part of their community? You bet they do. But these are people of strong tradition, and humor remains a valued part of this tradition. They still tell the story of the great raid. They never knew his real name, but the mock schoolteacher remains affectionately known to old-time Harkers Islanders as the Loon Ranger.

CHAPTER 9 CHICKENS, SAILOR GULLS, WITCHES, AND DEVILS

Over the years there have been a number of occasions when reporters have contacted me wanting background information about large numbers of dead and dying seabirds that had washed ashore. The events were always in early summer just as the tourist season was picking up, so there was considerable public concern as people logically assumed that the massive die-offs were related to some type of pollution. The birds involved were always greater shearwaters, and often their wave-washed corpses would litter the coastline for miles, sometimes washing birds ashore along beaches in several states simultaneously. It was not a yearly occurrence, and the reported die-offs ranged from a few hundred birds to estimates of many thousands. The calls and emails came from beachfront communities ranging from Florida all the way up to Virginia. One year, thousands of dead shearwaters were reported from beaches extending from South Carolina to the lower Delmarva Peninsula. The questions were always the same: "What's causing this?" and "What can we do about it?"

For years media reports suggested that scientists were alarmed and feared that these massive die-offs resulted from some unknown ecological disaster. These concerns were widely circulated over the Internet, and various research institutions encouraged people to salvage the dead birds so that they could be examined for contaminates and other signs that might explain the die-offs. Many causes had been suggested, including mercury poisoning, bacterial infections, and H5N1 avian flu. Necropsies of the dead shearwaters revealed little more than that the birds were very emaciated.

To dissect the problem it is first necessary to know something about greater shearwaters. There are dozens of other species of seabirds occurring off the Atlantic coast in June and they were not ever recorded in these die-off events. So it had to be something related to the biology of this one species of shearwater. Over the years, various wildlife rescue centers had saved dead shearwaters for our museum's collection. Looking back through these specimens showed all of them to be immature birds that had hatched

When flocks of Wilson's storm-petrels feed, they delicately patter on the water surface, appearing to walk on water.

that year. Looking at their weights suggested that all had probably starved, as their weights were far below those of healthy birds. For years captains of the Hatteras fishing fleet had told me about hungry shearwaters going after baits they trolled behind their boats. The mates would pull in the lines as soon as they encountered the birds in an attempt to prevent them from swallowing the hooks and entangling the lines. A boiling mad shearwater with a hook halfway down its throat is not easy to handle. Nearly every such encounter I personally witnessed involved a greater shearwater, and while I could not be sure they were first-year birds, by looking at their feathering I could see that they were definitely not adults.

Greater shearwaters are transequatorial migrants. They nest on islands in the sub-Antarctic off the tip of South America during its summer and then wisely depart to the Northern Hemisphere to enjoy our summer. For the most part they "summer" on the Grand Banks of Newfoundland, where long days produce vast plankton blooms that support massive numbers of fish that forage in the cool surface water. Nevertheless, modest numbers of these shearwaters occur off the southeastern Atlantic states throughout the warmer months; the Gulf Stream supports both migrant and summering individuals from May through November. While the bulk of the spring migration occurs along the outer continental shelf, much of the southward fall migration is over the mid- and eastern Atlantic.

Though the entire breeding population is restricted to just three small islands off the Falklands, the species is quite common, with a population in excess of six million nesting pairs. The average age of maturity and first breeding is believed to be between six and seven years, and survivorship from hatching to breeding age for similar species of shearwaters that have been intensively studied is 25 to 35 percent. Thus, the number of immature birds at any given time is likely to be far greater than the total adult population. These figures suggest that at any given time the greater shearwater population probably exceeds 20 million individuals.

Like many other pelagic birds, greater shearwaters produce but a single egg each year. After raising their chicks, the adults depart the nesting area and start to head north in April and May. The fledglings are well fed and actually weigh considerably more than their parents by the time the adults depart. The young shearwaters spend weeks alone at their nest sites shedding down feathers and exercising their wings. They do not begin to head north until sometime between May and early summer. Thus, the northward-bound young birds depart almost a full month after the adults.

Given the timing of the die-offs and the age and weight of the dead birds, I've concluded that the die-offs are most likely linked to the stress of northward migration. In order for the birds to reach the North Atlantic, it is necessary for them to cross the Doldrums, the same windless equatorial seas that in the past stranded large sailing ships for weeks on end. The shearwaters are dependent on winds for migration and the belt of low barometric pressure that often remains unaffected by both the northeast trade winds and the southeast ones in the Southern Hemisphere can create a virtual no-fly zone for some seabirds.

The influence of the trade winds in equatorial regions can be identified by, or measured by, decreased salinity, seawater density, surface evaporation, and barometric pressure, with increased precipitation and air and water temperatures. Combinations of these factors can increase or decrease the extent of the area affected. In the western Atlantic, the northern trade winds seldom extend south of northern South America. The winds of the Southern Hemisphere shift from south to north as the Northern Hemisphere spring changes into summer. At their peak, the northern extent of these winds occasionally influences Northern Hemisphere seas as far north as coastal Venezuela. During the remainder of the year this region is under a prevailing calm. The axis of this calm zone separating the trade winds of the two hemispheres is actually a few degrees above the equator. In that the northern shift of the southern winds does not begin until the northern migration of the shearwaters is already underway, any variation in timing or magnitude could result in many of the birds being forced to cross the Doldrums while the calm zone is still wide.

The problem of a seasonally enhanced low-latitude no-fly zone is made worse by a general lack of food resources for surface-foraging seabirds. The warm surface waters of the tropics hold little oxygen. Accordingly, measurements of plankton in the upper 150 feet of the western Atlantic are at their lowest between latitudes 10° N and 20° S. The westward-flowing Atlantic Equatorial and Brazilian Currents turn sharply to the north and south, respectively, in this same general area, thereby eliminating current edges and other opportunities for the formation of oceanic fronts along which the birds could feed. These windless conditions deplete the bird's energy reserves as the combinations of limited food resources, extra demands needed for flight, and increased time needed to travel through the area take their toll on the shearwaters. The result is shearwaters in stressed and starved conditions when they reach the patchy resources of the temperate North Atlantic. While it is not unusual for birds to have high mortality in hatching-year age groups, the seasonal mass die-offs that have been reported suggest that in this species they result from the instinctive timing of the young birds' departure as it relates to yearly variations in equatorial weather patterns.

While an explanation for the die-offs is now available, the real question is whether this is a problem resulting from human activities. While the Doldrums themselves are clearly a weather condition of natural occurrence, it seems strange that a bird would develop a migration pattern that would regularly put a significant proportion of its population at risk. Prior to the 1960s, a Florida-based ornithologist was able to document only 22 records of the species for the entire southeastern region, and most of these were of individuals that washed ashore here and there between 1879 and 1962. Greater shearwaters were considered to be of rare occurrence and museum curators were eager to get the beached specimens for their collections. Yet, the dates of collection were mostly outside the June period when the die-offs normally occur, and the majority were of single birds driven ashore during late-summer and fall hurricanes. The first die-off event was reported in the 1960s, and in subsequent decades the number of these events has continued to increase. Is global climate change affecting the weather patterns within the region of the Doldrums? It's hard to say, but something has changed and perhaps we would be too complacent if we simply regarded the shearwater mortality as a naturally occurring event. At what point will the change in ratios of surviving young, future shearwater generations, to those of the adults begin to affect the long-term stability of this bird's population?

＜

Like many second-generation charter-boat captains, Harry Baum, and his father before him, called all shearwaters "sailor gulls." He did not actually differentiate between any of the species of shearwaters, petrels, or fulmars; they were all simply sailor gulls. The smaller storm-petrels were "chickens." This chicken reference was obviously an abbreviated reference to Mother Carey's chickens, a name that was once used by sailors for all the various storm-petrels. Mother Carey is simply a corruption of Mater Cara, one of the many epithets of Maria, the Divine Virgin, and the guardian of all seamen. The Portuguese and Spanish, the first Westerners to venture on the high seas, named the birds based on their surface pattering and the appearance that they walked on water. Their name, petrel, is a religious reference to St. Peter, who walked on water with the Savior's help. To people totally unfamiliar with this history, there is the potential for confusion with the marketing strategy of referring to canned tuna as "chicken of the sea." While the simplified terminology of sailor gulls and chickens hardly does justice to such taxonomically diverse groups as the petrels and storm-petrels, it does show that both early sailors and modern-day charter-boat captains know the difference between these birds and gulls and terns.

The effortless flight of the "chickens" and sailor gulls sets them apart from the other species that occur over the Gulf Stream. For the most part they appear to glide on outstretched wings, with an occasional flutter when they need to make a change in direction or other major adjustment. These birds use only 9 to 13 percent of the energy needed by gulls for sustained flight. They come here from nesting grounds throughout the Atlantic basin. Some come from breeding sites that are relatively close by, such as the Bahamas and coastal Canada, but many come from distant places in the eastern and tropical Atlantic and, like the greater shearwater, the sub-Antarctic.

Let's take a look at these "chickens." There are a number of species that occur off the Outer Banks, and for the most part they are small, black, long-winged birds with white butts. Of the seven species documented to occur off our Atlantic coast, Wilson's storm-petrels are by far the most abundant. In fact, they are considered to be the most common bird in the world. I liked to tell Captain Baum this, and then add "well except for chickens." Actually, domestic chickens are clearly the most common avian species, there are a reported 1.3 billion of them just in our U.S. factory farms, but this additional fact neither amused nor confused Harry Baum, and usually in half an hour or less he would point out another flock of "chickens" off the port bow that he thought I might have overlooked. Despite their abundance, storm-petrels are seldom seen from shore, and even during major storms they are the least likely pelagic seabird to be blown inland or even to wash up on a beach. This is because they seldom fly more than a few feet above the sea, and are therefore not easily blown about by gales and hurricanes. They are actually sheltered by the waves; they ride the less turbulent air as they fly up and back within the wave troughs. The larger, high-flying petrels and shearwaters are much more likely to show up as beached storm wrecks, and sometimes they are even transported many miles inland within the eye of fall hurricanes.

The early naming of the storm-petrels had much to with their style of flight and their behavior. To the open-sea sailors who first proposed the names of petrels and Mother Carey's chickens, these storm-petrels were familiar birds, commonly following in the wake of ships. In light winds, they seem to drift just above the ocean's surface and can, when conditions are right, go for hundreds of yards without a single wingbeat. On outstretched wings, they patter their long legs and webbed feet across the sea surface, giving them the appearance of walking on water. As they skip along the surface, they give vigorous kicks whenever their feet touch the water. When they feed, they almost stand upright, their long legs keeping them well above the surface. The storm-petrels lock their wings and face into the wind as they extend their webbed feet into the water, the extra drag slowing them from being quickly pushed backward by the wind. Their alternate gliding and fluttering make Wilson's storm-petrels easy to distinguish from the other species of "chickens" occurring off our coast.

The incredible abundance of Wilson's storm-petrels is a direct result of their varied diets and feeding behaviors. They dine on creatures from various levels of the marine food chain and are efficient scavengers. Throwing almost any food item overboard is likely to attract them and even a spoonful of mayonnaise can bring dozens to the stern of a boat. They are quickly attracted to oily slicks, picking up the odors coming from upwind, and zigzagging back and forth into the wind until they locate the source. This behavior works well when schools of fish are feeding as they can efficiently hone in on the scraps. Cleaning fish at sea always attracts them, and in former days the numbers of Mother Carey's chickens reported to be swarming around whaling ships as the catch was being processed is legendary. While these birds are primarily surface feeders, they can dive to depths of several times their length to secure a sinking tidbit. They also forage on plankton, small crustaceans, squids, and fish. One of their major foods is oceanic waxes stored in the bodies of marine copepods, minute crustaceans. While a number of the copepods on which the storm-petrels feed are deep-water species, the adults can live at depths of over 1,200 feet. During the summer period when Wilson's storm-petrels are off our coast, the younger stages of the copepods move to the surface and feed on phytoplankton. The triglycerides and fats stored in the copepods are a key element of the pelagic community food chain. The waxes in some of these copepods can actually make up 70 percent of the creature's weight. Because of this diet, the tissues of Wilson's storm-petrels are extremely oily. Prior to the availability of electricity, sailors would gather up disoriented and dead storm-petrels that crashed onto the decks on foggy nights. Sticking a wick in their bill, the seamen made use of the volunteer candles. The oils in their bodies would burn for hours, providing light for the dreary below-deck quarters.

During the late spring and summer, Wilson's storm-petrels were by far the most common seabird encountered during my surveys. There were usually hundreds of individuals seen on any given day, and it was not unheard of to see 500 or more. On many days, their total numbers exceeded all other species combined. This situation is not unique to North Carolina. Between May and early September up and down the entire Atlantic coast this is typically the most abundant seabird.

All of the Wilson's storm-petrels nesting colonies are on islands in the sub-Antarctic, yet once their nesting chores are completed they head north, avoiding the winter of the Southern Hemisphere while taking advantage of the Northern Hemisphere's summer. While this bird nests across the ring of circumpolar Antarctic islands, for some reason they are far less common in the Pacific. In the western North Atlantic they are primarily found in the Gulf Stream, but they commonly range north to Canadian waters. Talk about frequent-flyer miles!

Nearly all of the Wilson's storm-petrels encountered off eastern North

America are adults. The younger birds, distinguished by whitish feathers on their foreheads and white borders on the feathering of their bellies, are all but absent. This of course raises the question, where do the young birds go during their first year or so? The adults undergo a complete feather replacement while they are summering in the North Atlantic. The molting process is rapid and is usually completed by mid-August to September, prior to their southward migration. The molting process not only replaces old feathers with new ones prior to their 8,000-plus-mile journey home, but it also partly rids them of various feather parasites. In the late 1970s I had a University of North Carolina student working for me who did his PhD work on external parasites of Wilson's storm-petrels. He compared their parasite loads to the bird's age, sex, date of collection, and wing molt sequence. He found varying numbers of four species of feather lice and three feather mites. This is of interest because the different parasite species live on different areas of their host. One of the feather mites lives near the end of the wings' long flight feathers. These particular mites make their living feeding off the diatoms (minute plankton) that get caught up in the feathers when the tips of the bird's wings dip into the sea. For the small fare of keeping the storm-petrel's primary feathers from being encrusted with diatoms, the mites get taxied all over the Atlantic.

～

Petrels are yet another group of specialized seabirds and in the course of my studies I discovered a number of them off North Carolina. None of the four species I was seeing were known to occur with regularity off our coast and several were essentially unknown from the western North Atlantic. The most commonly occurring one was the black-capped petrel. This species nests only in the Antilles, and we now know that they normally range at sea from Brazil to North Carolina. These petrels are uncommon in the Gulf of Mexico and appear to be uncommon in areas of the Atlantic not directly influenced by the Gulf Stream. This was the only species of seabird that I could see with regularity any month of the year, yet, except when displaced by tropical storms, they, like other pelagic seabirds, are almost never seen from land. Like the other petrels and albatrosses, they are strong, swift aerialists. While nesting and feeding chicks in the Caribbean, many individuals commute over 1,000 nautical miles to reach the productive foraging areas off North Carolina.

These comings and goings between sea and land are in and of themselves interesting events. As biologists, we get very curious as to exactly how these movements take place for particular populations. For example, the black-capped petrel is today a rare seabird that we see off our coast, but in the colonial period we know that it once nested on at least four islands in the Greater and Lesser Antilles. Within the historic period, these petrels were known to nest on Hispaniola, Martinique, Guadeloupe, and Dominica. Pre-Columbian man, and then later European colonists and their slaves, ate these birds on a regular basis. Populations were rapidly depleted, and today these petrels are known to nest only in scattered isolated sites in the mountains of Hispaniola. Other factors, all resulting from European contact, also led to the species' demise. The major issues were the introduction of predatory mammals such as dogs, rats, pigs, and mongooses, as well as deforestation and habitat destruction.

This species was once a superabundant part of the Caribbean landscape and is deeply ingrained in the history of the Antilles. At the time of European contact, black-capped petrels were still abundant. Deposits of sub-fossils found in caves in Haiti as well as the writings of naturalists from the 1700s tell us that at one time there were hundreds of thousands, perhaps even a few million, breeding pairs. People in the Antilles were protein deficient, and the birds were considered a necessity as well as a delicacy. As a consequence, these petrels were hunted throughout their winter and spring nesting season. Often, dogs were used to locate their nesting burrows. Enterprising French colonists on Dominica commercially exploited great quantities of petrels, exporting them to other French colonies in the Antilles. Into the 1960s, Haitian peasants built large bonfires near the nesting cliffs to obtain birds. Disoriented by the light, the petrels circled like moths into the flames, where they were captured, efficiently cooked on the spot, and eaten. That practice has mostly stopped, but only because the petrels are now so uncommon that the climb up the mountain is no longer worthwhile.

In 1724, Père Labat, a priest, provided an account of the bird's exploitation on Guadeloupe. "Those who read these memoirs will be surprised that we should eat birds for Lent; but the missionaries who are in these islands, and who [in] many matters exercise the power of bishops, after serious deliberation and consolation of a medical man, have declared that lizards and diablotins are vegetable food, and that consequently they may be eaten at all times." Diablotin is the name used for these petrels on the Creole-, French-, and Spanish-speaking islands. The name translated to "little devil," and is derived from the nocturnal cries the birds make while flying over their nesting colonies.

For some time, the bird was believed to actually be extinct, but active nesting colonies were discovered in remote mountainous regions of Haiti in the early 1960s. The discovery was made by none other than David Wingate, his knowledge of the nesting habits of the similar Bermuda petrel allowing him to figure out how to go about finding these petrels at their nests. It was a logical assumption, and probably a correct one, that the black-capped petrels I was seeing over the Gulf Stream were from this breeding population. But the question of their actual origin arose when fishermen reported hearing "brujas," or witches, off the southeastern coast of Cuba. In 1977, Nicasio Vina Bales, a biologist with the Cuban Academy of Sciences, following up on the tales of eerie sounds, added a new dimension to what was known of these birds. It turns out the strange vocal array was coming from petrels that were feeding just off the Cuban coast. Shortly after Vina wrote up his findings and shared this with one of the Cuban newspapers, the story was picked up by James Bond, a prominent ornithologist working at the Philadelphia Academy of Sciences. (Ian Fleming found his name while searching through documents pertaining to the West Indies and later borrowed it for his 007 character.) Dr. Bond had been working for years on an annotated checklist of the birds found in the West Indies and, sometime after learning of Vina's discovery, in his 22nd installment, he reported that black-capped petrels nested in the Sierra Maestra in southeastern Cuba.

The black-capped petrels I was encountering off North Carolina actually represented two plumage types, and later, through DNA studies, we learned that they are genetically different. Could it be that I was seeing petrels from both Hispaniola and Cuba? I made several trips to Cuba to try to confirm that the birds were nesting there, timing my visits to correspond with the onset of their early winter nesting. Their protracted incubation periods and the extended time it takes them to raise their chicks forces them to begin nesting earlier than other seabirds. This early nesting allows them to complete their nesting duties prior to the hurricane season. Together, Dr. Vina and I worked the coastal area where he had first found the birds. While we did see petrels at sea, we were unable to confirm that they were flying inland and nesting. The petrels may nest here, but the mountain range is vast, sparsely populated, and for the most part inaccessible. Since my visits in the early 1990s, several others have tried to verify nesting, but the Sierra Maestra is not giving up its secrets. Documenting a breeding population here would be a very important piece of information for planning the long-range conservation of this highly endangered seabird. I am currently working on obtaining DNA samples from the birds Vina collected in the 1970s, and we can see how they match up with our North Carolina series.

The sailor gulls, chickens, and witches, or shearwaters, storm-petrels, and petrels if you must, are all members of a distinct order of highly pelagic marine birds. They differ from gulls, terns, and other familiar species in a number of features, but the most noticeable one is their tube-like nostrils. The distinctive fused tubes extend out onto the bill. Excess salt is regulated through their kidney excretion, but when seawater intake is high, salt glands associated with these nostrils can eliminate 69 percent of the salt buildup in their bodies—a nice built-in appliance for creatures living far at sea. These birds are long lived—some may take 8–10 years to reach adulthood and come ashore only to nest. Pairs will occupy the same burrows for years. They lay only one egg per year and, like black-capped petrels, have extended incubation and fledgling periods. At their nesting grounds they are nocturnal, and many species, because of exploitation by humans and introduced predators, are also now restricted to inaccessible island nesting sites.

Quite a number of these tube-nosed birds have been discovered off the Carolina coast. Many of them occur quite commonly, depending on the season; others, many of which are rarely encountered in North American waters, are less predictable. Nonetheless, these are species of high demand for birders wanting to obtain as many species as possible for their life list. These tube-nosed birds include rarely encountered petrels, shearwaters, and storm-petrels, as well as two species of albatrosses. Many are ones that are far more likely to be seen in the Gulf Stream off Cape Hatteras than any place else in the North Atlantic. Offshore excursions from Cape Hatteras, run exclusively for bird watchers, are timed for the maximum likelihood to encounter these target species. Still it would take hundreds of one-day trips to have any hope of seeing all of them. Most are difficult to identify, but these trips are led by experienced people, and even a few of the boat captains are beginning to recognize that the sailor gulls and chickens come in a number of different flavors.

CHAPTER 10 GETTING TO KNOW
A GALLERY OF GULLS

Gulls are considered ubiquitous in maritime settings. It would be difficult to find a painting of a seascape that does not include the image of at least one seagull flying above a cloud-covered horizon, and every coastal scene on film includes a sound track with the distinctive vocal arrays of gulls. And how many seafood restaurants have we all been in where the restrooms are labeled buoys and gulls? Gulls are seabirds so common that they can also be readily seen mooching french fries in McDonald's parking lots of inland towns. That said, while people think of seagulls in a generic sense, for the most serious of bird watchers they are an interesting and challenging group, as there are a number different species. Some of these are rarely encountered in the eastern states. With proper identification being tricky, many of the rare ones go unreported.

While most bird watchers are lured onto pelagic-bird-finding excursions with the hopes of seeing rare petrels, gulls are actually the perfect birds for both novice and highly experienced watchers interested in species identification. As a group, gulls are common, widely distributed, and come and go at different seasons. They are often relatively tame and easy to approach, and in time, one is bound to encounter rare, out-of-season vagrants. If the number of species wasn't challenging enough, as the birds age, their plumage changes, so age-related wardrobe changes must be committed to memory if you ever hope to tell one gull from another.

When I was asked to teach NOAA observers to identify marine birds caught as by-catch on commercial fishing boats, my advice regarding the gulls was to learn the three to five most common species very well, then, if something different is found, to pull out the books and try to figure it out. There are some basics that help in the sorting process. Different species groups come in distinct sizes—basically, small, medium, and large. Knowing this, one can simply look at a gull and instantly rule out two-thirds of the species known from the western North Atlantic. There are a few where there is some overlap in the size categories, but basically this works. Then, by noting bill and leg color, the presence or absence of tail bands, head patterns,

Seagull identification can be confusing given the variety of seasonal and age-related plumages, at times confounding even the most knowledgeable birders.

and so forth, most of the time-identification choices can be whittled down to two species. When in doubt, assume it is probably the more common of the two gulls. This last piece of advice, while practical and useful to NOAA observers, really frustrates bird watchers, as the driving force behind bird watching is the discovery of new, or at least the most rarely encountered, species.

⤙

With this background in mind, let's first discuss the gulls—the perfect bird group for active birders. Because of their marine and coastal distributions, gulls tend to get around. Although they have a natural sense of direction, many gulls still end up as lost vagrants, displaced by massive weather systems. Others follow active fishing vessels for days and weeks on end and can wind up almost anywhere. While it is unusual to find Pacific-coast or European species along the Atlantic and Gulf coasts of the United States, it's not unheard of. Over the last few decades a number of species that were previously considered as ones of accidental occurrence have been reported almost every year from along the Outer Banks, and both herring gulls and great black-backed gulls, northern species that formerly only wintered in the Carolinas, now nest here. Surprises are the norm, but add to that the challenge of how the hell you tell one species from another and you have the perfect group of birds for experienced birders to sharpen their skills, make unusual finds of the type that will impress other birders, and cause highly heated debates. In addition, the members of the state and national bird records committees can make judgments on the identifications, cases that are not unlike some of the major decisions of the Supreme Court, as everyone is interested in the outcome.

Different species of gulls take different amounts of time to mature. Small gulls become indistinguishable from adults within 13–16 months, when they acquire their second winter plumage. Medium-sized gulls take 25–28 months before they wear the uniforms of the adults, and the largest species, such as glaucous and Iceland gulls, go through a fourth winter plumage and 37–40 months before they look like breeding adults. Serious birders must have an understanding of age terminology and a vocabulary of special terms that relate to feathering on gulls in order to make correct identifications. Flying birds will also look altogether different from those standing about on docks, as totally different field markings are exposed. While the basic field guides do a good job of describing how to differentiate the most common species, you really need to know your stuff before you announce seeing any of the more uncommon species to the skeptical birding world. As if that is not enough, there are different subspecies, some of which look just different enough to make you take a second look and get an outside opinion. And this is just the standard-issue birds! Several species of gulls hybridize, and in several regions the majority of some populations are hybrids. This has caused headaches for ornithologists as well, as birds once described as full species are later proved to be hybrids. As you might guess, there is no place for hybrids on personal life lists, and a number of birders had near fatal meltdowns when birds they had identified and ticked off years before were later recognized to be mere hybrids. The good news for me was that the less common species were seldom found well offshore with only wintering kittiwakes and Bonaparte's gulls regularly taking up residence along the outer continental shelf.

Because of their name, most people logically associate seagulls with the sea. Yet these are also birds often seen on inland lakes, at golf courses, around landfills, and in the parking lots of fast-food restaurants. While most species occur along our coast, they are not necessarily found far at sea. The various marine species tend to occur in predictable zones that can be expressed as distances going out from shore, and only a few wintering gulls actually exploit the open sea. In fact, many gulls seldom venture out of sight of land. For most seabirds these zonal distributions can, in part, be explained by differences in feeding modes, prey availability, and selection. In the case of most gulls, the preference to stay near land is attributable to the physical way in which these birds are put together. You would think, because gulls are such feeding generalists, that they would be able to make a good living all over the ocean. As it turns out, though, gulls in general, and the coastal species in particular, have very inefficient wing-loading ratios when compared to other types of seabirds. The overall weight of their bodies exceeds their wing area to the extent that flight is labored. To commute 35 miles or so to the Gulf Stream and compete for food resources with swifter shearwaters and petrels is not worth the effort. During the winter months, however, when the water in the Stream is so much warmer than the air above it, the heat rising from the surface gives the gulls additional lift, allowing them to soar effortlessly above the surface, and they become regular visitors to the Gulf Stream. Because of this gull invasion, the total number of birds encountered offshore in winter increases dramatically. The application of this flight advantage can be seen clearly while driving across some of our longer coastal bridges. Gulls take advantage of the additional lift provided by winds coming off the supporting structures of the bridge as they glide above the road. This same factor is also directly responsible for the large numbers of gulls that wind up as roadkill on bridges. Sorry, but rules are rules, and dead birds cannot be counted on personal bird life lists.

Like most seabirds, gulls are rather long-lived. Herring gulls are reported to live 15–20 years, a number that may be skewed because so many birds lose the bands that ornithologists use to track individuals. There is a record of one wild herring gull that lived to 30 years, and current literature documents that one captive gull lived for 40 years. The Bible-like bird publication that shared this tidbit overlooked our most famous North Carolina gull, Kaiser. Kaiser died on July 8, 1935, after being kept in an enclosure in Morehead City by Captain John E. Lewis and having attained an age of not less than 49 years. For several years, Kaiser was kept with another herring gull and together they produced two eggs and raised their young to maturity. This long-overlooked account of Kaiser's life can be found in the 1935 issue of *Bird-Lore*.

⤙

I started this chapter with the intention of providing information on gulls and the challenges in identification that they can present. It might be just as informative, though, to also address the nature of bird watchers. So to start off I need to get my nomenclature right. People who are serious about their bird-watching hobby dread the term *bird watcher*, a term that's suggestive of little old ladies who watch cardinals and sparrows land on back-porch bird feeders through kitchen windows, rather than of the adventurous, full-throttled, energetic pursuer of feathered creatures. Such a person is never more than 10 feet away from an array of three or more of the most recent editions of bird field guides. This latter group prefers the term *birders*. To call a true card-carrying member of the American Birding Association a bird watcher is like calling an exotic dancer a stripper—correct but insulting.

I should probably not discuss the little games we'd play with birders and skip the stories of seasickness, but some of them are too funny to omit. One mate that I worked with would stick squid tentacles up his nose and then go talk to seasick birders. On one trip, a lady in the group climbed up to the bridge to talk to the captain. Her husband, she said, was terribly seasick and she wanted us to turn the boat around and head back to shore. It was only about 10:30 in the morning and we still had much of the day ahead of us. She pleaded with the captain, "But he is so sick that he actually wishes he was dead." Big Al looked at me, thought for a moment, and politely said, "Yes ma'am, that's one of the symptoms," as we continued southward along the edge of the Gulf Stream.

And there are other stories that are simply fun to share. Some years back, word got out that there was a black-headed gull hanging out at one of the coastal sewage treatment plants. It had been there for a number of weeks. At the time there were very few reports of this species in the southeast and there were no specimens for North Carolina. After a day or so of thinking about it, I decided it would be important to collect the gull for the museum. With a few calls, I managed to get up with the person running the county treatment plant. I explained who I was and why it was important to obtain the specimen for our museum. We arranged an afternoon for me to drive down there. The bird was surprisingly easy to get, though I had to make a number of casts with a fishing rod to snag it out of the sewage lagoon. No one volunteered to wade in and get it. The facility staff watched in amusement, but eventually I got the bird. As I was preparing to leave, the plant supervisor came over to my car and thanked me. I must have looked a little puzzled, because he explained that bird watchers had been driving his staff nuts. They had been coming from all over the state just to see this bird, and policy prevented him from allowing the general public access to the site. When I inquired how word of its presence had gotten out in the first place, he didn't have an answer, but he said that for the last few weeks people had been sneaking into the plant and his staff was constantly having to run them off. They were on the verge of getting the town's police department involved in issuing trespassing citations.

~

One would assume, given the number of trips we made to the Stream and the many things that can go wrong at sea, that there would be some real adventure stories connected with our marine-bird studies. There are surprisingly few—occasionally the inlet would be fogged in on our return and trying to see the channel markers was a challenge, more than a few boats have run aground or collided with the Bonner Bridge over the years, and, once when I was aboard, Big Al's boat got struck by lightning, but there was no serious damage. There was, however, one very memorable whale-watching trip in the late 1980s. The North Carolina Museum and the North Carolina Aquarium had decided to cosponsor a bird- and whale-watching trip for the public. As one might guess, the majority of the participants were bird watchers hoping to add a few new species to their life lists. The night before the trip, I presented a program at the aquarium to let the folks know what they might expect to see and to give them some background on the natural history of the area we would be visiting. After the presentation, Al, his mate, and I shot pool and drank far too many beers at Drafty's Tavern, an establishment that Al just happened to own. Then, the adventure began.

The next morning, the seas were not calm, but Al knew the *Crystal Dawn* could handle them and we got everyone on board and set out just before dawn. This was Al's other boat, a 69-foot head boat that he used to take people bottom fishing, and which was the perfect size for our 67 eager passengers. By 10:30 we approached the edge of the Stream. Looking about I could see that most of the participants were not feeling well, and several were well into advanced stages of seasickness. I was on the bridge with Al and his mate when a well-plumaged adult pomarine jaeger flew across the stern. I announced the bird's identity over the speaker system but there did not seem to be much interest. The aquarium staff had invited several reporters and a TV camera crew, but they did not respond as they were mostly under the spell of the sea as well. Within a few minutes I spotted a large leatherback sea turtle off the starboard side. It was quite close to the boat and provided good views as it refreshed its lungs with air. This was actually an exciting find for this early in the year, but, again, there was little interest. Several flocks of Bonaparte's gulls could be seen feeding off in the distance. Normally, experienced birders would be carefully scanning the flocks with their binoculars looking for rare species of gulls that might be mixed in with the feeding flock. This time, though, no one was paying the slightest bit of attention, and as we worked farther offshore the swells got higher, the combination of wind and the direction of the current was producing large white caps. Nothing that unusual, but the boat was not riding well—something was wrong.

Al and the mate went down to check things over in the engine room, leaving me to steer. Now, these boats don't exactly have power steering, and I assumed the lack of response from the wheel was a result of my inexperience in running a boat of this size. By the time Al returned to the bridge, any ability to steer the boat had been totally lost. Al reported that a cooling hose had broken loose, and one of the engines had to be shut down to stop it from pumping in more water. Much of the hull was full of water. With little power, there was no way to steer and there was no power to the bilge to pump the water out. We were soon catching waves broadside and eventually the second engine overheated. Except for my wife and Charley Potter, a whale expert from the Smithsonian who I invited along to help lead the trip, no one seemed to be looking for whales and there was no interest in the few birds we were seeing.

By the time we were aware of our predicament we were nearly 40 miles out to sea. Due to the 18-knot winds, all the charter fishing boats had started heading in at least an hour earlier. The only option was to call the Coast Guard. Now the adventure starts to get interesting. Just weeks before, the Reagan administration had seriously cut the budget of the Coast Guard, and as it was a weekend, the on-duty staff had been significantly reduced. Al finally made contact with someone on duty at a Coast Guard station in Norfolk. The radio connection was poor, and Al and the person on the other end, in part due to the static, and in part due to the Coast Guard employee's strong southern accent and Al's Down-East dialect, could barely communicate. We knew there was a problem when he repeatedly referred to our SOS as coming from the "Crystal Gale." Except for my wife Mary, Charley, Al, and myself, everyone on board was now in some stage of seasickness. This included the mate. I went below and got Mary. My wife grew up in a small southern town, and because she had been on enough of these trips to know the drill, she had taken enough Dramamine to remain functional. She did an outstanding job as our radio interpreter. After what seemed like an hour, Mary was finally and absolutely sure that whoever the guy was on the radio got our coordinates and the name of the boat right. Help was on its way.

By late afternoon a Coast Guard helicopter deployed from Elizabeth City was hovering overhead, broadcasting out directions that somehow could be heard even above the sounds of the sea and the noise of the helicopter. Apparently, everyone on board was required to put on a life vest before the Coast Guard could proceed. Not an easy task as there were few participants that were able to be of much help, and putting life jackets on limp or curled up people while trying to remain balanced on a rolling boat and dodging projectile vomit, sometimes successfully, was not a minor task. Once that was achieved, we made various hand gestures to the Coast Guardsmen to let them know we were ready. They threw us a rope. Charlie and I used it to haul in a pump that they dropped into the sea. It was a large pump in a big bobbing bright survival-orange metal barrel, and with no way to control the boat, or the waves, the water resistance made this a major undertaking. Additional deck hands able to stand upright would have been most welcome. Once aboard, Al fired up the pump and the water in the boat's hull was pumped back into the sea in short order. The bad news was that now the *Crystal Dawn* floated higher and with no power, the roll of the boat became even more noticeable. The helicopter remained hovering above until a Coast Guard cutter from the Oregon Inlet station showed up. By now it was dark. The tow back to the marina was uneventful, but it was well past midnight before we reached the dock. Mary radioed ahead and got a nearby motel to hold a number of rooms and have someone available to check people in for the night.

Perhaps the only thing worse than seasickness is enduring it for 18 hours. Al, being the enterprising boat captain that he was, had brought along a number of cases of beer, hoping to sell it to the participants on the way back in. Needless to say there was not much interest, and Charley and I got dirty looks from a number of passengers as we stood in the stern seeing how much we could consume before reaching the dock. The first bird- and whale-watching trip sponsored by our museum also doubled as the last, and the day's event was featured in the *News and Observer* a day or so later after the reporters had stopped swaying enough to punch out a story. The TV camera crew did not get any useable footage, so we were spared that humiliation. I forgot to ask, but I don't think any of the birders on board got new lifers for their list.

The mixing of serious amateurs and professionals in any field always results in amusing stories, the details of which often reveal the seriousness of what an outsider assumes is simply an interesting and fun hobby. On one of my earliest trips out to the Gulf Stream, Paul DuMont and I chartered a boat. He was out there watching birds and wearing his birding gear and I had brought along the 12-gauge just in case there was something we needed to document and work into our museum collection. Not too far into the trip, a mixed flock of gulls appeared behind the boat. They were checking us out to see whether there were any fish scraps being tossed over the stern. In turn, Paul and the friends he'd brought along were checking out the gulls. At the time, I was on the bridge with the captain trying to figure out our best course for the day. Paul yelled up to us that there was a glaucous gull off the port side that I might want. We collected the bird and the mate netted it onto the boat. Within a few minutes someone shouted, "Iceland gull!" "That's one you have to get," Paul informed me. The captain was impressed with the shot, as there must have been 30 gulls of three to four different species trailing our boat by this time, each soaring at different heights and speeds, crisscrossing each other's flight paths—a living cloud of gulls. With one shell, the Iceland gull dropped into the water and not a single bird in the rest of the flock was touched. Most of the boat captains were also duck hunters, and I had successfully dropped two flying birds from a rolling boat in a fairly good wind with just two shells. I was not sure if the look I was getting was disbelief or admiration. This story gets richer.

For the better part of a decade the presence and identification of Iceland gulls had been a contentious subject in North Carolina. For years, Paul and other birders from the Virginia and D.C. areas had been reporting Iceland gulls from various locations on the state's coast. Glaucous and Iceland gulls are difficult to distinguish from one another, but for people who are familiar with both species it is not an impossible task. Overall size and the proportionate bill size are the main field marks as the plumages of the various age classes are similar. Paul had me pull the first bird out of the ice chest, and there on the deck, side by side, were two gulls of very different size and with different bills. Cameras appeared and everyone photographed the two gulls side by side. "There!" (he named several people) "can all take that Iceland gull and stick it . . ." The birders were sick of the people in North Carolina who were in charge of keeping records of the state's avifauna repeatedly rejecting every Iceland gull sighting that had been reported, simply saying that in view of the similarity of appearance of glaucous gulls no one could ever be sure. The North Carolina birders, meanwhile, thought of the D.C.-area birders as outsiders and poachers of birds that they as residents of the state should be the first to see. You don't insult a hardcore birder by saying something off color about his mother, you do it by rejecting one of his sight records, and no love was lost between the two groups. I had only recently moved to the state and was a member of both worlds, and fortunately did not know at the time that I would soon become the chairman of the state's bird record committee, a job that makes overseeing church politics seem simple and straightforward.

Back in Raleigh with the specimens in hand, using my library and my growing reference collection of seabirds, I carefully studied the two gulls. They were both glaucous gulls. It turned out that this gull was known to come in two distinct size classes, the smaller one approaching Iceland gulls in both size and bill structure. Today, some ornithologists suspect that these smaller versions of glaucous gulls may actually represent hybrids. The gull wars only lasted another year or so as true blue Iceland gulls were soon documented as part of the official and growing list of North Carolina birds. We now know that while they don't show up every winter they are actually relatively common, at least when compared to some of the rarer gulls.

To most people, bird listing seems a little bizarre, but it's probably only a small step beyond bribing birds with seed and birdbaths so you can spy on them from your kitchen window and catch them in the act of eating and bathing. The earliest "listers" were actually collectors, and the concept of looking at live birds through spy glasses did not really catch on until the early 1900s. The earliest field identification guides, ones that allowed people to identify species other than common backyard birds, did not appear until the 1930s. Previously, people who were fascinated by birds collected them with guns and had their own personal collections. Others collected eggs and nests and some of these private collections were extensive. These later proved to be valuable libraries of information as to what occurred where and when, and the egg sets were useful in determining the historic breeding distributions of many birds. With the passage of the various migratory bird acts and treaties, private collections were made illegal and over time many of the more important private collections were merged with ones in accredited museums. Prior to field guides and the availability of binoculars, it was generally believed that birds could only be properly identified in the hand, but this quickly changed. In the back of the first guides there were actually little blocks next to the birds' names where you could check off each species as you saw them, and from this we see the origin of listing.

By the mid-1970s, when I started up my seabird research, the sport of listing birds was well advanced, and birders already had their own magazines, conventions, and lists of who's who in the birding world. I was impressed with their organized approach to fieldwork. Many of the birders who accompanied me on my day trips to the Gulf Stream had those little pocket protectors that held pencils and pens. There would be a number of different colored pencils and I watched in amazement as they used different ones to color-code sightings as they checked off each bird. A regular lead pencil tallied each species they saw that day, but if it was a new one for the year, or a new one for the state, specific colors were used, and the red one was reserved for new birds for their life. These guys were keeping up to four lists at once while standing on a rolling deck and watching for additional new birds! All this has changed; technology has taken over the world of birding. You can go online and see by location and date what species have been seen in the last seven days and read descriptions and blogs about what people think of an individual sighting of a rare bird or the person reporting it. Conversely, you can stand on the Outer Banks and with your cell phone inform birding list servers and announce to every serious birder on the continent that you are watching a mew gull in second winter plumage. If I were running a motel or a restaurant on the Outer Banks during the off-season, I would be checking the beaches and inlets every day for unusual vagrant gulls. By reporting unusual birds to the e-mail lists of bird clubs, the local establishments would be filled to capacity for days on end.

Partly because of this organized reporting, the birding community has, over time, made a tremendous contribution to the total body of knowledge of North American ornithology. For every professional degree-carrying ornithologist in our universities, museums, and agencies, there are hundreds of others out in the field seeing birds and reporting on what they find. In addition, there are any number of citizen-scientist type programs where individuals can collect data in a manner such that it can be directly entered into computer programs that monitor changes in bird populations and their migratory movements. Some birds may be rare along the mid-Atlantic coast, but we are learning that others actually appear on a regular basis. In the case of gulls, of the 14 different species now known from the state, birders were originally responsible for first finding and documenting all but the five or six most common species. Knowing your second-summer and third-winter plumages pays off.

—∽—

Times may already be changing for birders and regional committees respectively keeping track of their personal and official bird lists. In the past century we progressed from the need to collect birds to determine their correct identity to binoculars and field guides, digital photography, and vocal arrays captured on tape to vouch proper identification, and for reviews and approval by bird record committees. It was just a matter of time until we moved to the next logical step—tracking bird occurrences on our laptops. Not only is the technology readily available, it is well used by amateurs and professionals. For a number of years now various websites have been providing up-to-date bird lists for most states. And now ornithologists are tracking individual birds with geolocators and satellite tags—lightweight, electronic tracking devices that allow researchers to follow the movement of individual birds. The more advanced tags, when fitted on a bird, can calculate its exact position to within meters, and some of the tags continue to work for up to five years.

Currently there are various species of seabirds—frigate birds, boobies, tropicbirds, terns, murres, and puffins, as well as a number of species of petrels and shearwaters—that are carrying around geolocators and satellite tags. The tracking devices, which communicate with satellites, transmit locations of individual birds directly back to websites that can be accessed through your laptop. In the near future birders will be able to see what birds are offshore without ever leaving home, and bird records committees can instantly confirm the presence of species new to their state even when no one has actually seen them. Field guide and binocular sales will drop, no one will worry about seasickness or their lack of knowledge of those damn field markings, plumage variations will be irrelevant, and the need for the verification of bird sightings can become a thing of the past. Our computers can manage our personal bird lists and bird record committees will no longer even need to meet. Birding can become a reality video game.

Lines of Sargassum can stretch for miles along the ocean surface of the Gulf Stream, providing hideaways and food for many marine species.

The thick masses of Sargassum are home to distinctive and specialized marine animals that live among the branches of this pelagic surface seaweed.

Tunas are fast, powerful fishes that provide exciting action for the sport fisherman. Here, the author's wife, Mary Kay Clark, holds her catch.

Sport fishing in the Gulf Stream is an important business along the Atlantic Coast. After a successful day of Gulf Stream fishing from Big Al's Country Girl, the catch is displayed on the dock before being divided among the fisherman.

Rudolph Inman shows off a big catch from the Cape Fear River. Shad fishing, a favorite pastime, is exciting and rewarding; for several weeks in the early spring the fish flood into coastal rivers from the Atlantic Ocean, moving toward their birth waters to spawn. (Photograph by Melissa McGaw)

The elegant white-tailed tropicbird breeds on tropical islands, but it is a powerful flier that spends much of its life far out at sea.

The author holds an adult tropicbird taken from a nesting burrow during a breeding bird survey in the Caribbean. The dependence on both islands and offshore waters makes understanding their biology and protecting their habitat a special challenge. (Photograph by Mary K. Clark)

Dr. David Wingate's lifelong efforts to bring back the cahow from near-extinction led him to undertake the holistic restoration of Nonesuch Island. His efforts included creating artificial nesting burrows that provided critical sites for seabird nesting after natural burrows were destroyed by storms.

Audubon's shearwaters nest in colonies on rocky islets with both parents sharing incubation duties. The single egg laid is brooded for about a week. Then the hatchling spends much of its time alone in the burrow while the parents forage offshore to feed their voracious offspring.

Horseshoe crabs live on sandy or muddy bottoms, coming ashore to mate in the spring. Large mating aggregations produce millions of eggs that are a rich food source for migrating shorebirds.

Scientists use submersible machines fitted with bright lights and large glass windows to study life at the mid-water depths and below, all the way to the ocean bottom, where light becomes scarce, and even nonexistent.

Marine mammal diversity is high in North Carolina's waters, the result of the state's latitude, where both boreal and subtropical species overlap. The bottlenose dolphin is perhaps the most recognizable of the 27 marine mammals that occur in inshore and offshore waters.

PART III **LAND AND SEA**

Unexpected Connections

The high tide line—is this where the sea begins or where it ends? For centuries beachcombers have taken delight in finding shells, pieces of coral, sponges, driftwood, sandblasted glass bottles, and the seeds of tropical plants that become stranded on our shores. Objects from the sea lay scattered along the tidelines of the world, intermixed with things that originated on land, washed out to sea, and after a time were carried off and returned to distant beaches. But the relationship between the two worlds of sea and land, marked by these tide lines, goes much deeper.

Take birds for example. Seabirds are obligated to return to land, even if just to nest. Other birds that for much of the year we regard as terrestrial and freshwater species—loons, jaegers, phalaropes, and even the Bonaparte's gull (a tree-nesting species from the far north)—spend their winters far at sea. Just as many sea creatures have subsequently evolved to live in freshwater and on land, a number of freshwater and terrestrial species have returned to the sea. Sea turtles, whales, and seals are descendants of land-dwelling animals that in turn had past distant connections to amphibious creatures originating in prehistoric Devonian seas (360–420 million years ago). There are numerous examples of creatures that, primarily because of physical restraints in their reproductive cycles, don't break free of their dependence on one world or the other. Horseshoe crabs and marine turtles, while capable of being entirely seagoing for the vast percentage of their lives, are obligated to return to shore to lay their eggs. Conversely, the ghost crabs that run about on the beaches of the Outer Banks must return to the water's edge to deposit their eggs, thus dispersing their aquatic larvae.

For most humans, our connection to the sea goes unnoticed. Yet the sea has a tremendous influence on our weather. Our vast oceans are the world's thermostats. Because of their volume and the ability of water to retain heat, the trade winds and oceans temper seasonal extremes. Just as important are the rich blooms of phytoplankton in our oceans—they nourish 85–90 percent of the world's oxygen needs. To this list perhaps I should add commercial trade routes (two-thirds of the items you purchased at the mall last month were likely shipped here from overseas), the inspiration for tales of ancient mythical monsters, fodder for literature dating back to antiquity, and topics for so many of those nature specials that have proliferated on cable television.

Commercial and industrial fisheries of the world are obviously dependent on the sea. This dependence and interconnection can be experienced not just in the frozen food departments of your coastal grocery stores, but also in seafood restaurants in downtown Omaha. Now with our global economy it is not unusual to find seafood that has been harvested, for lack of a better term, overseas. I recall purchasing a bag of frozen shrimp lo mien in a Walmart in southwestern New Mexico. The frozen dinner was labeled as a complete meal for two, ready in 14 minutes, and with no MSG added. Somewhere on the back of the bag, in the smallest of print, was noted the fact that the shrimp were from Thailand.

Global currents warm our coast, allow species like the shad and eel to move freely from one world to another, and support valuable (if overextended) international fisheries. But unfortunately, they also transport all kinds of waste and pollutants throughout the North Atlantic. Acid rain, which has seriously degraded northern freshwater ponds and lakes to the point that we are seeing high mortality in loons, is now affecting our seas. At least this pond is bigger and the process more gradual; still we are already reading about how the pH of the ocean is changing and affecting coral reefs.

There are international agreements about disposing of plastic in the ocean, ones that have been in effect for decades. During my research I became involved in a study to assess the amount of plastics ingested by seabirds. Not only did we find plastic in the digestive tracts of 21 of the 38 species examined, but it had increased significantly in quantity over 14 years during my study. While much of the plastic particles are doomed to forever ride oceanic currents, the same currents, winds, storms, and tides that build and nourish our beaches now deposit more plastic objects than (the occasional) dead fish upon our shores. Perhaps we should take some comfort in the fact that given the right opportunity, the sea manages to regurgitate our trash.

Before you put this book aside, take note. The five chapters that follow are not about how we contaminate the sea with our waste products; they provide examples of the biological connections between land and sea. These chapters celebrate natural examples of this connection within the biological community. To us these connections may seem subtle, but they are important. Ocean currents transport marine life to estuaries that function because of the combined input of freshwater rivers and the energy of moon-induced tides. Freshwater fishes going to sea to spawn literally pass marine species migrating up inland rivers on their way to lay eggs. The majority of our songbirds that winter in the tropics take shortcuts by migrating directly over the open ocean. Even small seeds, ones passively transported by the sea, can be cast onto the Outer Banks and similar barrier islands; they occasionally germinate and over time dictate the nature of the vegetation growing on the dunes. In many ways, the flora and fauna of the land exploit the oceans much as we have—for transport, colonization, and its rich and dependable food resources. In turn, we too have come from the sea, and over time developed lungs, learned to walk upright, use two-ply bathroom tissue, and invent microwave ovens that allow us to cook frozen shrimp from Thailand.

CHAPTER 11 DONKEY'S EYES, SEA PURSES, AND FAIRY EGGS

It was midday, and as usual there was a lull in the offshore seabird activity—time for another break from the marine-bird surveys to grab some lunch, apply a new coat of sunscreen, and do a quick check of the radio for the marine weather forecast. Light winds from the southeast had flattened the sea. Enjoying the calm, I was so into my relaxing mode that at first I did not realize I was staring at a drifting coconut. We were 40 miles off Cape Hatteras. How far had it drifted in its northward circuit in the Gulf Stream? The nearest coconut palms were in the Bahamas and south Florida. The large gooseneck barnacles hanging from the husk indicated that this particular coconut had been floating for a long time. I have no idea how long it takes a gooseneck barnacle to reach maximum size, but certainty longer than the few days required to drift up from Florida. Did it come from the Lesser Antilles? Perhaps this was not its first time passing North Carolina? Small, colorful, striped jacks of several size classes swam below the bobbing coconut, finding shelter in the drifting patch of shade. As the coconut drifted past, the barnacles cast and recast their purple feathery nets into the blue Atlantic.

If this particular coconut had the good fortune to break free of the grasp of the Gulf Stream current and be washed ashore, would it grow? A coconut without its surrounding husk can remain afloat in saltwater for over 19 years, and there are reports of coconuts found in Britain and Ireland that actually germinated. However, coconuts remain as viable seeds for only about 100 days when immersed in seawater, so the ones that germinated on European coasts were perhaps simply thrown overboard from passing ships.

The trip from the tropics to North Carolina is much shorter and faster. When passive objects are caught up in the Gulf Stream, it does not take them long to find their way northward. This current flows north at a rate of about 100 miles a day. For germination, however, the seeds need temperatures of 77–86° F, and night temperatures cannot fall below 65° F. Thus, we are not likely to find coconut palms growing on North Carolina's beaches.

A personal collection of sea beans is a collection of ties to exotic locales. These drifting seeds of various species may be carried hundreds of miles, floating for years before washing ashore.

Coconut palms are actually native to Southeast Asia. They were distributed by indigenous people throughout the tropical Pacific prior to European contact, and in the 16th century throughout the tropical Atlantic by European colonists. The seeds of the coconut palm are large and take 9–12 months to ripen on the tree. The coconut has three embryos (the "eyes" on the hard shell of the inner core), two of which abort. This leaves the remaining one with a huge food reservoir; the young palms get a real jump-start from all this nourishment. It is this same food reservoir that makes coconuts such a popular food in the tropics, while the arching trunks of the coconut palm give added grace and charm to tropical beaches. Though widely dispersed by man, the seed itself has evolved for open-sea transport. Many a small cay has been colonized by drift coconuts tossed high onto tropical beaches by storm surges.

⌒

Coconuts are but one of many seeds commonly transported by oceanic currents. These seeds, as well as other flotsam, are often blown inshore and washed onto Atlantic beaches by storms and spring tides. Tidelines of *Sargassum*, eelgrass, and other marine plants mark the upper reaches of these storm surges. Mixed among the *Sargassum* line is a strange assemblage of marine debris, woven and rewoven by the sea's dynamic and endless energy. Bones of fishes, feathers of birds, and legs of crabs can be found beside pieces of sponges, egg cases of skates and whelks, colorful shells of marine mollusks, and the barnacle-encrusted timbers and other various floating debris discarded or lost from ships.

The supply of new material is as endless as it is varied. Exploring beach tidelines after a strong winter storm can be a rewarding experience for anyone curious about the sea. On the shortlist of the most interesting objects to be found in tide lines are floating tropical seeds, which, like coconuts, are often transported well north of the regions where they normally grow to be cast upon foreign shores. These seeds, representing 50 to 100 species that have been recovered on North Atlantic beaches, are collectively referred to as sea beans.

A winter walk on a Carolina beach in search of sea beans—I can't think of a better way to squander time. The solitude alone makes such excursions worthwhile, and let's face it, one does not need to have his or her brain in fourth gear to comb beaches. Looking through the tideline of brown decaying *Sargassum* and eelgrass leads to all sorts of unexpected rewards: broken flip-flops, Styrofoam cups, pieces of long-forgotten wooden boats, and innumerable bits of marine life driven to shore and onto land by tides, waves, and wind. Each has its own story, but none is likely to be as good as that of a tropical seed that found its way from a nameless remote South American river to the Outer Banks. Individually these seeds have traveled farther and longer than most circus elephants. Holding one of these seeds in your hand does not transport you to some tropical paradise, but it does connect you to one.

Sea-bean devotees have formed societies where members share information through newsletters, and meetings are held to share about the sea beans themselves, ocean currents, and delivery schedules. These same people also record movements of floating trash. Specific loads of plastic toys and other floating objects lost from cargo ships tell interesting stories when their origins are known and when a number of points of recovery are recorded. Plastic toys of a certain type lost at a specific place and time have a lot to tell us about the speed and direction of currents when enough of them are retrieved.

A personal collection of sea beans is a collection of ties to unknown places. You might find nicker beans, likely from Florida or perhaps from the West Indies. Then you can add crabwood seeds and sea purses from tropical America, sea hearts from South American vines, and horse-eye beans, coral beans, ivory nuts, and seeds from any number of species of tropical palms, each from different places, and each with its own unwritten travel log. The itineraries of individual seeds recovered on our beaches are unknown and thereby fuel our imaginations.

All drift seeds are not of foreign origin. The seedpods of red mangroves, a common estuarine tree of south Florida, are designed to float. Water transports them to mud flats, and with the long growing season in the tropics these trees colonize the tidal flats rapidly. Mangrove seeds that get caught up in the Gulf Stream drift endlessly. Meanwhile, seeds of water hickories and pecans, washed downstream by the Mississippi into the Gulf of Mexico and then northward by the Gulf Stream, find their way onto beaches as far away as England. Those found closer to home are unremarkable and for the most part go unnoticed. The hickory seeds can remain afloat for over a year. Seeds of both trees that wash ashore in the southeastern United States are often viable.

Drift seeds have strange names, given by people who knew only that they came from the sea. Donkey's ears, sea purses, and fairy eggs are but some of the names applied to these castaways. Sea beans became components of medieval folklore and were given names that translate into such things as "supernatural kidney," suggesting that people not only had no idea where these objects originated but also that they had no clue as to what they actually were.

Sea beans have been known to societies for thousands of years. As early as the first century AD there were written accounts of sea beans, but the Greeks who wrote of them had little idea about their real nature. Pliny, in his *Naturalis historia* wrote of "eagle stones," stones that eagles kept in their nests. Without these stones it was said the bird's eggs would not hatch, and the stones were worn as charms by pregnant women to prevent miscarriage. What Pliny described as stones inside of other stones was actually the seeds inside the pods of sea beans. The speculations of Pliny and other Greek scholars persisted well into the 16th century as scientific fact and the true nature of the eagle stones remained masked.

Only recently has it been shown that the eagle stones are occasionally found in the nests of fulmars, boreal seabirds that nest on cliff faces in England, Iceland, and other northern locales, are actually sea beans. The fulmars forage southward to the Gulf Stream off North Carolina in winter. They ingest the floating seeds and later regurgitate them when feeding chicks. I have examined the stomachs of fulmars, both ones collected far at sea and those that are sick and dying that have beached. I have yet to find a sea bean, but fulmars have one of the highest instances of ingestion of floating plastic of any seabird I have examined. One hundred percent of the fulmars examined had plastic of some type in their digestive tracts. Snatching up floating sea beans does not seem that far-fetched.

Strange alien objects cast onto beaches had quite an impact on medieval European societies. Sea beans became the focus of much folklore, superstition, and myth. One must keep in mind that people of the time neither had access to the Internet nor did they know about oceanic currents, that there was another side to the Atlantic, or that tropical jungles existed. Drift seeds were considered floating stones, and they have been referenced in historical English-language documents for several centuries. Much of the sea bean folklore that developed centered on fertility and childbirth. Perhaps this was a logical connection, considering the fact that these floating stones always had a little stone inside.

In Iceland, midwives would chant prayers with drift seeds clenched in their hands. The tradition was tolerated by the Roman Catholic Church, and sea beans used to ease the pain of childbirth were often consecrated on the altar. Mary's bean, from a tropical American vine, was so named because of its use in similar prayers directed at the Blessed Virgin Mary. In some societies these seeds were worn by female children to guard their chastity. Go figure! The same seeds often have an indented cross on one side, and in some regions they are referred to as a crucifixion bean.

Much sea-bean folklore developed in isolated places, and it is now hard to pin down which species of drift seed was believed to have which superpower. But drift seeds placed under pillows are reported to keep away evil fairies and other creatures that are often up to no good. In Scotland sea beans were placed in barns and in water troughs to prevent sickness in cattle. Some beans were worn as amulets against evil eyes and witchcraft. In the medieval period, when magic, sorcery, science, and religion were interwoven, the seemingly supernatural presence of sea beans was used to support wild theories. Sea beans became important artifacts for cult religions, and in some cases, mainstream ones as well.

Some seeds, called Molucca beans, thought to be from the Molucca Islands in the East Indies, were considered as evidence of a yet to be discovered Northeast Passage. Columbus knew of sea beans, and the seeds of unknown plants that washed ashore in the Azores and on other islands in the eastern Atlantic were important in forming his belief that the East Indies could be reached by a western route. Among the Portuguese names for various sea beans are ones that translate into "Columbus's bean" and "Columbus's chestnut."

The first factual written accounts of sea beans are from Cornwall, England, in the 1500s. Even 400 or 500 years ago people had a good idea about the nature of these floating pods. It was "the faith of the Cornish folk that dwell by the English sea," they said, "that these seeds had been driven from the New World under the influence of southerly or westerly winds because no one could recall any ship being wrecked on local coasts." The essence of drift seeds was accurately captured in this one sentence, but not until the late 18th century were various sea beans matched to known living tropical plants.

In the 19th century, naturalists came to recognize the role of drift seeds and their relation to oceanic currents. Most of this information came from English scholars, because the Atlantic coast of England was the final destination of a number of sea beans washed northward by the Gulf Stream. New World ship captains returning to Europe had known for decades the advantages of following oceanic currents, but it was the sea beans that provided compelling evidence of the actual extent of influence of the Gulf Stream.

Charles Darwin's book, *On the Origin of Species*, includes a brief comment on drift seeds. The single paragraph is just a summary of Darwin's interest in the link between oceanic currents and the distribution of plants and animals. After years of correspondence with botanists about drift seeds, Darwin had done some experiments on their ability to float and, to the astonishment of botanists of the period, proved that they could germinate after floating in seawater. The discussions and disagreements about the nature of drift seeds and the establishment of new colonies of plants on distant shores became amplified by the fact that Darwin was looking at this from a global perspective. The British botanists of the time were focused simply on demonstrating how these tropical seeds failed to thrive on European shores.

∽

How long does it take for a seed to passively drift from the American tropics to the coast of Europe? It's a question with an open answer, like "how long is a piece of string?" Information obtained from marked drift bottles helped to determine the minimal time, about 400 days (a little over 13 months). Though this is a long time for a seed to remain in seawater, the seed will remain buoyant if its density is less than pure seawater. Seeds that are adapted for oceanic transport need only to remain intact and retain a density that is a small fraction less than seawater. Seawater, because of variations in density caused by temperature and salinity, is normally 1.02 to 1.03, so even an object with 1.0 density will float.

For some seeds the passive transport adaptations are conspicuous. Seeds that have empty air-filled cavities increase the volume, but not the weight, of the seed, thus decreasing the overall density. Some just have air spaces inside the seedpod, while others have lightweight corky and spongy tissues and do not require the additional flotation of air sacs. The living tissues of all these floating seeds need protection. Most of us have seen seeds like those of common garden vegetables, that when exposed to water, absorb what they can, start to swell, and sprout. If there was no protection for ocean-dispersed seeds, then the additional water would change their density and they would sink. And seawater is an efficient herbicide. Thus, the successful drift seeds are all encased in very tough, nearly impenetrable, waterproof coats. (Ever try to open a coconut?) Within the seedpod, the embryo must also have the ability to remain dormant. Some sea beans can remain dormant for years.

What types of plants cast their seeds into the sea in the hope that they will arrive on some remote shore and establish new nations of vegetation? Few, if any. Most are species of tropical plants that benefit from seed transport across freshwater lagoons, lakes, and rivers. The fact that they get washed out to sea and end up far from the tropics by oceanic currents is not really part of the master plan. Most seeds that end up far out at sea are doomed. It helps to understand the biology of the parent plants that allows for such a wasteful dispersal of their seeds.

Many of the hard and shiny sea beans cast up on our beaches (sea heart, Mary's bean, sea purse, and the hamburger bean) come from jungle vines. All of these vines are long lived, often outliving the tropical hardwoods that support them. They tend to reproduce primarily through vegetative means. Once these vines start growing, they climb rapidly and cover so much area that even when major parts of a vine are killed the plant survives, and then quickly they reclaim their share of the jungle. Pollination and seed dispersal are for the most part unnecessary. Seeds washed downstream or across lakes can start new tangles of vines well removed from the parent stocks. It is only necessary for these vines to reproduce themselves once over many hundreds of years for the species to survive. It is easy to see why it would be wasteful for plants such as this to produce vast numbers of seeds since few could survive the competition for light and nutrients from the parent plants. Thus, these species are prone to produce small numbers of well-encased seeds that are capable of remaining dormant for long periods, giving them the ability to be transported well away from the parent plant.

Many of these plants, striving for light, grow on trees angling out over the shores of rivers and lakes so it is very likely that many of their seeds will fall into water. And in gallery rain forests where the entire forest is half submerged by swollen rivers for a large portion of the year, what better dispersal agent could a plant ask for than flowing water? These seeds not only have a woody outer protective layer, but each seed also has a large food supply, so when the proper growing situation is reached the young plant can make the jump from a seedling to a climbing vine even in the deep shade of the forest floor. Under competitive conditions, a few large seeds are of more value to plants of this nature than hordes of small seedlings with limited food supplies. It's almost a mathematical certainty that the parent plant will replace itself through its seeds. If one takes the total number of seeds produced each year and multiplies this by the centuries during which the vine will live to produce seeds, something will grow. Unlike annual plants, where successful germination of seeds is needed every year, the seeds of the perennial tropical woody vines are little more than a long-term insurance policy—a policy that in most cases is not really needed. Most of the seeds will end up in inhospitable places—doomed to float the seas for the remainder of their existence or land on Carolina beaches only to become stored in the collection boxes of beachcombers or to be sold in shell shops.

A botanist traveling through Florida in the late 1800s wrote of a thriving sea bean jewelry business in the St. Augustine area. Seeds collected from tide lines on central and north Florida beaches were fashioned into watch charms and buttons, monogrammed and otherwise embellished. The seeds of the sea heart were carved into snuffboxes and marketed in the British Isles. Global marketing started earlier than many suspect.

This business took off because most sea beans (at least those easily recognized as something foreign to our shores) are woody, and because of the actions of the sea and sand, they are often quite well polished. They take on the appearance of mahogany while the seed remains protected. The round and flattened hamburger bean is typical of a polished, mahogany-like sea bean. It gets its name from differential coloring in the central part of the seed coating, with the upper and lower wood being lighter and looking not unlike hamburger buns. When the seed first falls off the vine it is covered with a leathery, thick, hairy covering. The seed is about four inches long and shaped like the openings of the sound holes in a violin. The seed's hairy coat gives the plant another name—cow itch. It's said that the hairs, when mixed in a brew, can be consumed to get rid of certain types of intestinal parasitic worms. Apparently the prickly hairs stab the worms to death. (I wonder if Blue Cross covers that one.) The seeds are also said to have properties that cure hemorrhoids, paralysis, and urinating disorders; some also claim they are an aphrodisiac. So there you go: a trip to the beach may do more for body and soul than a trip to the doctor's office or a prescription for Viagra.

It is generally believed that having a sea bean of any sort in your possession brings good luck, or conversely, prevents bad luck. Not unlike rabbit's feet and four-leaf clovers, sea beans are regarded as lucky charms. In Europe sea beans were made into brooches and lockets so they could be worn regularly and bring constant good luck. Often they were passed along with Bibles from one generation to another. In present day they may be found for sale in shell shops and similar beachside operations. To me, though, the true luck associated with these beans is finding one, and their purchase is degrading to the whole point of beach combing.

The message in a bottle concept fascinates everyone. We have all read stories of messages found 20 years later on some distant shore, usually heartwarming stories that connect the message sender and the person who found the bottle. According to the *Guinness Book of World Records*, the longest period a message has been cooped up in a floating bottle was 97 years and 309 days. The bottle, recovered from a fishing net, was tossed into the sea by Captain C. H. Brown of the Glasgow School of Navigation on June 19, 1914. The note inside the bottle promised six pence to whoever found it. In 2014 this record was surpassed when a German fisherman recovered a message in a beer bottle from the Baltic Sea that was set afloat 101 years previously.

The exciting part about bottled messages is not what is written on the note inside, or that corked bottles can float for long periods and distances. How the messages are transported is the real story. Sea beans, like bottled mail sent to anonymous places, are a great way to track currents and in reality represent a vast number of current-delivered messages, if people know how to read them.

These types of oceanic journeys are not limited to seeds. The pads of prickly pear cacti (genus *Opuntia*) can survive in seawater for about three months and the presence of six species of cacti on beaches ranging from Florida to Cape Cod may be the result of sea drift. Prickly pears growing on Bermuda and islands in the Bahamas and Antilles may likewise have been dispersed by currents, but the records are poor and it's hard to tell on oceanic islands that have been colonized by man for hundreds of years what was intentionally introduced and what arrived by natural dispersal agents. For the cacti, at least, it seems unlikely that pre-Columbian man or even early European colonists would be interested in intentionally moving them about.

Henry David Thoreau once said, "I have great faith in a seed . . . and I am prepared to expect wonders!" Seeds represent the future; perhaps this is the root of the fascination in sea beans. Some may think of sea beans as misplaced objects from the tropics, but many, many sea beans are distributed by oceanic currents within the tropics, and the natural distribution of the plants that sprang from them was established long before people thought of such things. This makes it difficult to illustrate specific distributional patterns that have benefited from oceanic currents or even to say with certainty the place of origin of parent stocks. Understanding the native distributions of plants and animals constantly plagues naturalists. Are seeds that find their way to foreign shores by natural means native plants? What about ones moved about by pre-Columbian man? The chance is astronomical that one drift seed would survive an oceanic journey, germinate on a foreign shore, and start a new colony. But the number of seeds finding their way into the ocean is astronomical too, and the few drifting ashore over time becomes significant. The edge of the sea remains a strange and fascinating place; even the common seaside plants characterizing our barrier islands have their secrets.

CHAPTER 12 UP FROM THE SEA

We all look forward to spring. It comes in bits and pieces. Puddles of singing chorus frogs, restless movements of wintering waterfowl, the locked-winged courtship flights of doves, and the sequential appearance of buds and blossoms on any number of plants each give the message that winter's end is near. Many of the natural signs that mark the coming of spring are short lived. Blink and they have gone. Yesterday the wintering juncos at my bird feeder were the most common bird in the yard; today there is not a single one. With spring comes a gradual increase in fluctuating air temperatures and the longer days of late winter result in a steady rise in water temperatures. Once these temperatures reach about 41° F, the spring migrations of the American shad begin. And unlike the explosive nature of most vernal events, the migration of shad is quite protracted. By the time river water temperatures are 55–61° F, the shad migration is at its peak.

For those who cannot be bothered with sticking thermometers in rivers, there are other signs the shad are running. In Maryland I knew that the arrival of spawning shad was more or less timed with the blooming of the shad bush, a plant that originally got its name from those in tune with the out-of-doors. But there are slight variations in the theme as spring progresses northward with different speeds, and along the Atlantic coast not everything is on the same schedule. In southeastern North Carolina when the dogwoods peak and the swallows return, the shad runs are running full throttle. While the peak is more or less in mid-April, our regional spawning run of American shad extends over several months.

What follows is not just about commercial and recreational fishing or your Friday-night church shad fry—for people who fail to understand how tied we are to the sea, shad may best make my point. Even well inland the sea continues to have important cultural and economic impacts. Hopefully, we are all aware of the importance of estuaries where the freshwater from inland rivers feeds into the sea. Whole worlds of creatures are dependent on estuaries, and their comings and goings benefit both marine systems and major coastal fisheries. Estuaries are nurseries for everything from oysters, crabs,

American shad are anadromous fish—that is, they spend most of their lives in saltwater, but spawn in freshwater. Their annual spring spawning runs upriver are much anticipated by fishermen.

and flounder to larval marine fish that are of major economic importance. But added to the equation are species such as shad, fish that mostly bypass the estuarine system altogether and get on with their business elsewhere. Shad are marine fishes that spawn in freshwater—swimming far, far inland and bringing the productivity of the sea much farther into the interior of the continent than most would expect. It is interesting to contrast the ingrained differences between nations, various religions, and other matters of opinion that are in constant disarray with something as seemingly incompatible as oceanic habitats and freshwater Piedmont streams. They have for eternity contributed to each other's well-being. Nations comprised of different creatures function far better than those managed by our governments. The interactions of the seemingly opposing forces of land and sea and salt- and freshwater are well governed and time-tested and became agreements of natural order well before the advent of human nonsense. And the neat part of all this is that the shad runs have become symbolic of spring, combining forces of nature's renewal that are easily appreciated.

Except for their spawning runs and the migration of young to the sea, shad spend the majority of their life in marine environments. But even at sea these fish continue to undertake extensive migrations. During the summer and fall they live in relatively shallow waters such as the Gulf of Maine, but they winter in deep offshore waters. It has been estimated that the average shad travels 12,000 miles in its lifetime. While the spawning runs of shad are well known and outright remarkable, these fish have a totally unrelated and unexpected aspect of their life history—hearing. They are the only fish known to have the ability to detect ultrasound (frequencies above 20 kHz and above the limit of human hearing). The enhanced hearing is not used for hunting the plankton on which they feed (marine copepods, amphipods, shrimp, and shrimp-like crustaceans) but for predator avoidance. This superpower enables American shad to detect, and help them in avoiding, foraging dolphins. The dolphins use echolocation to locate schooling fish. Shad's enhanced hearing ensures that significant numbers of the stock will survive their five-year residence at sea and be able to contribute to the spring spawning. Marine mammals are credited for having an impressive intelligence, so perhaps they are aware of the American shad's scientific name—*Alosa sapidissima*. This name was assigned in 1811 and I would bet that most dolphins are aware that *sapidissima* actually means "very delicious."

The fact that shad spend almost their entire lives at sea was actually a major factor in its popularity for its human predators. The fish's oily salty flesh permitted it to be preserved by adding additional salt, allowing them to be stored and shipped without ice or refrigeration. Shad caught in North Carolina's Albemarle Sound, for example, were regularly shipped to markets in Baltimore, Richmond, Petersburg, and Norfolk. Between 1890 and 1970, average landings from this one sound exceeded millions of pounds per year.

Since I wanted to experience the totality of our local shad run, I needed a reliable indicator to inform me as to when it started. Unlike the action-packed salmon runs of the Northwest, shad don't have waterfalls to leap or brown bears intercepting their movements up freshwater rivers to reach their spawning grounds. The upstream movements of shad are more subtle and known mostly to ardent fishermen. My wife's cousin informed me, "If Rudolph Inman's boat and trailer are not behind his house, the shad are back. You'll find him fishing below the locks." Sure enough. And he was out there every day from early March through the first week of May. If looking for his boat is not enough of a sign, on evenings during peak season his yard fills with curious people waiting to see what he caught that day and to hear his stories.

One spring I accompanied Rudolph on a number of his fishing ventures. If I was going to learn about shad it might as well be from a person with many years of experience. At eighty something, Rudolph had experience. Wishing to tag along, I would inquire as to when he was going; after a few days of this, I figured it out—he went every day. Every day? Pretty much. The exceptions were after heavy rain events; an inch and a half of rain would make the river too high and the current too strong to secure the boat. But we could go the next day. While Rudolph worked the lines and fish, I worked Rudolph for fish stories.

Rudolph, it seems, led the way for shad becoming a sport fishery in North Carolina. In the 1950s, while he was commercially fishing shad with nets in the lower Cape Fear River, he continued to hear stories of people catching shad on rods in Florida's St. John's River. On a whim, he gave a friend heading to Florida five dollars and asked him to buy some of whatever it was that they were using to hook the fish. His friend later returned with a box of assorted darts. The next spring Rudolph gave 'em a try and he has been catching shad on lines ever since. What makes the story interesting is that shad do not go after baited hooks. They are plankton feeders and during their spawning runs don't even attempt to feed. Why do they get hooked on darts? They probably just see the darts as an annoyance and in nipping at them to get them to move out of their way they can get snagged. But the why is not important, and I think we all know how useless it becomes trying to figure out what makes a fish respond to anything. The point is it worked. Rudolph told his friends, and they told their relatives. Other fishermen saw people returning to the boat ramps with coolers full of shad and in no time the rivers became filled with recreational shad fishermen. The drill is not to figure out what the fish are eating that day, the success of shad fishing is to get the shad to snap at your dart. And to do that you need to get the dart right in its face. Sounds easy enough until you see the murky silt-laden Cape Fear River. Successful fishermen need to have a rather good idea as to where to work the darts and annoy the fish. Shad darts are now standard issue; last spring I saw that even the local Elizabethtown WalMart carried an impressive assortment.

Fishing stories, ones actually rivaling Big Al's, were endless. There were not just standard-issue big-fish tales. Rudolph told me one from a few seasons back where someone borrowed a friend's boat. He had all of his poles rigged for shad and in the excitement of the day shoved off before he fired up the outboard. Well the motor wouldn't crank, and the spring currents soon carried everything over the locks. Rudolph pointed to the spot where the boat was greeted by the rock dam. There was not much left of the borrowed boat and motor, or the fishermen's pride. On the boat ramp chatting with a wildlife officer while Rudolph was off-loading his boat, I retold that story. In a whisper the officer cut me off and motioned that the guy fishing behind him was the one responsible. At least he had learned to do his shad fishing from the bank, or as Rudolph later pointed out, "I don't think anyone is going to be lending him a boat." The days were rich with stories; many were not about fish. I listened with awe as he recounted his experience storming the beaches of Normandy in World War II, and then there were ones about the Cape Fear itself, including the big flood in 1945. I smiled when he told of the time he shot a quail that fell squarely on the head of a very surprised raccoon.

Except as a fresh target for his fishing stories, I was no help at all with the shad fishing. Rudolph let me tie the boat to various objects and deploy and retrieve anchors, but he was fishing by himself. He would nose the boat up current into position, and by the time I was finished looping rope over some stationary object he would have four lines over. The current held the lines taut; the darts rode the currents with teasing motions below the surface. Rudolph fishes three darts to a line, each separated by a number of yards from the next, allowing the gear to simultaneously annoy shad at different depths. I thought that four lines might be a little much for one person to watch. Apparently not, the next boat was just a few yards farther downstream, and that guy had 11 rods out.

Some days Rudolph fished from the same spot, on others, he moved his johnboat two or three times. Often he would take over a spot vacated by a boat that had caught its limit (10 per person per day), but sometimes we would just untie and move to a new spot for what seemed like no apparent reason. It took me a few days to see a pattern. We were fishing where the current was strongest and the water was deep. "Some holes below the locks are 58 feet deep, but in most places we are in 10–12 feet of water," Rudolph shouted above the noise of the river rushing over the dam.

We were fishing below the no. 2 lock, one of the three locks constructed between 1917 and 1919 to enable barges to work the Cape Fear between Wilmington and Fayetteville during periods of low water. Of course, with the development of the interstate highway system, river transportation is not as important now as it was in the past. Nonetheless, the locks continue to allow boat traffic to move up and down the river by maintaining high water levels. Of course, the locks also prevent migratory fishes such as shad from moving freely through the river. This was a concern when the locks were first built, so fish ladders were provided. Unfortunately the engineers in charge did not do their homework; fish ladders, which are readily used by species such as salmon, were totally ignored by the shad. During the spring shad run the personnel assigned to the locks open them every three or four hours to lift the shad to the next higher stream level. Even so, the migrating fish are confused by the dam and tend to accumulate below the locks while they try to figure out how to get past them. The recreational fishermen figured this out too. Rudolph's boat was not the only one out there, and, though a number of fishermen worked the river farther downstream, a disproportionate number crowded just below the no. 2 lock.

In November 2012 the Army Corps of Engineers, with the help of $13 million in federal stimulus money, reconfigured the face of the first dam. Lock no. 1 is 39 miles upstream from Wilmington, near Riegelwood. They piled several hundred feet of boulders below the 11-foot dam, converting it into natural-looking rapids that the fish can jump. The project was successful, and in the spring of 2013 not only were more fish making the 33 miles to the no. 2 lock where Rudolph fishes, but they were arriving earlier. In previous years the first fish were showing up in mid-March. The first shad caught near the Elizabethtown lock was hooked on February 27. Plans are now underway to retrofit similar man-made rapids below lock nos. 2 and 3. This should help get more fish to their spawning grounds, an upstream area in the Piedmont section of the Cape Fear—the rocky bottomed section of the river where the females lay their eggs.

In addition to efforts at river restoration, many states, North Carolina included, have established hatcheries that raise shad fry and release them into drainage systems where the fish was formerly abundant. Historic records provide key information that helps to direct these projects. In the mid-1840s northeastern North Carolina, for example, the shad fishery supported approximately 1,000 workers. Now the state's Wildlife Resources Commission is releasing a significant number of fry in this region annually. With individual females able to produce thousands of eggs, the local hatcheries raise and release 2 million fry each year. Normally, about 70 percent of the young fish die before reaching the sea. In that the hatcheries protect the fry for some time before their release, the young fish can gain weight and grow before being released, reducing mortality. While American shad are unlikely to ever reach levels of former abundance, the efforts of fishery biologists look promising.

⤳

When Rudolph was catching fish, success came in spurts. Well, the shad were hooked in spurts; some days, when I could look down in the shadows and watch them swimming below me, it seemed as if they were there all the time. Nosed into the current, they mostly held position. The darts were playing 20 yards or more behind the boat, but it would have been informative to see how the shad interacted with the darts. Rudolph's intuition, however, was in constant play. He thought the ¼-ounce darts were best, but occasionally he would shift over to ⅜-ounce or 1⅙-ounce darts. "The color doesn't make much difference." He would say this each time he changed out one color dart for another.

I had not given the sport of it much thought as my previous experiences with shad had been on the end of a fork or seeing their compressed bodies stacked on ice. For a rod and reel fisherman, a hooked four-pound roe shad puts up a darn good run, but even the smaller "bucks" give quite a fight. The females were much stronger, of course, and on occasion ones are caught here that would go five or six pounds. A male averaged two and a half pounds. The difference was obvious to Rudolph; he would say, "This is a nice roe," within seconds of hooking into one and long before the fish was in sight. Rudolph would position the line so it was clear of the boat and then gradually work the fish. Once it was close to the boat, and while holding the rod high with his left hand, he would net it with his right. Shad don't surrender, and a number of them shook the darts within the first minute of being hooked, others got away just as the net was scooping down. The daily limit was 10, so as the day went on often the bucks were unceremoniously released so that the fishing could continue until late in the day. The bucks are really second-class fish, at least on days when the darts were most annoying.

⤝

There are guys fishing for shad with fly rods who are clearly on the river for sport, others that are out there for the fish, and there are many who are just happy to be on the water on mild spring days. Rudolph is out there for all of this. Toward the end of the season he starts stocking up on shad and in early May my wife's father and uncles host a shad fry. Rudolph supplies and cooks the fish and the other hundred or so folks bring their appetites. Bankers, plumbers, lawyers, policemen, auto mechanics, and insurance salesmen catch up on their versions of the local news, swap stories, and devour shad and hush puppies. And, of course, there is more fish information than one could imagine. "You know we haven't caught any hickory shad here since the '60s?" "Yeah, they used to be a lot in the river before the paper mill went in." I find myself spending much of the evening trying to discreetly pick shad bones out of my gums. When I was growing up in Maryland we just ate the roe, but now with umpteen North Carolina shad fries behind me I still have not mastered eating the damn things.

American shad are anadromous. This is a 46-cent word used by stuffy scientists to indicate that shad spawn in freshwater and grow up at sea. Other anadromous fishes include sturgeon, salmon, and some of the other species of shad. American eels are just the opposite; they grow up in freshwater and breed far at sea. They are catadromous. OK, so now that your vocabulary is 92 cents richer, think of the eels and shad passing each other with our rivers simultaneously being the eastbound and westbound interstate highways from the sea. Shad migrate farther upstream than any other anadromous fish. Prior to dams some were reported to ascend over 300 miles up Atlantic coast rivers. Once the rivers warm up, their migrations are rapid. Years back, at the no. 2 lock, Rudolph hooked a shad that had been tagged. Soon after reporting the tag number, he learned that the fish had been caught and released by commission fisheries biologists just 26 hours earlier. I don't know if he was more surprised about the male shad's 33-mile upstream movement or the fact that the fish had been tagged and released by his good friend Jimmy Davis. Jimmy is now retired and in the spring can often be found fishing from the stern of Rudolph's johnboat.

A ripe roe shad produces anywhere from 1,000 to 6,000 eggs. Soon after spawning most of the adults die, but a few Cape Fear shad have been recovered while spawning for a second season. Depending on water temperatures, the eggs hatch in three to eight days. Young of the year shad remain near the mouths of their home rivers or in nearby estuaries until the fall and then migrate out to sea. In four to five years, when most reach adulthood, they return to the same rivers where they first hatched. Because of this, the rivers with the fewest dams and other obstacles, and those with the least pollution, support the best shad runs. Shad migrations bring a huge amount of biological mass far inland. This is a key energy source for the rivers. It's not just the returning adults, the millions and millions of fry are also important direct or indirect food sources for everything from dragonfly larvae to kingfishers. Yes, shad support an important commercial and recreational fishery, but they also help feed the river.

The shad industry in North Carolina and elsewhere along the Atlantic coast at one time was one of the major fisheries in the New World. The American shad was an important species for both Native and Colonial America. The massive spring spawning runs brought a marine resource inland where the shad were easily captured in mass. They arrived at a time of year when winter food stores were largely depleted, and nearly everyone became involved in some aspect of the fishery. This is likely why the Native Americans mythologized shad. Their March spawning runs were a key part of their calendars, and studies of New England Indian middens show that coastal tribes were living off shad, not salmon. The stories we learned in school about the Indians teaching Pilgrims at Plymouth to fertilize their crops with dead fish were true, and we learn from writings of the original settlers in 1621 that the fish used were shad. In Philadelphia, barrels of shad served as currency. Owners of downstream farms built dams to prevent the upstream migrations of shad and enable them a larger catch. In return, owners of upstream sites raided their neighbors, starting feuds that created a lawless American society like the one we now associate with the Wild West. These fish played major roles in the lives of George Washington and Thomas Jefferson, both of whom maintained riverside shad fisheries as a major source of income. Henry David Thoreau was the first to become alarmed about the effects of dams on shad migration. Because of the shad fishery, land along rivers became worth much more than nearby agricultural lands. Generations of commuting shad shaped not only our history, but our economy as well.

Populations started to decline by 1850. The Bureau of Fisheries kept records of the landings of American shad starting in 1880. During this record keeping, in North Carolina alone the harvest peaked at nearly nine million pounds in 1897. By 1947 the harvest had dropped to only nine hundred thousand pounds. This is about 12 percent of the peak harvest. Overharvesting by commercial fishermen both at the mouths of rivers and at sea over the intervening years took its toll. In the mid-1900s Russian fishing fleets annually harvested tons of shad from off the Atlantic coasts. However, pollution of estuaries and rivers, and more importantly dams that prevented successful upstream spawning runs, caused the populations to crash. Today the Delaware River is the only major river on the Atlantic seaboard that remains free flowing and it is this river that has become the mecca for shad sport fishing. Additionally, our taste has changed. Shad roe and scrambled eggs have been replaced by supersized egg McMuffins and today many people consider the shad itself to be too strong for their taste. For a number of reasons shad will probably never occupy their former importance as a major commercial species.

For Rudolph, his commercial shad fishing days ended decades ago. One spring, about 30 years back, while checking his nets at the mouth of the Cape Fear, he discovered he had captured a submarine. The sub had strayed out of the main shipping channel. It was a U.S. one so Rudolph let it go, but his nets were beyond repair. Sport fishing with a rod and reel was more fun anyway; he let his commercial license expire, and now he waits for any sign of spring and a reason to be back on the river.

As the fish swims, it's over a hundred miles inland to lock no. 2; Rudolph and I not only benefit from the mild spring weather generated by the Gulf Stream's influence on the Atlantic's temperate waters, but also from a friendship we built around the dart-induced bounty. And, by the way, the Elizabethtown shad fry is not limited to just fried shad; the roe is the star. Over the years, I have been promoted from just another hungry invitee with gums full of sharply pointed shad bones, to the chief chef in charge of cooking the roe. While not my favorite, compared to collards, turnip greens, chitlins, green bean casseroles, ramps, and most other southern dishes, shad roe, even when I cook it, rates a 9.3. While I probably should not share secret family recipes, this one can't fail. The major flavoring ingredient is good old bacon grease—lots of bacon grease—to cook anadromous fish ova. How can it not be good?

CHAPTER 13 SLITHERY, SLIMY, AND ELEGANT—EELS

They're hiding under rocks, far up the Mississippi basin, beyond Baton Rouge, Vicksburg, Memphis, and Louisville, and well past Cincinnati and Huntington, West Virginia. In fact, they're slipping under rocks in the New River, almost to North Carolina's western border. Though the common freshwater eel, *Anguilla rostrata*, can be found in nearly every body of water draining into the Atlantic and Gulf slopes of North America, its presence this far upstream still seems astonishing.

Laying out a piece of string on an Exxon road map (this was in the days before Google Maps), I once tried to simulate the snaking route these eels followed to get them all the way up from the Gulf of Mexico to the New River. Making tight turns secured with tape, the string twisted all the way back toward the spawning grounds in which the eels were conceived. Measuring the string against the scale of the map, I estimated a crude distance of the eel's migration, roughly 1,000 miles from the Gulf of Mexico to the New River, and that's after coming 3,000 miles from the Sargasso Sea. Other eels take even longer routes to reach Kansas, Nebraska, South Dakota, Minnesota, and even central New Mexico. All those miles and then the eels have to retrace their travels back to somewhere in the Sargasso Sea where their lives begin and end. The migration of eels is a fascinating business, and not just because of the distance traveled.

The comings and goings of eels have perplexed humans for centuries. Aristotle was one of the earliest writers to present observations on European eels, and he was also the first to recognize that the young eels, called "elvers," came from the sea and return to it as adults. Nevertheless, in the centuries that followed, some of the most preposterous fish stories ever told have been about eels.

The sudden appearance of young elvers in the spring—strange-looking creatures by anyone's standards—caused some people to believe they came from the "entrails of the earth." Others suggested that eels emerged from the skin of large "worms" (the classification system of animal life did not have

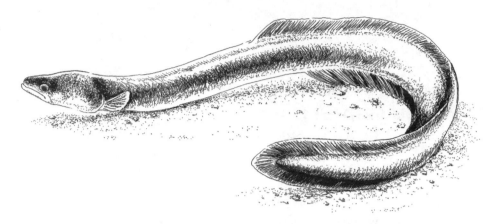

American eels begin life as eggs in the Sargasso Sea, hatching into larvae that drift with the Gulf Stream. It takes years for them to reach the U.S. freshwater streams and estuarine habitats where they mature, changing color and form as they reach adulthood. Completing their life cycle, they return to the birth waters of the Sargasso Sea to spawn and die.

the constraints it does today). When these worms were torn apart, little eels could be seen inside. Another theory was that shreds of skin left by adult eels rubbing themselves on rocks somehow turned into little ones. One of my favorite myths comes from Italy, where, shortly after the birth of Christ, it was said that Roman eels "drunk with desire" came from the sea to mate with snakes. The snakes were supposedly so enamored that they vomited out their black fatal venom, so as not to harm the love-struck eel, and headed toward the beach while whistling a love song. The eel swam toward the shore to meet the snake as the snake threw himself into the sea to meet her. Panting with pleasure, the female drew the snake's head into her mouth. Somehow, this satisfied the creatures' passion and contributed to the next generation of eels, after which the snake and eel returned to their proper elements. The snake of course did not forget to re-absorb the black poison after it crawled ashore. Italians are such romantics!

American versions of eel folklore are no less bizarre. Even the fish stories of modern-day bass fishermen pale in comparison. Tales of romantic encounters between male eels and female catfish border on the pornographic. Other lore involves supposed aphrodisiac powers possessed by eels. (Strangely enough, if one were to compile a listing of all food items with reported aphrodisiac powers it would read like a menu of things most people would normally avoid eating. The early history of marketing strategy, I suppose.)

Fantasies aside, by 1684 biologists had again correctly guessed that fresh-water eels lay their eggs in the sea. Then in 1692, Antoni van Leeuwenhoek, most remembered for his early version of a microscope, described the swim bladder of an eel as a womb because it contained what were actually parasitic worms. This one dissection set the knowledge about eels back at least 100 years. In 1777, the ovaries of eels were found and described; it took another 100 years before the existence of male eels was confirmed, when a specimen with testes was reported. Male eels never obtain the length that females do, and apparently it took some time before scientists bothered to poke around in eels under 20 inches in length, as they assumed they were not mature. Although larval eels were found in 1856, the German naturalists that discovered them thought they were a previously undescribed species of fish. In the 1890s, researchers keeping these fish in aquariums accidentally stumbled upon the fact that the "new" species persistently transformed into young eel elvers.

With the question of where little eels come from and how they reproduce finally resolved, attention turned to finding the larvae in the sea. In a study that lasted from 1904 to 1922, Johannes Schmidt, a Dutch biologist, collected eel larvae from throughout the North Atlantic and Mediterranean. He mapped the catches by size and season and found that the smallest eels represented two distinct populations that drift as plankton in the currents of the North Atlantic. The larvae of the European eels complete a circuit around the gyre of the Sargasso Sea in approximately two and a half years. The American eel larvae have a similar journey, but it only lasts one year.

The exact spawning area has never been discovered, but it is assumed that adults of both American and European eels breed in the Sargasso Sea and then die. The fact that the exact breeding site, if one exists, has not been established is not, in itself, surprising. The Sargasso Sea is rarely visited. Furthermore, a complex gyre of currents, one of which is the Gulf Stream, and countercurrents would disperse eggs and larvae quickly.

One April, I watched faint shadows dancing on a sandy coastal-plain creek bottom. Puzzled, I dragged a net through the water and, to my surprise, caught dozens of glass eels, the elvers of *Anguilla*. They had been temporarily stalled by a wooden dam for a small millpond. I had never seen them before. I wanted to see for myself how they got around the dam, having read that on rainy nights they will swim through wet grass, and across stones, or wiggle their way up the sides of small dams. Was this feat the basis of the myth that young eels come from the sloughed-off skin of adult eels?

I ran my hand up the alga-covered surface of the cypress boards forming the dam, and, when I looked down, the cup of my hand was full of transparent two-and-a-half-inch elvers. There was no need to wait for night or rain—the elvers were on the move. I don't know how long it takes for young eels to assume their adult characteristic build and color. These were 20 to 30 miles inland, as the fish swims, and except for their eyes, they were still transparent. Hemoglobin, which would eliminate their transparent cloaking device, does not form until the eels are older.

Once past this stage in their tortuous life history, eels are known to eat a variety of freshwater fishes and invertebrates. While food habits vary from place to place and with the season, generally, 90 percent of their diet consists of larval aquatic insects such as mayfly, stonefly, and dragonfly nymphs.

The freshwater behavior of eels further complements the mystique surrounding them. They swim freely in the muddy, silty bottoms of lakes and among stones in rivers and creeks, generally lying buried during the day and throughout the coldest parts of winter. Experimentally displaced eels returned to home creeks from distances of up to 50 miles. Individuals kept out of water survived for 48 hours. Researchers have heard chirping, note-like sounds and sucking noises coming from eels on warm August evenings, and mature eels during migration have been found entwined in balls of up to 6 feet in diameter.

～

Worldwide there are about 20 families and several hundred species of eels, but the common eel of the freshwater genus *Anguilla* (16 species) is the eel familiar to most people. The American and European eels, the only two species of freshwater eels in the North Atlantic basin, are similar, differing only in the number of vertebrae (103 to 111 for our species and 110 to 119 for its European counterpart), in color and duration of the larval stage, and in a few other minor features, apparent only to attentive ichthyologists. In fact, some researchers now believe that both types are really just one species. American eels are larger than the European ones. Females 48 inches long and weighing as much as 16 pounds have been reported. Males, however, rarely exceed 24 inches.

There is no precise answer as to how long individual eels live in freshwater before returning to the sea. Generally, the females leave freshwater after about seven years, and males, which mature in estuaries, return in four to seven years. Nevertheless, the growth rates and ages of freshwater eels, like most aspects of their life cycle, are not well known. Some females will remain in freshwater 15 to 20 years before maturing, and individuals trapped in landlocked lakes have been known to live there 35 to 40 years. A European eel kept in an aquarium in Sweden, unable to complete her spawning run, lived for 88 years.

I've seen lots of eels, but only once have I encountered a full adult. It was dead and rigor-mortised into a snake-like posture near the high-tide line of the lower Chesapeake Bay. Three to three and a half feet in length, it was not brown or yellow but a silver color, like the dull side of a piece of aluminum foil. Its large eyes were sunken, indicating that it was not exactly fresh. I resisted taking it home. There was no question that it was *Anguilla*, but the appearance was so striking that I had to make a quick mental tally of the marine eels of the area to convince myself that my identification was correct.

In preparation for its marine journey, this one eel had made its final transformation, not as spectacular as a caterpillar becoming a moth, or even an eel larva becoming a full red-blooded fish, but a striking change nevertheless. The eel's scales become firmly fixed and the skin toughens and grows thinner, creating a silver, metallic sheen. The lateral line, a sensory system, increases, and nostrils dilate. The eyes are most striking. They double in size, giving a totally different set of proportions to the head. Biologists studying changes in the eel's eye have shown that the area of the retina quadruples, with the total volume of the eye increasing eight times. A change in the retina color allows for the absorption of blue light, the only wavelength that penetrates the sea. The digestive tract shrinks, and by late summer the homeward-bound eel ceases to feed. Its body is programmed for only two goals—movement toward the spawning grounds and spawning.

Once an eel leaves freshwater, no one really knows where it goes or how it gets there. Only a handful have been captured at sea, only one has been photographed in the ocean, and the eggs have never been found in all the thousands of North Atlantic plankton studies. To some extent *Anguilla* is still the mystery it was in 350 BC. However, the silver color of the eel, the increase in their eye size, and a change in the size of their swim bladder all suggest that eels probably migrate through the sea at a depth of about 500 feet.

Researchers who have tagged eels have determined that migrating eels can cover 30 to 40 miles per day. Knowing this, we can project a travel time of 80 days to the Sargasso Sea for European eels, and less than that for ones leaving the American coast. Though this might seem like a long journey to be covered without food, 80 days is a relatively short period for fasting migratory fish. Atlantic salmon, for example, may fast for 10 months before completing spawning runs.

Based on the size of the smallest larvae, and assuming egg development of only seven days, biologists believe that the adult eels spawn in winter and early spring, leaving their progeny to ride the currents. Actual counts of developing eggs in mature eels exceed 2.5 million. The whole process seems terribly inefficient, but like primitive plants with wind-transported spores, eels persist.

~

Despite 30 years of fieldwork in the Gulf Stream working in a current that must transport untold billions of larval eels, I have never seen one. Nevertheless, here they must drift and perish in astronomical numbers. They are as common as raindrops, and most are as short lived. Biologists collecting the larvae have found them to drift at depths of about 1,000 feet, moving upward, like so much of the Gulf Stream's euphoric fauna, to 500 feet at night. I have looked unsuccessfully for their small, transparent, leaf-shaped bodies in the stomachs of seabirds I collected off North Carolina. We know that a number of mid-water-column organisms are forced to the surface by the strong upwellings along the Stream's western front. These patchy food sources provide livelihoods for entire communities of marine birds, and the eel larvae must be forced up to the surface as well.

Unless they swim under it, the strong northbound current of the Stream presents a formable obstacle for minute fish larvae genetically programmed to move toward shore. Larvae would be swept northward at a rate of at least 100 miles a day, and perhaps half that again. How many days would it take one to swim across a current that is 70 miles wide at Cape Hatteras? How do any of them make it? Probably the small percentage of the larvae that survive to change into elvers do so after they reach the rather quiet waters of the continental shelf. Perhaps the ones that complete their journey are carried toward shore by the giant warm-water eddies that periodically break free of the Stream and drift lazily northward over the continental shelf. Some eddies persist for months and would provide efficient, if not safe, transport for planktonic transforming larvae.

In their transformation from larvae, elvers actually decrease in size. Yet, compared to the larvae, they can swim better and now have direction in their life. Still, it's hard to imagine how they can cope with the tides, long-shore currents, and the downstream rush of coastal rivers. Starting in late winter they begin to arrive in freshwater, but, unlike shad, they are not believed to be programmed to find parental rivers.

A spring visit to almost any small creek near the coast will yield a number of elvers, and their presence is a testament to the driving force of migration. The odds of any given eel larvae getting this far in life must be phenomenal; the fact that they arrive at all suggests that the spawning output of the adults is beyond comprehension. But many do survive, and, in places, they are found in great numbers. In good years the elver fishery on the Severn River in England may be as great as 50 tons. That's a lot of eels for one river system. In some areas of the world elvers and the eels themselves are an important seafood.

Although skinned eels are a delicacy fried or smoked, few are eaten in the Western Hemisphere. Those caught on a hook and line are generally considered an annoyance by fishermen who must face untangling both the twisting, knotted fish and the line and removing the swallowed hooks. That said, because their flesh is so firm, eels are often used as bait for catfish and crabs. And eels may soon find themselves off the hook and in the frying pan in North America. Considered a delicacy in Europe and Asia, eels and eel elvers are increasingly caught in the United States and Canada, frozen, and then exported. Jellied eel is a connoisseur's delight in London and east England. The jelly is produced when the boiled skin slime jells. I have never had any, but to be honest, the thought of eel jelly makes me quite supportive of the eel export business.

⤛

How did such a lowly, primitive fish develop such a strange, seemingly backward, and taxing migration? Salmon, shad, marine lampreys, and other anadromous fishes have a lifestyle that at least makes sense. Adults funnel their reproductive energy into the headwaters of rivers, where the concentrated adults have an increased chance of finding mates. Eggs can be hidden in gravel, and young are protected until they have a chance to grow and have the strength and wit to live in a chaotic, predator-filled ocean. But eels are forced into currents of the sea and against the downstream flows of rivers when it seems they are at a size least able to cope with those hazards.

Many ichthyologists now suspect that eels, both American and European, originally bred in a small sea, perhaps a river, which once separated North America from Africa. At one time the coast of Europe fitted against North America, and Brazil nested into the Gulf of Guinea on the African coast. Two hundred million years ago, during the Triassic age, a crack split the land-masses. As the crack widened, water filled the void. Eels moving upstream from the spawning areas came from an inland sea, which eventually grew into the Atlantic Ocean. The eels remained loyal to their spawning grounds and returned to the same general site, generation after generation. The eel's homing behavior has a built-in loyalty, not much different in concept from a pigeon to its roost.

At first such a theory seems preposterous. Yet, it has been discovered that eels, like many other migratory animals, have bits of magnetite in their heads. Perhaps this enables them to maintain migration routes that relate to advancing magnetic plates. As I write this, the Atlantic continues to widen. Continents continue to move apart at a rate of about three-eighths of an inch per year. That's four inches in an average eel's lifetime, thousands of miles in the history of the species.

The migration of *Anguilla* is simply an extension of a global pattern in many types of eels. All their spawning takes place in warm marine waters at considerable depths. Some species live close to their breeding areas; others travel to grow and mature in inshore areas. Some travel to lagoons and estuaries, and, in the extreme case of *Anguilla*, into freshwater. The fact that some American eels spend their adolescent period in the New River of Virginia and North Carolina, believed by some to be the second-oldest existing river in the world, makes the story of these ancient fish a little richer. Time, the key factor in the formation of rivers, oceans, and eel biology, is the one aspect of all of this that is most difficult for us to comprehend.

No human was around to predict the scenario of this migration as it evolved in a changing world. From before the time of Greek philosophers until the beginning of the previous century, all the yarn tellers combined were unable to concoct a tale that could compete with the story that the reality of eel biology and time has fashioned. The epic migrations of this fish are unmatched and, even after centuries of curious probing, still not entirely understood.

CHAPTER 14 COLD WAR, WARM WATERS

If you think the Gulf Stream's waters matter little to the health and happiness of everyday people, you might be asking the wrong people. Instead of locals, ask a citizen of the former Soviet Union.

Most people are unaware that at the height of the Cold War, large fleets of Soviet vessels regularly fished off our coast. For a period of about 20 years, an extensive Russian-based fish industry explored and worked the waters of the outer continental shelf between Canada and Cape Hatteras. This was not Billy Bob trying out his new Bass-o-Matic—it was a huge industrial exploitation of marine resources. In design, it had all the strategies of a large military operation. The expeditionary oceanic fishery conducted by the former Union of Soviet Socialist Republics was a pioneering effort that did much to shape the development of present-day commercial fishing. The Soviet concept of commercial fleets and industrial fishing was unprecedented; their far-reaching effort exploited all of the world's prolific fishing areas. Many of these rich fishing grounds were unknown prior to the Soviets' systematic explorations. The significance of their exploitation of the coastal waters of the eastern United States and Canada and the new technologies they developed for open ocean fisheries between the 1960s and the early 1980s cannot be overstated.

The fishery relied on a large number of vessels of various sizes and classes, each with a different task, deployed in groups to major fishing grounds. The Soviet Union's close state control and integration of systems for production, distribution, and monetary exchange was the underlying reason it could successfully expand its commercial fishing fleet on such a scale. Efforts to better organize the oceanic fisheries began in the 1940s. It was a grand plan with a clear goal—conduct expeditionary fishing in all parts of the world's oceans, freeze the catch aboard ship, deliver the products to home ports, and create onshore bases for distribution. The structure of the fleet was based on "weatherproof" ships of medium and large tonnage, mother ships, transport refrigerator ships, tankers, and rescue ships. All were tied together with land-based communication systems. In the early years available information

At the height of the Cold War, for about 20 years, large fleets of Soviet vessels regularly fished the prolific waters off the North Carolina coast.

on the ocean's resources was scant, the open sea was common property, and the pioneering explorations discovered many large, often previously unknown, fish populations. The Russians scanned the available literature, produced detailed maps of the bottom topography, and staffed their exploratory voyages with research biologists, hydrologists, and oceanographers. It was a venture of unequaled scale.

One of the major interventions of the expanding global Soviet fishery was the harvest of small pelagic schooling species that occurred abundantly over continental shelves. This was particularly true of the waters of the western North Atlantic. Species such as herring, shad, mackerel, and menhaden, considered to be of low marketable value, were a key part of the new fishery. These were fishes that represented a high potential source for protein, and they became the basic component of the harvest. The Soviet fishery had found a vacant niche in the world's fish market.

It was this thinking that led to the expansion of the fishery to the east coast of North America. The newly developed market was so novel it was difficult to believe. The vessels typically remained at least 40–50 miles offshore, and the fleet made no ports of call in the United States or Canada. Even at the height of the Cold War, most Americans had no idea that major Russian fishing activity was taking place within a few miles of our shores. While the fleet never visited U.S. ports, the Soviet fishermen frequently took shore leave in Cuba where Castro welcomed them.

There was one notable incident that could have changed public awareness. When one of the fleet's sonar operators was taken seriously ill and it was determined that he needed immediate hospitalization, the nearest mother ship was 600 miles away, but the U.S. port at Atlantic City was only 60 miles. The huge rust-covered factory ship was escorted into port by the Coast Guard. Suspicious that the ship was on a spy mission, military personnel equipped with various instruments descended on the ship, searching every cabin and locker and measuring everything for levels of radioactivity. A representative from the Soviet embassy arrived and translated the demand that one of the barrels in the hold be removed for examination. It was filled with salted herring from the Georges Bank, east of Cape Cod. This did little to alleviate the suspicion—what's a ship like this doing 5,000 miles away from her home port? Where does it refuel and how do the sailors get their food and water supplies? And what was such a large ship doing transporting herring—a fish that few Americans would consider eating? But the U.S. public was less concerned. The crewman was returned from the hospital in two days with stocks of medicine and piles of get-well cards and letters from Americans who saw an opportunity for a little soft diplomacy. The ship headed back out to sea.

⤳

To appreciate all this, one must have an understanding of the Russian palate, culture, and the political and economic background leading up to their massive offshore harvest. To most Americans, herring, shad, and menhaden are fatty, oily, and full of bones. They are the poster children for "fishy taste." To Russians, however, salted herring are a mainstay, not just for meals, but also as a finger food served in neighborhood bars. For Russian settlers who inhabited the coast of the White Sea from the 12th to the 18th centuries, herring was the primary commercial fishery. In time, with improved transportation, salted herring began showing up in inland markets, and by the pre-Revolutionary period the fishery had shifted to the Caspian Sea and eventually also expanded to the Russian far east into the Seas of Okhotsk and Japan. But the European herring fishery peaked by the early 1900s. World War II led to a breakdown in the herring supply. Overfishing was a major contributing factor; from 1954 to 1962 the eastern North Atlantic stock had a fourfold decrease. To the fishermen it seemed impossible that such a vast and widely distributed stock could have been all but exterminated. A new source of herring-like fish was required.

In his historical 1945 speech, Joseph Stalin defined the future of the socialists' community: "50 million tons of cast iron, 60 million tons of steel,

500 million tons of coal, and 60 million tons of oil must be secured against any eventuality." In a series of successive five- and seven-year plans the Communist Party achieved its goals, but with an unexpected result. While the industrial output had improved by two and a half times what it had been in the previous decade, the revitalization of agriculture turned out to be a difficult task and showed little growth. The postwar Soviet Union was facing widespread hunger. The disproportionate development between agriculture and industry, a result of war-years strategy, was increasing. Agricultural production continued to decline through the mid-1960s. With a surplus of steel and oil and a hungry nation, thoughts turned to the production of a massive fishing fleet to harvest the world's seas. While the new super fleet of trawlers with built-in freezing capacity was being constructed, the existing fleet that would otherwise have been laid-up was deployed to New World fishing grounds.

The exploratory venture of the 1950s and early 1960s discovered a major untapped commercial resource that the Soviets efficiently exploited in the decades that followed. The fishery developed around small schooling fishes that were low in the food chain but extremely abundant. The fleets were large and the task of the different ships diverse. These were floating cities. They tracked everything and constantly analyzed the data. They quickly discovered that the movements and concentrations of herring and similar fish are largely dependent on the mix of cold and warm currents and could be best fished where the countercurrents came together and formed gyres. Forecasts of the fish abundance and locations of the fish stocks were accurately determined three months to a year in advance. The schedules of the fleets could be arranged to accommodate this and tactics for maximum efficiency of capture, storage, and transport could be determined. The scouting ships informed the fleet of the precise whereabouts of fish, and the groups of fishing ships maneuvered into position. The captain was to keep his ship continually on fishing grounds that had dense concentrations of the abundant species. Furthermore, the level of fishing was dictated by economic forecast, which in turn was driven by the government's marketing. The Soviet Union's annual consumption of fish and fish products increased between 1950 and 1980 from 15 to 40 pounds per person.

While the effort revolutionized open-ocean fishing from an industrial perspective, it did little in regard to the long-term management of the fish stocks or the sustainability of the fishery itself. In the 1960s and early 1970s the average number of medium-tonnage Soviet fishing vessels off our area was 20–29, and in peak years the annual catch in our region was 100–130 thousand tons of mostly herring, menhaden, and mackerel. In some years the number of active ship/days fished was 7,500–10,500. Still, the actual amount of fishing conducted off the Carolina coast, while significant, was small compared to the effort the Soviets had made at fishing stations farther north, such as on the Grand Banks and off New England. This was largely a factor of the location of aggregations of the commercially important fish species. Yet, in terms of impact on our local fish stocks, most of the surface and mid-water species are highly migratory. In other words, shad caught off New England would include ones that spawned in North Carolina rivers, as well as other highly mobile species that were also more easily captured during periods when they concentrated around summer plankton blooms in nutrient-rich waters over the Grand Banks. In many cases they represented individuals that swam off the Outer Banks at different seasons or at a younger age. Like the fish, many of the seabirds that followed them made up the same flocks I observed regularly foraging off the Outer Banks. Research using small satellite tracking devices has recently shown that even tropical seabirds such as Audubon's shearwaters and white-tailed tropicbirds will follow the migrating fish stocks into Canadian waters.

All this is to say that the statistical data collected by the Soviet fishery may have supported economic decisions about where and when to fish, but it said very little about the depletion of the fish stocks as one moved from north to south. The Soviets were fishing and overfishing the herring and other schooling species that for most of the year concentrate their activity within the closed circulation systems of the continental shelf. As the fish stocks were affected, so surely were the seabirds. Although there were no programs to measure this, we know that marine birds suffer considerable loss because of drowning in nets as a part of what's called by-catch. Moreover, many of the petrels and storm-petrels of the western North Atlantic are attracted to lights at sea, making them especially vulnerable to the night fishing activities of the vessels. Seabirds' recovery from the period of the western Atlantic Soviet fishery would be even slower than that of the fish. Most are long lived, taking five to seven years to reach breeding age, and many lay but a single egg per year. Fulmars and some of the more common species of gulls would actually benefit from all the food scraps dumped on the surface from the trawlers, but other seabirds would experience a decreased prey base, as the pelagic fishery and the birds competed for the same resource.

In the mid-1970s when I was first starting my pelagic seabird studies I recall seeing large fishing vessels as they worked the offshore waters of the Outer Banks. The Soviet fleet worked closer to land here than elsewhere in the western Atlantic because the continental shelf is narrower and the Outer Banks themselves project out to sea. The charter-boat captains called them factory ships. They flew flags that no one seemed to recognize and many bore the names of various East European republics across their sterns. Generally, they fished inshore of the Gulf Stream, and some seemed as large as the tankers and container ships that used the Gulf Stream current as a northbound shipping lane. At the time sport fishing along the outer continental shelf and inner edge of the Gulf Stream was relatively new. While a number of Hatteras- and Oregon Inlet–based charter-boat captains had made experimental excursions to these deeper waters, in the previous decades their boats were mostly too small and lacked the speed needed to make it that far out and back again in a single day. Prior to the mid-1970s most of the charter fishing was inshore and targeted bluefish, migrating tuna, and bottom-dwelling fishes.

Some days we would come across ships as the crew was washing the unwanted by-catch over the stern. The seabirds were very intune to the timing of the seine hauls and would begin to concentrate behind the ship even before deck cleaning was underway. This provided a massive feast, and thousands of various species and age classes of gulls, kittiwakes, and gannets would converge at these sites. In hindsight I wish I had understood what was taking place. It would have been very informative to study the impact of this fishery on the seabirds. Were the birds shifting their seasonal patterns of movement and areas of concentration to take advantage of the fishing activity? If so, how did all this "free food" effect the composition of the scavenging species over the outer continental shelf? I recall a trip when one morning we encountered a large actively working fishing vessel that was surrounded by massive amounts of floating whale blubber. It extended out half a mile or so from the ship. The ship had no identification that we could see and flew a flag that we did not recognize. The charter-boat captain called a report in to the Coast Guard, but by then the ship was underway, and I don't think anything came of it. On most days we just worked around the ships as they fished, recording the assortments of birds attracted to the ships' activities. I always wondered what went through the minds of Soviet fishermen as they looked down from their high decks and saw us with our binoculars scanning the flocks of seabirds that were attracted to their processed fish scraps that they were washing overboard.

The Soviet fishery was methodical. Researchers tracked the catch/effort statistics and with this information they constantly shuffled vessels to new sites, fished at different depths, and shifted to different species as various stocks became depleted to the point that it was not likely to remain economically productive. The fishing techniques were diverse, allowing ships to shift gear types and to continue to exploit areas they had already overfished. Drift nets, purse-seine fishing, and pair trawling were all used, often with different mesh sizes and at different depths and seasons. Ships could rapidly change from bottom trawls to nets set for mid-water and surface pelagic species. And while the fishery focused on small schooling pelagic fishes they also could rig to catch swordfish, marlins, tunas, sharks, king crabs, squid, and even krill. With various mesh sizes and hulling depths, these ships could catch anything from bottom-dwelling flounders and sea robins to eels and needlefish living higher in the water column. The Soviets even tried electric-light fishing, but this never got past the experimental stage. The fish stocks with the highest abundance and greatest densities of concentration were harvested to the maximum, with thoughtless disregard for future catches. Harvest effort typically declined in years following peak catches. The most spectacular catches off the North American coast were in 1965 and 1966 and between 1971 and 1973.

In 1977, the United States, Canada, and the European Economic Community introduced 200-mile fishing zones in large part due to the Soviet fishery. Not only were local fishermen being deprived of income, but a number of the fish stocks themselves had been greatly depleted. Eventually, new international laws regarding the enforcement of fishing zones, combined with the changing political and economic structure of the Soviet Union, resulted in the decline of its fisheries operations in the North Atlantic. But the ministry overseeing the fishery took a number of steps to avert the crisis and retain the scope of the global industry they had established. In that the fishery was run as a business venture of the Soviet Union, very detailed records were maintained as to the locations, seasons, and the catch, and the fleets were constantly shifting operations. They shifted to shelf waters off West African countries that had not defined protected fishing zones, and the Soviets were able to secure other areas with bilateral governmental agreements. The fishing fleets also began to explore new fishing areas on the high seas. As a result the fishery shifted focus to the open ocean (50 percent), the Antarctic (12 percent), and to unregulated shelf waters (16 percent), and their total catch actually increased by 4 million tons in the first five years. The exploratory ships discovered major untapped jack mackerel stocks outside the 200-mile zone off Peru and Chile. The fleets were now sailing farther and cast their trawls ever deeper in their quest. In the second half of the 1980s a total of 10.5–11.3 million tons of fish were harvested annually and in 1989 the Soviet fleet had surpassed Japan as the number one country in commercial fish harvest.

The end came quickly, however. In just the first four years of the 1990s the total catch dropped by over 50 percent. Unanticipated changes in the structure of the Soviet Union itself during the previous decades had been the major contributing factors. The fisheries branch was structured to function under the socialist-run state with a centralized system of planning. The system depended on state allotments of funding and a fuel supply that was provided below cost. The shift to more open-ocean fishing resulted in a massive catch of pelagic fishes of low commercial value. The new, more distant, fishing grounds resulting from the closure of the 200-mile zones led to escalation of costs, not just of fuel, but the need for use of foreign ports also came with a price, and rights to fish within the 200-mile zone had to be paid to the host countries. The annual catch included tons of small species with little commercial value and no dependable market. Much of the catch was processed for industrial purposes. State subsidies were no longer practical. By the time the Soviets had become the world's leader in oceanic fisheries the subsidies had reached a level of five to eight billion dollars a year and the industry was clearly no longer sustainable. These problems were developing even in the early 1980s as the economy of the U.S.S.R. was already deteriorating.

Soviet earnings from oil operations were noticeably reduced by the mid-1980s and the old administrative system was becoming dysfunctional as its financial stability decayed. By the time of the breakdown of the U.S.S.R. and the union's governing bodies, the government's debt had climbed to 60 billion dollars. The reforms were built mostly on liberalization of prices and privatization of markets. During the transition and the shift of most of the state's property to private enterprise, the various ministries' centralized control of the economy weakened, destroying the government's fishing industry. By 2000 the non-state sector made up 93 percent of all enterprise and nearly all of the production output. Once Latvia, Lithuania, and Estonia withdrew from the Soviet Union, the large coastal fishing complexes were lost. By this time 70 percent of the ships had been in service for over 10 years and were destined to be reduced to scrap metal. The Russian fleet abandoned its productive southeast Pacific fishery and the distant portions of the Atlantic to concentrate on the economic zone of Russia and nearby areas of the northeastern Atlantic. The possibility of re-opening the more distant large-scale open-ocean fisheries has been considered, but calculations show that losses would greatly exceed profits in today's market.

Duplicating the Soviets' innovative technologies allowed other countries to quickly move into the void left by the decaying Russian fleets. Calculations show the larger Russian trawlers capable of capturing and processing 6,300–10,000 tons of pelagic fishes in a year. Today's Dutch super trawlers only need 20–30 days to produce the same volume of frozen fish. The Russian ships are physically outdated and have no future. In the Pacific, Russian fishermen now only work areas within their economic zone, and the fishery is failing. Alaska pollock, the most important fish stock in the region are decreasing. Poaching Asian fishermen and foreign firms are now moving into the region to exploit the resource.

—

For nearly 40 years, thousands of Soviet ships and hundreds of thousands of fishermen explored the world's seas and harvested untold tons of seafood under what was the most ambitious far-reaching commercial fishery ever developed. Its decline was a combination of changing international law, internal political change, and overexploitation of a resource that is sustainable only when properly managed. The collapse of this industry obviously was a benefit to our local fisheries, but it also allowed for a partial recovery of western North Atlantic marine ecosystems. The Soviets' take of vast quantities of small seemingly unimportant fishes was quite disruptive to the population stability of the larger species that preyed on them. For example, the Soviets were removing tons of menhaden a year; in some years the catch was as high as one million tons. This obviously had a negative impact on the species, but, once the menhaden stocks began to recover, brown-pelican populations also increased and their breeding range expanded northward. These pelicans for years had been on state and federal endangered species lists, and it had always been assumed that their decline was largely due to DDT in the marine environment. In that menhaden are one of the primary foods of these seabirds, it probably is not a quirk that the pelican's recovery corresponded rather closely with the demise of the Soviets' commercial harvest.

The Soviet program did much to add to our knowledge of oceanic resources, their systematic mapping and tracking of fish populations later became key in the International Commission for the Northwest Atlantic Fisheries database for their marine atlases. Their efficient industrial plan for a high-seas fishery paved the way for today's modern fishing fleets, and the overexploitation of our offshore waters forced attention for the need to form international treaties to protect them. The success of the program also eventually led to the formation of a joint fishery effort between the United States and the U.S.S.R., one of the first cooperative programs between the countries during the Cold War era. Unfortunately, these methods of mass exploitation have now again become widely used and collectively have become a significant factor in the decline of commercial fish stocks.

CHAPTER 15 MIGRANT CLOUDS AND RADAR DOTS

For a captain of a lost ship, an empty horizon can be a lonely place, particularly if he must answer to a disgruntled crew. For one such captain, the appearance of songbirds restored hope and some sense of harmony to the nearly mutinous crew of 87 men. The date was September 20, 1492. The troubled captain was, of course, Christopher Columbus. After seeing the birds, Columbus and the three ships under his command sailed onward with renewed confidence.

The birds are a great part of the story that many may remember from grade school history. Omitted from the version I was taught was the fact that the birds were sighted 22 days prior to sighting land, placing Columbus and the flock in the middle of the Sargasso Sea. In these remote, mysterious waters, Columbus reported seeing ducks, doves, and "singing birds" that had no reason to be there. Yet, his log also mentions more land-bird sightings on subsequent days. For years natural history scholars have puzzled over Columbus's log entries. Some of the more presumptuous flatly announced that Columbus deliberately erred in his statements. They speculated that his crew was so irritated that Columbus was forced to keep two logs, one for his personal calculations and one to appease the crew.

Were the bird entries simply a ploy to quiet the crew? The answer is no, but it was well into the 1900s before ornithologists began to document the magnitude of oceanic migrations of our North American land birds.

The annual fall migration saga starts sometime in early August, peaks in October, and continues through November. Millions of songbirds completing their summer nesting duties, triggered by shortening day lengths, move toward the coast. Fifty to a hundred miles inland they stop and wait, sometimes for days, constantly feeding to keep up fat reserves. When cold fronts pass through they depart, trailing the front. Gaining altitude, they fly out to sea—strange behavior for three-quarter- to one-and-a-quarter-ounce birds that seem ill equipped to handle the rigors of the open water.

Songbirds annually cross the Atlantic Ocean during fall migration, sometimes opportunistically taking a break from their long journey by resting on ships at sea.

The evidence for a North Atlantic migration route is now rather extensive, yet it was well into the 1970s before the cumulative body of information was put into perspective. In the past, common sense led to one of two assumptions—either the birds following this seagoing route perished (and such confused migratory instincts were not typical) or the birds swung southwest and made landfall farther down the coast. Early evidence for land birds at sea suggested that when sailors encountered those birds, they were indeed lost. For instance, photographs taken aboard the steamship *West Quechee* in the eye of a hurricane in the Gulf of Mexico on August 27, 1927, were used as sure evidence that the birds were lost at sea. When the wind in the hurricane's eye declined to the mild rate of five or six mph, the migrating birds filled the air. Live birds were so thick on the ship's deck that they could be scooped up by the armful. The photographs show swallows, thousands of them, closely perched on rigging and railings. These birds had been swept into the eye of the storm and probably had been transported for hundreds of miles.

Similarly, on October 9, 1979, two hours after sunset, large numbers of small birds were seen far at sea flying around lights on the USSR R/V *Belagorsk*. The evening North Atlantic sky was overcast and the wind southwesterly. By nine o'clock, an estimated 700 birds, attracted like moths, were swarming around the ship's lights. Sixty-six dead or stunned birds were picked up on the deck of the ship. All but two were blackpoll warblers, and 68 percent of these were adults. Most of the birds (84 percent) had high fat reserves and appeared to be healthy. Apparently, they were simply confused by the lights.

Yearly, large numbers of tired North American birds find their way to Bermuda. It is not believed to be a scheduled stopover, but instead a refuge for a few emaciated land birds lost at sea. Strangely, some years, healthy birds, still loaded with fat reserves, have been found dead after having struck the lighthouse in Bermuda. The presence of significantly small numbers of emaciated birds compared to those with plentiful fat reserves seemed contradictory. To add to the confusion, a modest number of the misguided North American birds find their way in autumn to the European coast where they are eagerly tallied by local bird watchers (oops, excuse me, "birders"). It was inevitable that the pattern of open-sea migration of land-based birds would be recognized as more than an aberrant phenomenon.

I have talked to many North Carolina charter-boat captains who, knowing of my interest in birds, never fail to provide stories of small exhausted birds that land on their boats each fall. Many refer to the songbirds as canaries, but captains familiar with birds have also reported rail, ospreys, eagles, teal, doves, shorebirds, and herons—all far offshore. On one of my offshore excursions, accompanied by several enthusiastic bird watchers, all hoping to add rare seabirds to their life list, one lady erupted, "Oh my! What is that?" Captain Al leaned over from the bridge and announced in a loud voice "Ma'am, back on shore we call 'em swallows."

Early one October I recall a male yellowthroat landing on Captain Harry Baum's charter boat. The bird was exhausted and easily captured by hand. We gave it some water and put the bird in a paper bag, assuming this would quiet him and allow him to regain strength. Early in the afternoon the captain caught a fly, which the yellowthroat devoured with enthusiasm. Late in the day, as we were coming back through the inlet, we released the bird. Land was less than 200 yards off our starboard and I was curious to see the direction it would take. The bird launched itself from my hand, but before he had flown more than 10 yards from the boat, it was grabbed and devoured by a laughing gull.

Gulls, and particularly jaegers (seabirds that have a migratory schedule similar to that of the land birds), must consume a large portion of the weakened birds that are unable to maintain speed and altitude. The individuals that land, or try to land, on ships at sea must represent a very small fraction of the annual casualties. Some of them cannot even catch up with charter boats moving at trolling speeds, and I have seen weary birds fly through the crest of waves presumably too weak to avoid them. These birds must be easy prey for the keen-eyed jaegers. I once found an Acadian flycatcher in the stomach of the first long-tailed jaeger ever collected off North Carolina.

But eventually, people began to see something other than accidental behavior in the patterns of open-ocean migrations by land-based birds. Impressed with the consistency of the migratory pattern, researchers in Bermuda focused radar units on songbirds. World War II was long over, and the people running radar units needed a new purpose to justify their program. This exercise revealed that great numbers of birds flew directly over the island. At the outer range of the radar the birds were still flying east-southeast. Most ornithologists of the time still believed that the oceanic flights were nothing more than very large numbers of genetically misinformed land birds on a suicidal flight.

During the 1977 fall migration, researchers from Woods Hole Oceanographic Institution in Massachusetts stationed a radar unit aboard a ship southeast of Bermuda in the Sargasso Sea. They were 1,000 miles from mainland North America. As expected, they intercepted vast legions of birds flying at altitudes of a few hundred feet to ones at the upper limit of radar detection, one and a half miles overhead. At the same time, radar units on Antigua picked up high-flying birds coming from the Sargasso Sea and heading for the South American coast. The last link in the journey was confirmed. The open Atlantic was indeed an important fall migration route for North American songbirds.

Researchers soon established a network of stations using narrow-beam radar in an attempt to better understand the nature of the migration. The birds appeared as small, slowly moving dots. The radar showed that the birds depart at night, but only when winds were favorable for the preferred direction of migration. The birds did not depart from any specific point but formed a broad front all along the coast. Observers at Cape Cod were fascinated by the numbers of birds moving into the Atlantic in the early hours of darkness. They established that from the Cape alone, up to 12 million departed on some nights. There was much variability in direction, speed, altitude, and the size of the migrant clouds of birds. The bulk of the migrants flew below an altitude of one mile. Birds flew at air speeds of 19 to 38 mph, but, with favorable winds, a few groups were clocked at speeds of over 60 mph. The radar dots did not pay any attention to Bermuda or the Caribbean islands as they blipped across the monitoring screens. Somewhere over the Sargasso Sea birds changed direction and their flight shifted to the west, ensuring landfall on the northern South American coast.

Migrants use favorable weather conditions to initiate their flights over the Atlantic. Over land the bulk of the migration takes place at night. Cold fronts that trigger departure rarely penetrate far into the Atlantic and they usually become stationary 300 to 600 miles offshore. The birds eventually overtake the front and fly through it. Why the birds fly at such high altitudes, where oxygen is about half what it is at sea level, is open to speculation, but radar information from Antigua, at least, showed more favorable winds to be present higher up. To further complicate the story, birds over the Atlantic fly considerably higher during the day than at night. Perhaps they are avoiding predators.

~

It is well known that birds can travel long distances on fall fat reserves, but most of the early studies were on large species, and it remained difficult for people to visualize that small warblers, sparrows, and thrushes could go the distance too. Lesser snow geese fly about 1,600 miles in less than 60 hours, traveling from James Bay in Canada to the coast of the Gulf of Mexico. Brant fly almost 2,500 miles across the Pacific Ocean from the Alaska Peninsula to the southern California coast. The overwater distance covered by the passerines (songbirds) migrating from North America to South America is between 1,800 and 2,500 miles. In terms of wing-loading ratios, fuel supply, and other factors important to avian flight, it should not be any more stressful for a small bird to migrate than it is for a large one.

Small birds increase normal fat deposits with the pre-migratory reserve representing 35 to 40 percent of the bird's total weight. For some species it is as high as 50 percent. To show the effectiveness of fat as a fuel, Timothy and Janet Williams, two researchers involved with open-ocean migration studies of land birds, calculated that a warbler burning gasoline with the same efficiency as fat would travel 720,000 miles on a gallon. Their fat is high octane, I suppose. Based on fat-weight loss of blackpoll warblers, researchers estimate that they can fly for more than 95 hours, and their flight range without wind has been calculated by calorie consumption to be 2,153 miles. Using an average distance of 2,175 miles and a flight speed of 30 mph, I come up with a required flight duration of three days. What that means is the birds are perfectly capable of completing the trip, but the margin for error is small.

Flying with small fat loads would have advantages. The birds would simply need to travel a more conservative route and make a few additional stops to refuel. However, studies show there are drawbacks to this alternative migration; migrating songbirds do not start to regain weight until several days after arrival at each temporary stopover. Northern water thrushes, for example, establish territories on stopovers. Like many songbirds, water thrushes who don't establish a territory actually lose weight, and normally it takes two to three days before even temporary territories can be won. The migrants not only lose time, but also expose themselves to risk in an unfamiliar environment.

Additionally, migrants traveling the shorter overwater route get to their winter quarters faster than those birds that hug coastlines and island-hop from Florida through the Greater Antilles. The ocean route's distance is 40–50 percent shorter depending on their place of origin. The overseas migrants should have considerable advantage in locating and establishing winter homes.

That said, both routes can work. Some birds that are coastal migrants their first season may take the shortcut as adults. In the 1960s, as part of a network study of coastal migration patterns, my students and I assisted Chan Robbins of the Patuxent Research Station and Gladys Cole of the Maryland Ornithological Society in a banding study of fall migrants occurring along the Maryland coast. After untangling thousands of first-year warblers from mist nets I began to wonder about the near absence of the adults. Even in the late 1960s the extent of open-ocean migration was unknown.

~

While the occurrence of fall migrants landing on vessels is common enough, only rarely have the details of the event been recorded. The documentation of the migration route was now well established, but the species composition of the migrant clouds detected on radar screens remained unknown. Radar could often identify the larger non-passerines (dot echoes) from passerines (scintillation echoes), but otherwise the species remained anonymous. During the course of my 30 years of studying seabirds in the Gulf Stream off Cape Hatteras I kept records of the land-based birds encountered at sea. The cumulative records provide some insight into the specifics of the

Atlantic migration. Nearly 100 species belonging to 12 orders of birds were seen. Over half of the species were passerines and 90 percent of the individuals encountered were seen in the fall. Only 11 species were seen in the spring.

The fall migration is not serendipitous. The basic pattern was shorebirds in August and early September with land birds to follow later in specific temporal slots. During the early portion of the migration non-passerines, such as shorebirds, outnumbered the song birds two to one. The passerines present were species such as prairie, prothonotary, and Kentucky warblers, yellow-breasted chats, Acadian flycatchers, and orchard orioles. All were birds that originated from breeding grounds in southeastern states. These were followed by songbirds originating in northeastern North America: bay-breasted and blackpoll warblers, for example. Birds seen in both periods were ones that nest in intermediate latitudes or ones, like American redstarts and common yellowthroats, that breed over broad latitudes. The late season species were mostly short-distance migrants—wrens, catbirds, kinglets, and sparrows. Most of the latter group came in mid-October and by the first week in November the migration was complete. The last group of birds may not represent open-ocean migrants, but simply short-range migrants blown out to sea by fall storms.

Peregrine and other falcons also migrate at sea. For them, the weakened songbirds provide convenient in-flight snacks. Most surprising was the fall appearance of cattle egrets and European starlings far out at sea. The starlings were introduced from Europe while the cattle egrets worked their way from Africa to the New World as landscapes were altered to accommodate grazing stocks. Individuals of these species were discovering the convenience of the Atlantic migration route despite their recent arrival in the New World.

Birds are not the only travelers to have discovered the shortcut. Far at sea I have seen red bats, sulphur and monarch butterflies, several types of dragonflies, and a number of smaller insects. The globetrotter, *Pantala flavescens*, is a commonly seen dragonfly that, as its name implies, is a notorious wander. It is found throughout the world. Adults seeking temporary rain pools for their quick-growing larvae migrate with the winds. Eventually they arrive at the convergence of wind currents where large-scale precipitation is dependable. Thus, adult globetrotters are not only in the right place for breeding in newly forming rain pools, but other individuals of the same species delivered to the same region assure that most will find mates.

In addition to the obviously hazardous potential of strong Atlantic weather systems, the fall migration coincides with the late summer and fall hurricane season. For migrating passerines, the Bermuda Triangle must take its toll. In fact, the reputation of the Bermuda Triangle may, in part, be attributed to the millions of migrating birds passing through it. John Teal, one of the pioneers in the use of radar tracking of bird migrations, correctly points out that several of the small naval planes that disappeared without a trace were ones that could have sustained damage from striking flocks of unexpected fall migrants. And the impact from a great blue heron on a plane moving at 200 mph, a mile and a half above the Atlantic, could explode the windshield. For the birds, however, the problems are not as dramatic as one might suppose. By waiting for cold fronts to move to sea, the birds can depend on a favorable northwest wind during the early part of their flight. A passing front is also a good indication of fair weather from the coast to at least the Sargasso Sea. Hurricanes approaching the Atlantic coast will usually stall the southeast movement of the cold fronts. Once over the Sargasso Sea there is little concern for navigational calculations. If the birds continue to fly to the southeast, the trade winds will correct the track and carry the birds to their destination. It has been estimated that over 100 million birds undertake this journey each fall—the majority being successful.

It's a delicate system, demanding relatively predictable fall weather patterns, food resources for fueling up prior to transoceanic flights, and programmed avian instinct. Not that we need another one, but here is one more reason to be concerned about global climate change. Even slight shifts in North Atlantic weather patterns could have disastrous consequences for neotropical migrants that are already stressed from a continuing loss of habitat both on their North American breeding grounds and on wintering sites in the tropics.

After leaving the Canary Islands on his first voyage, Columbus and his crew were out of sight of land for 35 days. Following his instincts, he simply sailed into the wake of the setting sun. In the late 1400s it was unknown that a compass points slightly differently at different places, and the crew was in a panic by the time they reached what was later to become known as the Bermuda Triangle. Huge mats of floating *Sargassum* added yet another unfamiliar and eerie element to their fears.

The appearance of the land birds and the direction of their flight caused Columbus to adjust his course slightly to the south. What effect this had on the history of the New World can only be speculated. The original course would have delivered his ships to the mercy of the Gulf Stream, and, depending on the winds, the stream may have moved him far north of his historic destination in the Bahamas. Perhaps he would have discovered the Carolinas. Charleston could have become the hub of the Spanish conquest. The ramifications of this would affect every aspect of the 500-plus years of European inhabitation of the New World. Who knows, maybe I would be writing this in Spanish and Mexicans would be speaking French. Our entire history may have been determined by a few exhausted songbirds from Vermont.

PART IV   BENEATH ALL THE BLUE

Below the surface, the ocean consists of two basically separate, and quite different, parts: the water column itself and the ocean floor. As the water gets deeper across the continental shelf and down the continental slope toward the bottom of the Atlantic, conditions change, and the creatures that dwell in the depths become stranger and stranger until they get to outright weird. The marine oddities found here are remarkable creatures, programmed for making adjustments to decreased levels of light, increased pressure, and limited food resources.

In the inshore waters over much of the continental shelf, the marine life is mostly what one would expect. Many of the bottom creatures are adapted to bury themselves in the sandy bottom. Hard-bottom areas are patchy, but, where they are present, they provide support for all the sorts of life forms that require some type of attachment to prevent being whisked about by currents and tides. A number of fishes and invertebrates typically associated with tropical coral reefs reach the northern limits of their distribution off the Carolina coast because of these scattered hard-bottom features. These are particularly popular waters for visiting sport fishermen; head boats (so named because passengers are charged by the head) carry anglers 12 to 20 miles offshore to fish adjacent to known hard-bottom sites, where grouper, snapper, and other sport fish are abundant. The head-boat captains carry with them personal notebooks with exact coordinates of wrecks that often prove even better for bottom fishing.

Hooking fish from the deeper wrecks gives some added perspective on the conditions found even in these relatively shallow waters. When brought to the surface, many of the fish will have hemorrhaging eyes poking from their sockets and bloated swim bladders and stomachs protruding from their mouths. There's an easy explanation: a significant change in water pressure as these deeper-dwelling fish are pulled to the surface in relative haste. Fish adjust their swim bladders so that they maintain a similar specific gravity to the surrounding water. Fish living at even modest depths have compressed swim bladders, allowing their specific gravity to decrease to the point where the fish can retain neutral buoyancy. A change in depth of just 33 feet represents a difference in one atmosphere of pressure, resulting in a 50 percent change in the volume of the swim bladder. This is a difference of about 15 pounds of pressure per square inch and the bodies of most fish are not rigid enough to control the decompression and the expansion of the swim bladder, even when pulled up from this modest depth.

Now imagine the difference in pressure at 1,000 feet or half a mile down.

Leatherback sea turtles and some whales dive to depths exceeding 3,900 feet, where pressures reach levels of 1,800 pounds per square inch. Welcome to the world beneath the sea.

Declining levels of light create another set of challenges for deep-water creatures. In the relatively shallow shelf waters the obvious solution is bigger eyes to increase the amount of light that can be absorbed. The fishes hooked from reefs and wrecks often have eyes that are obviously larger than those of related forms that live closer to shore. The real issue, however, is that in the dimming light, marine plants and planktonic algae become increasingly handicapped in their ability to carry out photosynthetic processes. A number of the marine algae have made compensations by adapting optimum growth rates for the wavelengths of light reaching the sea floor. Nonetheless, on a community level, as the water becomes deeper, the photosynthetic process breaks down even faster. In the absence of photosynthesis the food resources shift from ones of self-sustaining mid-water and bottom communities to ones dependent on currents and other outside forces providing a food delivery service. And let's not forget the effects of low oxygen. Dissolved oxygen is in ample supply on the wave-swept surface waters. In deep water, with an absence of photosynthetic plants, oxygen production stops.

Because food and oxygen are scarce in these deep-water environments, the biodiversity is generally lower and less dense than what one finds closer to the surface. The underwater creatures that do live in this zone have responded by modifying their lifestyles. Many lead lives of slow, deliberate motion to conserve energy. Seldom do the species here pursue their prey; instead, it is simply ambushed. To further conserve energy the marine animals of the deep are generally smaller than their shallow-water counterparts, and many that walk about the bottom do so on long energy-efficient spider-like legs.

⤳

As you think about these peculiar, rarely seen life forms, keep in mind that relatively shallow shelf waters make up only about 8 percent of the total area of the world's seas; 84 percent of our oceans exceed 21,000 feet in depth. When you move farther offshore of the Outer Banks, you encounter not only the Gulf Stream but also the slope of the outer continental shelf. Here the water becomes deeper yet, descending downward to depths of over 6,000 feet, deep into the abyssal zone. Here, the red end of the light spectrum is absorbed quickly and the heating effect of the sun is totally lost. These depths are well below the threshold of light penetration. From a biological perspective it is not quite total darkness at 3,600 feet—enough light still penetrates to stimulate the eyes of some crustaceans, and photographic plates are able to register exposure to light. From a biological perspective, the fauna found in this deep-water zone is of immense interest. It's home to everything from marine plankton and swimming octopi with inter-arm webbing that makes them look like pale umbrellas, to fish that sport built-in headlights and long dagger-like teeth. To compensate for the protracted periods between meals and the unlikelihood of between-meal snacks, a number of these deep-sea fishes have super-sized stomachs that allow them to accommodate prey that are larger than themselves.

The conditions are basically stable, and the sea creatures are in zones where water temperature, salinity, and all the other physical and chemical variables remain constant over time. The food that is available is outsourced from above—drifting downward to supply a food chain, not unlike rain bringing needed moisture to our crops. The sea floor itself is composed of various clays, muds, and oozing sediments that slowly accumulate on the sea's floor. Scientists studying such things note that the accumulation of the ocean's bottom sediments can be extremely slow. They estimate that in some cases it takes about a 1,000 years for three- to four-tenths of an inch to accumulate. Many of the deep-water inhabitants are burrowing creatures that live within this layer of ooze. It's a quiet place; change is all but nonexistent, while there are seasonal changes in the amount of "raining" detritus and phytoplankton, there remains a constant demand for dietary restraints and a need to conserve energy. This is definitely life in the slow lane.

Along the continental slope off Hatteras, many of the characteristics of the abyssal zone become lost, or at least extremely modified by the Gulf Stream. The Stream runs deep and in this particular area rushes over the middle levels of the shelf, stirring up sediments and bringing in nutrients and food sources atypical of deep-water seas. It's apparently this combination that drives the biological community top to bottom, from birds and porpoises to small bottom-dwelling crustaceans, the diversity, and in some cases density, is as good as it gets anywhere in the North Atlantic.

From the surface we can watch whales and marine turtles as they rest and replenish tissues drained of oxygen from their deep dives. Yet, seeing them at the surface tells us little about what they are truly about and how they manage to successfully navigate the depths of the sea. It is like trying to understand football by only viewing the halftime show and the commercials.

The marine biologists who study these creatures have learned much about how they go about mastering the abyssal depths, overcoming all the sundry problems that most other air-breathing creatures never have to endure. Their dives, descending thousands of feet below the surface, make the ordeals of our early maritime explorers seem trivial.

CHAPTER 16 PODS OF POTHEADS

From the distance it appeared that there were logs floating in the sea, huge logs. But these logs had big bulbous foreheads all facing in the same direction. The short-finned pilot whales were lined up, evenly spaced, their backs and dorsal fins exposed, reflecting black in the sun and air. We were able to bring the boat slowly alongside the pod. The nearest whale rolled just enough so that it could look at me with a round, dark, unblinking eye. Although short-finned pilot whales, subtropical cetaceans, are common in the North Carolina offshore waters, they seldom behave so cooperatively. I wanted to reach over and stroke the melon-shaped head of the closest one, but the distance was just about a yard farther than I could reach. So we just stared at each other. Then without effort or sign of alarm she descended, and in the clear water I watched the dark form slowly disappear beneath the boat. The others held their positions as the current of the Gulf Stream moved us northward away from the group. While this was not an experience filled with excitement, to me it was quite meaningful. Science-fiction writers describe encounters with aliens and the frustrations of being unable to communicate with them. Perhaps they too have met pilot whales eye to eye.

In times past, pilot whales were harvested off the North Carolina coast for whale products. Nineteenth-century whalers called them potheads. The bulbous head of each animal contains 20–25 liters of very fine oil that was used as a lubricant in watches and other items that have delicate gears. The flesh was salted and later traded for fresh food during the long voyage. Even though pilot whales are small compared to some other species, rarely exceeding 18 feet, economically, the small size was offset by their abundance—so much so that whalers from New Bedford and other North Atlantic whaling centers would harvest the summer herds that populated the outer continental shelf off North Carolina. Detailed harvest records are few—the numbers taken are unknown. Whaling vessels did not wish to share the location of productive areas with others, and from ships' logs we can learn the volume of take and little else.

The Hatteras grounds, in fact, were well known to New England whal-

Pilot whale pods are often seen on charter fishing trips in waters offshore of North Carolina. The curious cetaceans come close to the boat, rolling over to better see the occupants of the boat.

ers as an ideal hunting ground. In route to the lucrative Pacific and Indian Oceans, captains could stop and give untested crew members the opportunity to practice the basics on pilot whales. Manning the small chase boats and positioning them for the kill required precise timing and teamwork. Stalking the highly prized sperm whales that were the main quarry in the distant seas was a very profitable but risky business and captains could ill afford an inexperienced crew.

Eventually it became known that the Hatteras grounds also had a small resident stock of sperm whales. They too, were heavily exploited by the New Bedford whalers. In fact, my family four generations back were whalers. Benjamin Beal Howard owned the whaling ship *John Coggeshall*, and during the 1840s and 1850s he held shares of ownership in over 30 other whaling vessels. From existing records it is unclear whether Captain Howard personally participated in the hunting or simply ran a business from his New Bedford home. His life, 1788 to 1867, spanned the heyday of New England whalers. His were only part of a large fleet of Yankee ships that patrolled the high seas, harvesting the giant whales in the post-colonial period.

The world's stocks of sperm whales were quickly overexploited by my family and their New Bedford contemporaries. Fortunately for the whales, in the second half of the 19th century the whaling industry started to decline. Captain Howard had been a leader in its re-establishment after the War of 1812. The British Royal Navy blockaded American ports and the whaling ships with their stashes of oil were captured as they returned home from long voyages to the Pacific whaling grounds. Several decades after the New England whalers rebuilt the fleet, it became clear that it was more economical to work the vast Pacific sperm whale stocks from the west coast. San Francisco became the New Bedford of the Pacific. This too was only temporary. By 1849 the lure of the California gold rush made it more profitable to transform whaling vessels into passenger ships. The whaling crews often deserted to try their hand at mining. What was left of the diminishing rebuilt Yankee fleet was lost in the Civil War. Southern privateers captured many ships and word spread that the whaling grounds off the southeastern United States were unsafe to hunt. In 1861 40 New Bedford whaling vessels, Captain Howard's among them, were loaded with rocks and the "Stone Fleet" sailed south and was sunk in the Charleston harbor to discourage blockade runners.

After the Civil War, small numbers of whale ships continued to sail out of New England and Pacific ports. The discovery that mineral oil converted to kerosene (1895) and could be used in lamps helped to erode the whale oil market. The Yankee sperm whalers eventually died out and the books closed in 1925 when the two remaining ships returned to New Bedford from their last cruise. Most whale stocks, at least those in U.S. waters, now receive near complete protection from hunting. So despite the commercial interests of my ancestors, the opportunity to encounter these creatures off our coast continues.

$\smile$

Pilot whales are small, as whales go, or at least compared to the popular perception of whales. Females average only 14 feet in total length, males 18 feet. Exceptionally large males reach 22 feet. Perhaps they are better thought of as really big porpoises. The classification of whales and porpoises has nothing to do with length. There are a number of different families of whales and porpoises divided into only two major groups—baleen whales and toothed whales. The baleen whales include most of the really large species, the giants. These are the filter-feeders that use their large brush-like baleen plates to filter small marine animals from the water. These whales range in size from the 102-foot blue whale to the 16-foot pygmy right whale. The toothed whales include various cetaceans that are individually referred to as whales, porpoises, and dolphins. They are predatory and hunt and feed, actively pursuing fish and squid. While the maximum size is 65 feet, for sperm whales, most of the toothed cetaceans are small- to medium-sized porpoises. There are but two species of pilot whales. The short-finned pilot whale, a subtropical species, is present off the North Carolina coast throughout all of the warmer months. During the winter, the other slightly larger species, the long-finned pilot whale, occupies these same waters while its subtropical counterpart migrates southward.

Over the years I have encountered thousands of pilot whales off North Carolina. On calm days their spouts can be seen from a mile or more. Probably 95 percent of my sightings have been along the edge of the outer continental shelf and within a quarter mile of the 500-fathom contour. I assume that their association with this water depth corresponds to their feeding habits. Short-finned pilot whales hunt mostly at night. The major component of their diet is squid, and they probably wait until the squid make their nightly vertical migrations toward the surface before starting to feed. An average-sized adult will consume as much as 100 pounds of squid a night. During the day, pilot whales rest at or near the surface and ones I see on the move are probably making short-range movements to be in position by evening in order to hunt new deep offshore areas. Often they are motionless, expending only enough energy to maintain position or to keep out of the way of our charter boat.

Whenever we approached a pod, they usually submerged as we cruised across their path and surfaced again, without disruption, behind us. Every so often we would find a curious individual that would surface beside the boat and roll its eye out of the water to see what we were about. Whales' eyes are on the sides of their heads, and their lack of frontal vision makes for awkward head movements that are real giveaways as to what they are trying to position themselves to see. Several times I took Blacky, our aging golden retriever, along on my offshore excursions. The whales and the dog would always strike up quite a rapport. It was hard to tell which was the more curious (or confused) about the experience. Short-finned pilot whales are quite vocal and make a popping sound that can be heard distinctly even above the drone of a boat's engine. Underwater the sounds are more like a chorus of bird-like twitters in several different keys. I'm not sure what part of the "song" Blacky was hearing, but he felt obligated to answer. His barking seemed to stimulate another long volley of vocalizations from the whales. Not without some envy I watched as our tail-wagging, barking dog communicated with the singing whales; somehow he managed to convey "happy," "wanna play," "glad to see ya," and "where the hell have you been" with just tail motion and barking. In contrast, as scientists, we make the simplest of our observations seem so damn complex.

Pilot whales are extremely inquisitive and like to investigate everything that goes on around them. This has long been known to sailors, who still tell the story of "Pelorus Jack," a New Zealand pilot whale who accompanied ships traveling between Wellington and Nelson almost every day for 32 years. The animal became so well known that between 1904 and 1914 it was protected by special legislation.

To people unaccustomed to seeing pilot whales, they at first seem very stiff, lacking the agility and personalities of flipper and the other trick-performing cetaceans seen on TV and in public aquariums. The heads of all cetaceans are fused with the trunk of the body, but bottlenose dolphins can move their heads to a near 45° angle. It is largely this movement that gives them their TV personalities. Pilot whale's heads are, for all purposes, immobile, and this in turn limits their personal appeal—at least the way most humans would score them. My dog knows better, and so do people who have worked with pilot whales, both in captivity and in the wild. In terms of overall size, pilot whales' brains weigh about four and a half pounds. When the anatomy of a pilot whale is compared to that of other animals and biologists compare the weight of the brain and the brain stem with the total weight of the animal, pilot whales and other toothed whales group out with elephants and humans. The baleen whales, apes and monkeys, horses and other ungulates, and seals make up the next highest group. Blacky and his friends, like most other mammals, are grouped even lower. We won't even bother to categorize opossums, toads, and sponges. Most people become uncomfortable thinking about animals' intelligence, especially when the latter are perhaps the smarter. Those of us who are outright defensive are quick to point out that whales have not invented pantyhose, lead-free gasoline, or Thighmasters or discovered how to make plastic hula hoops or to split atoms. In the defense of whale intelligence, I would say that is correct. Furthermore, it is probably the anatomy of whales not their overall IQ that has limited their "achievements."

The elongated flippers of pilot whales seem far out of proportion to the rest of the body. Examination of the skeleton of a pilot whale, or any whale for that matter, reveals that these fins are formed and supported by a large number of various-sized bones. For years, well-meaning educators have tried to impress the public with the simple, and true, fact that the fins of a whale have a skeletal structure similar to those of a human hand. For some reason they expect people to gasp in amazement that the paddle-like structures contain bones like the ones in our fingers and wrist. This, I suppose, is to support the idea of some common relationship between them and us. Actually, the flippers are so highly modified that one could more easily show similarity between the hands of man and a paw of a Norway rat. What is fascinating about the fins of a whale is not so much their similarity with our hands, but the modifications. A whale's flipper is not just a hand, it is a whole arm. The arm bones are shortened and flattened and the fingers elongated. In typical mammals, man and rats included, each finger has three phalanges (the thumb has two). Cetaceans have extra ones and the pilot whales have even more than other species. The second and third fingers have 14 and 11 phalanges, respectively. The fingers are enclosed with an enveloping sheath that gives the flipper its flat shape and stiff but elastic properties. The shoulder is the only joint that is truly moveable.

People mistakenly assume the flippers are used for swimming—a simplification that allows their real purpose to be lost. Cetaceans swim with stiff up-and-down movements of their tails and bodies. The flippers are held at the side and used for balance and steering. Why the pilot whales have such extraordinarily long ones is unclear; presumably this has to do with underwater maneuvers used when capturing darting squid. Perhaps they need additional turning ability because of their stiff necks.

It takes female pilot whales 6 years to mature, 10 to 13 years for the males. This whale has the longest period of adolescence of any cetacean—long association with a parent results in the development of strong social units. Pilot whales mate in the fall and have a 13–16-month gestation period. Because of the long gestation period, there is a two-year period between births. Females are reproductively active for about 25 years and typically produce five to six calves in their lifetime. The young are six feet long at birth and grow fast. They have a brief nursing period because the females have milk rich in both fat and protein. Most mammals produce milk that is relatively low in fat (2 percent in humans to 17 percent in reindeer) with moderate amounts of sugar (3–8 percent). Pilot whales produce milk with 40–50 percent fat that has no sugar.

Pilot whales are so named because of the fact that they have established leaders, usually the dominant male. A pod consists of ten to several hundred individuals. At times several pods converge on the same neighborhood and scattered groups of these whales can be seen for miles. Smaller satellite groups of females with calves or young males are usually found in the vicinity of the main pod, but often the pods are broken up into so many scattered subgroups that it is hard to tell how, or if, the groups are related. Often pilot whales are found in the company of other species of large whales or dolphins. The most common association off North Carolina is with offshore pods of bottlenose dolphins. One time in early April I came across a huge school of long-finned pilot whales accompanying an even larger group of fin whales. Altogether there were thousands of whales, and scattered among them were numerous pods consisting of dozens of bottlenose dolphins. The whales went on for miles and eventually I gave up trying to estimate their numbers. We watched them for several hours, and before the day was over, I was able to locate several minke whales mixed in the group. At the time, these were the first minkes ever reported in North Carolina waters.

⤙

To encounter whales, one does not always need to be miles offshore. Pilot whales, more so than other species, often become stranded on our beaches. Aristotle wrote, "It is not known why they sometimes run aground on the seashore; for it is asserted that this happens rather frequently when the fancy takes them and without any apparent reason." This is no longer exactly true. Researchers have gathered much information to help explain whales beaching themselves. I collect news clippings of mass whale strandings, and by far pilot whales are the species that most often appear in media print. What makes them so vulnerable? One can't learn the answer from the papers. For years the media has led the public down the same path. While they feel compelled to report strandings of whales, they always work in that mode of "scientists remain puzzled by what causes strandings." Of course researchers would like more information, but researchers always want more information; this amounts to an easy way out for the journalists, who as writers seldom take the time to work through the details of the explanation.

The nature of strandings is complex, but here are some things you need to know.

First is the nature of the word *stranding*. A dead porpoise on the beach is not necessarily a stranding. Dead things, some of them anyway, float. Many of these wash ashore. The detailed facts of currents and tides that carry them to beaches may be complex but there is no mystery here. The same can be said of an obviously dying whale or porpoise, one too weak to swim. In fact, because they are air-breathing mammals, sick or injured whales and porpoises sometimes move into shallow water where getting to the surface to breathe requires less energy. As the animals get weaker they get closer and closer to shore where the bottom helps to support their mass near the surface. Tides and currents often then bring such animals onto the beach.

Strandings, however, are a biological phenomenon that typically involves several seemingly healthy marine mammals. Sometimes the whole pod comes ashore. Attempts to turn them back to sea are seldom successful and the animals keep beaching themselves. Why do these animals leave the safety of the sea? First, it should be noted that nearly all mass strandings are of open-ocean species, healthy inshore and coastal species of whales seldom strand. This suggests that the deep-ocean species are confused and may not understand the nature of the shoreline; indeed, shallow waters may have never before been encountered. Second, the species that strand regularly are highly social and travel in moderately sized schools. Trial-and-error attempts to get stranded groups back out to sea indicate that the whales are following a leader. If the leader goes back to deep water, the rest of the school will follow. The problem, of course, is to identify the leader and make sure that that animal is rescued first. But how? Additionally, the bulk of the whales and the cycles of the tides make the rescue of most stranded whales impractical.

A well-documented stranding of false killer whales on an island group off the Florida Keys provides much insight into the nature of whale strandings. False killer whales are a deep-water tropical species that occurs regularly in the Gulf Stream off North Carolina. In 1976 a group of 30 of these medium-sized whales went aground in Florida. They were able to return to the sea on the next high tide, but three days later this same pod became stranded on a bank of coral 160 miles away in the Dry Tortugas. One of the whales lay tilted to one side, bleeding from his right ear. The others formed a tight wedged-shaped group around him. Several people tried to push individual whales into deeper water, but the whales became agitated and they could not be prevented from rejoining the group.

The tidal range in the Tortugas is only about two feet so not only were none of the animals left high and dry, each had the option of returning to deeper water at any time. Many became severely sunburned, but all remained with the injured male supporting his head above water. People who were present report that it was clear this whale would have toppled over and drowned on the first return tide if it had not been for the support of the group. The third night the injured male died. The pod of whales slowly dispersed and by the morning of the third day all had returned to deeper water.

During the process, people witnessing the event did everything possible to keep the whales wet and to protect them from the sun. One person swimming near the whales found that whenever he breathed through his snorkel one of the whales would break out of the group, swim under him and rise slowly so he was lifted almost out of the water. He was carried to the beach and "rescued" several times. Strandings are not the result of blind self-destructive urges, and the careful recording of facts associated with a particular event will often explain it. In this case the entire pod was looking after one of its members that had become ill.

The real question in strandings is not what causes all of them, but what may have caused a particular one. Illness, parasitic infection, disorientation during storms, confusion caused by gently sloping beaches that are inadequate for reflecting echoes, stray calves, and group leaders panicking in shallow water have all been shown to be factors that contribute to strandings.

Only a small percentage of the whales that come ashore are true strandings, most are ones that wash up individually because they are sick or dead. Because the Outer Banks accumulates dead cetaceans, over time the compiled records have provided the state with the largest documented marine-mammal diversity in this hemisphere. This is a result of our latitude, as well as the local convergence of two major oceanic currents—the Gulf Stream and the Labrador Current—bringing whales to our waters. For these reasons this large variety of cetaceans has been documented from North Carolina. Twenty-seven species of marine mammals are known from the state.

The great whale of Moby Dick fame, the sperm whale, is certainly the most notorious of the whales that are found regularly off North Carolina's coast. The females are year-round residents of the deep-water zones and are seen commonly near the edges of the outer continental shelf. They live just north of the area where the warm waters of the Gulf Stream take an abrupt turn toward Europe. These whales favor the edges of ocean trenches and areas where strong ocean currents flow in opposite directions. Thus, the offshore area east of Nags Head is ideally suited for them, and based on early records of my great, great grandfather and other whalers, this has always been an important whaling ground. It is the place to go if you want to show someone a sperm whale. Sperm whales, first captured off the U.S. coast in 1712, became the mainstay of the whaling industry. This is a whale that can eat up to a ton of squid each day. It specializes in the large deep-water squid but is also an opportunist. Over 49 species of squid have been documented in its diet; one individual whale was found to have 28,000 tiny surface squid in its stomach. They also eat a number of other types of prey. Some of these show up often enough to indicate that they are not simply ingested accidentally. The menu includes long-nosed skates, snappers, angler fish, cod, ocean perch, lobster, and other bottom-dwelling species. Their large size, males have been recorded at 65 feet, allows them to consume large prey. A fourteen-foot shark was once found in a sperm whale stomach. Random samplings of stomachs of sperm whales harvested in the past revealed that they also consume boots, wire, buckets, plastic bags, jellyfish, large deep-sea sponges, and quantities of sand.

Studies of these whales show that they can make round-trips to depths of 3,300 feet in less than 15 minutes or stay on the bottom, hunting for prey for 45 minutes. They usually surface very near where they sound so it seems likely that sperm whales simply descend and lie in wait for their prey—schools of luminous squid. Locating prey in the dark is certainly facilitated by the squid's luminescence, but the sperm whale's sonar system is probably more important than sight for hunting in the ocean depths. There is one record of a completely blind adult sperm whale in good condition that was captured alive with a full stomach.

Adult male and female sperm whales have distinct lifestyles, so different that one might think they were different species. In the summer, males leave tropical waters and head to subpolar regions. The females and young are seldom found more than 40 degrees from the equator (the latitude of New Jersey). In the winter the sexes meet in warmer waters where the largest rival bulls, individuals who are at least 25 years old, battle for control of harems. The nursery pods of mature females and young usually number from around 20–30; most of the adults are already pregnant or caring for young. Because gestation lasts for 14–16 months, and the care of the young continues for over two years, the entire breeding cycle covers four years, and only a few females are available for breeding in any year. At the time of birth other females in the harem become helpers. They form a tight protective ring around mothers giving birth and they take turns nudging the newborn calf to the surface so it can breathe. This supportive behavior of sperm whales was well known to whalers and they ruthlessly exploited it. Despite the whale's ability to dive and remain submerged for long periods, they would stay at the surface to protect young or injured members of the group. The whalers could pick them off one by one.

Deep dives are well documented in sperm whales, and, based on prey items consumed, even deeper dives are suspected. Records from Western Union Telegraph and other companies that provide cases of entanglement in deep-sea cables, indicate that sperm whales were regularly recovered from depths of 3,000 feet. There is one record from 3,720 feet. These entanglement records support the conclusion that the whales were caught up in the cables while searching the sea floor, rather than being caught in mid-water as the cables were being placed. In fact, the presence of bottom-dwelling sharks in the stomachs of sperm whales captured in an area where the depth was more than 10,000 feet attest to their diving ability. The sperm whale's ability to exploit deep-water areas is important. Most of the other great whales limit their areas of activity to the relatively shallow waters of the continental shelf, or to regions where krill is abundant in surface waters. Over 90 percent of the world's seas, however, are more than 1,000 feet in depth. The sperm whale is clearly the master of the open sea.

The oil stored in the heads of both the sperm whales and the pilot whales is somehow related to their deep-diving behavior. The oily substance is called spermaceti, so named because early whalers thought it was a store of male sperm cells. The substance is a fluid when the whales are alive, but after death it becomes solid. Deep-diving species have more spermaceti than other whales, strongly suggesting that the substance is related to diving, but exactly how it is used is understandably difficult to prove. It may be related to pressure, somehow allowing the whales to withstand the tremendous pressures of the deep, or it may act as a heat reservoir and help the whales to maintain their body temperatures in the cold deep waters. In sperm whales the right nasal passage is big enough for a man to crawl through. It is 15 feet long and 3 feet in diameter and passes through the spermaceti case terminating in a large dead end sac. It is suspected that when sperm whales lie in wait for prey they draw water into the right nasal passage to cool and condense the spermaceti wax just enough to increase density to the point that the whales achieve neutral buoyancy. This, in turn, enables them to wait on the bottom, or at any depth, and not spend energy trying to maintain position. It is likely that the spermaceti, however, has more than one purpose.

A real puzzle about whale biology is how sperm whales can survive their long deep dives. It is well known that human divers who descend to even modest depths may incur decompression sickness if they ascend too quickly. Pulmonary gases are dissolved in blood and distributed to tissues. On ascent, the ambient pressure falls quickly and there may not be enough time for dissolved gasses, particularly nitrogen, to be carried to the lungs and discharged. The failure to clear blood of inert gases results in the formation of gas bubbles, causing damage to capillaries, serious injury, and often death. So, why don't deep-diving whales get the bends? A number of interesting, but not necessarily correct, hypotheses on how marine mammals avoid decompression sickness have been developed. One of the earliest suggested that whale blood contained organisms, possibly bacteria, that absorbed nitrogen. It was later discovered that these organisms were present as a result of blood samples being contaminated. The remaining theories only explain parts of a physiologically complex problem. These include circulatory redistribution during dives, the collapse of the whale's lungs reducing the rate of diffusion of nitrogen from the lungs to the blood, and the presence of fat droplets in the sinus and trachea of whales that somehow capture the nitrogen. All of these theories have at least one major weakness, and none of them really addresses the problem of how whales avoid the bends. The question may never be adequately answered because it will be so difficult to obtain experimental verification. Nevertheless, the topic is one that deserves study and the answer could provide important information for undersea research programs.

Because whales are air-breathing mammals like us, much attention has been given to the diving/ breath-holding ability of these animals. Cetaceans, despite their high metabolism, appear to have a low respiratory rate. And, relative to body size, the volume of air inhaled is no greater than land mammals and some species of cetaceans exhale before diving. Experimental studies show that even species that have inflated lungs when they dive receive little benefit from the air reserve. Below 300 feet the alveoli collapse, effectively preventing gas exchange. In whales, a specially modified diaphragm and thorax provide a 90 percent air exchange at each breath. In comparison, land mammals have only a 20 percent efficiency of exchange of tidal air. The whale's air exchange is also facilitated by the considerable amount of elastic tissue in the lungs. Whale lungs expand easily and respond quickly to pressure changes.

⌇

The whale stocks of the Hatteras grounds are still intact, inhabited all these years by pods of summering potheads and a resident group of female sperm whales. I had to consider that the ones I was seeing were likely descendants of the local stocks my ancestors had hunted in the mid-1800s. Four generations later, perhaps five or six for the sperm whales, we became re-acquainted. Naturalists always seem to be searching for common bonds with nature. Mine swam before me, their wrinkled bumpy backs glistening in the sun. I asked the captain to hold them off to our starboard. While the boat idled in the water we watched for half an hour or so as the sperm whales swam, eyeing us, spouting and replenishing air supplies to oxygen-hungry tissues. Surrounding both the fleet of sperm whales and our charter boat, the scattered schools of pilot whales remained basking in the summer sun and enjoying the warmth of surface waters. I felt no need to apologize for my ancestors' means of livelihood; it was a different time. I was simply pleased to think that our respective generations can now see eye to eye. For the moment at least, the sea seemed calm and content—with both whales and today's whaler of a different sort appreciating calamari, though I prefer mine cooked.

CHAPTER 17 A HIDE OF LEATHER
AND A WARM HEART

Leatherbacks are but one of four species of marine turtles that I have encountered in the waters off the North Carolina's coast. They exhibit the most bizarre lifestyle of any sea turtle, perhaps of any reptile. Leatherbacks are spectacular and specialized, and as far as I'm concerned, if the zoological world had its own tabloids, these creatures would appear regularly on page 1.

The immediate striking feature is size. Not only are they larger than other sea turtles, they are, in fact, the biggest living reptile. A leatherback seven feet long has flippers that spread nine feet from tip to tip. True, anacondas, several pythons, and various crocodilians can surpass the turtle's record length of 10 feet, 3 inches, but in total mass leatherbacks win. Even extremely large crocodiles, ones that reach lengths of 20 feet, seldom exceed 1,500 pounds, and only an occasional giant would match the record weights of leatherbacks. The largest leatherback that hit the scales weighed in at 1,902½ pounds. The biggest individuals have never been weighed. The problems with lifting and transporting these turtles to scales that would register in thousands of pounds have prevented researchers from obtaining this type of information. Louis Agassiz, a 19th-century biologist and founder of the famed Museum of Comparative Zoology at Harvard, claimed he saw leatherbacks that weighed over a ton. While modern specimens of this size have not been confirmed, Agassiz was not one to misrepresent biological facts. I fully expect that one day, someone will weigh an individual leatherback that weighs more than a ton.

Leatherbacks range widely, occurring throughout the waters of the Atlantic, Pacific, and Indian Oceans. In the Atlantic, they have been found north to Labrador, Iceland, the British Isles, and Norway and to Japan and Alaska in the Pacific. In the Southern Hemisphere they are found off Chile, Australia, and the Cape of Good Hope. This composite distribution makes them the most widely distributed reptile, and it could be argued that they are the world's most widely distributed animal. Not only is the species cosmopolitan in distribution, but, as adults, individuals regularly migrate across oceans

Leatherback sea turtles, the largest of all the living sea turtles, are the most pelagic of the turtles, rarely seen in inshore waters.

from tropical nesting beaches to subpolar seas. Sites where adult females were tagged on nesting beaches show little relationship to where individuals were later recovered at sea. One of the most extensive tagging programs has been continuously run in French Guiana since the late 1970s. Female leatherbacks tagged there have been recovered off Florida, Georgia, and South Carolina. The farthest distance covered in the western North Atlantic was of a turtle caught off Newfoundland in September 1988, four months after being tagged in French Guiana. Other tagged females from this same nesting beach were reported from Spain, Morocco, and France. Some of these localities represent multiple captures of different females, suggesting that these movements are not exceptional, but the norm.

These giants are said to be the most aquatic of turtles and the most pelagic. Unlike other marine turtles, they are not obligate bottom-feeders. They can feed on the sea floor, from the surface, and within the water column. Because of this, unlike other marine turtles, their ties to shallow shelf waters are all but broken. They are among the deepest diving of air-breathing vertebrates, with recorded dives to depths of over 3,900 feet. Because of this they are prime subjects for physiologists interested in studies on respiration. The problem, of course, is how to conduct the studies. By placing respiratory masks over the heads of females captured on nesting beaches, and calculating factors for differences in size, scientists learned that leatherbacks had respiratory rates that are 22 percent lower than that of active green sea turtles. During dives, their heartbeats slow to one beat per minute. Researchers also learned that leatherbacks' tidal-air volume was twice that of green sea turtles. Their lung capacity, however, is only 25 percent greater than would be predicted if they were of comparable size to other reptiles. Monitoring lactic acid levels in blood of resting versus active leatherbacks showed a minimal increase. Compared to active alligators, lizards, and other reptiles that go anaerobic during even brief periods of intense activity, leatherbacks appeared to be able to increase activity and still supply oxygen to muscles through normal breathing. And these calculations alone do not tell the whole story. Their sustained deep dives and respiration biology could not be explained through what was known about reptilian physiology. Researchers concluded that leatherbacks had independently developed respiration adaptations for diving that exist in deep-diving air-breathing marine mammals. These deep divers store oxygen in active muscle tissues, have enhanced circulatory systems, large tidal-air volume, and important adaptations in blood chemistry such as high hemoglobin concentrations. Blood is important in oxygen storage during deep dives, and to help accommodate their need for dissolved oxygen leatherbacks have the highest red-blood-cell count of any reptile.

All this is necessary for the turtle's lifestyle. These turtles are constantly diving, and sometimes stay submerged for nearly half an hour. Active around the clock, they are not your typical torpid, backyard reptile. They spend as much or more time diving as they do at the surface, and conduct as many as 50 deep dives in a 24-hour period. They have developed a chemical physiology that allows them to maintain a constant metabolic rate in their muscle cells. If leatherbacks were forced to run on an anaerobic metabolism, like other reptiles do when they are highly active, they would need to spend the majority of each day just resting on the surface to allow time for their tissues to rid themselves of lactic acid.

Snow leopards, giant pandas, Komodo dragons, various whales, well, in fact, most of the great animals of the earth, can typically be seen in some zoo or public aquarium, not so for the leatherback. They are seldom kept in captivity at all, and when attempts have been made to do so the turtles do not fare well. The record longevity for a captive is just over three years, and few survive more than a few months. Leatherbacks are constantly in motion, and in their world there are few barriers to movement. In captivity, leatherbacks spend every moment of the day and night swimming full speed into the sides of their containers. They acquire contusions and abrasions that never heal, and eventually infections take hold. In the late 1960s I once saw a small number of hatchling leatherbacks on exhibit at the Miami Seaquarium. To protect the turtles from hurting themselves, the curators had lined all but the front of the aquarium with an air-filled plastic liner (it looked like a modified air mattress) and the little turtles were all swimming at high speed, bouncing about like half a dozen ping-pong balls.

Specimens are also seldom exhibited in museums. The flesh and skin, even the skeleton, are all saturated with oil. Mounted specimens drip oil for decades, and eventually what remain look like large misshapen, black pieces of turtle jerky. Today a number of museums have produced high quality fiberglass models that look for all purposes like the real turtle. The North Carolina State Museum of Natural Sciences is the only place I know where you can view an actual leatherback. It still drips grease despite a collection date of 1897. I can find no record as to how the animal was prepared, but, despite showing its age, it has held up rather well and remains one of the most interesting specimens exhibited there. If you look closely you can still see a few grease spots.

The oil has uses beyond the destruction of museum specimens. In Indonesia, ritual and sustenance hunting of leatherbacks still occurs, and as is typical with ancestral rights practiced in a modern world, the hunts blend ancient ritual and the use of 21st-century equipment that eliminates any competitive edge the turtles may have had in the past. In addition to the meat, the oil is an important byproduct for the villagers participating in the hunts. In fact, the use of oil from these turtles was first described in 1554 by Guillaume Rondelet in a volume that contained the original published description and illustration of a leatherback. "I saw a turtle of this sort that had hung in the sun for several months, and a pound of oil dripped out of it every day," he wrote. "The fellow who had caught it used this oil for his lamps." This report probably came from the French Mediterranean coast where Rondelet lived.

To say that leatherbacks grow rapidly is an understatement. Reptiles in general, and turtles in particular, are renowned for their slow growth, while leatherbacks exhibit incredibly rapid skeletal and body growth. Their growth rates are more like mammals than reptiles, and some researchers suspect that they may reach sexual maturity in three to six years, while others believe it takes 5 to 15 years. In either case this is very rapid growth; a hatchling weighs only 1.06 ounces but by maturity it achieves an 8,000-fold increase in body weight. The pattern of bone and cartilage growth is not only unlike that of any reptile, it is totally different from any vertebrate. These turtles have vascularized cartilage superficially similar to birds and mammals. The supply of blood into cartilage and bone allow for very rapid growth, and detailed study of the cellular structure show the growing tips of bones are unique to leatherbacks. Cell biologists are preoccupied with the origins and formation of the different cell/tissue types and careful study of leatherback tissues has led cellular biologists in many directions that have in turn spawned many unanswered questions.

Scales, one of the prime characteristics of reptiles, are completely lacking in leatherbacks. Actually almost invisible, small scales do cover the shell and extremities of hatchlings, but these disappear almost immediately. Leatherbacks are the most streamlined of turtles. Peculiarities in shell structure make comparisons with other types of living turtles nearly impossible and the relationship of leatherbacks to other turtle families is unclear. The external and internal anatomy of leatherbacks, combined with their bizarre physiological adaptations led some herpetologists to suspect that leatherbacks were an independent evolutionary line of some freshwater ancestor. The species is so odd that in the past herpetologists placed it in a sister group to all other turtles (suborder Athecoidea). The superficial resemblance to other marine turtles, both in shape and nesting behavior, may simply have been a result of the influences from making a living in the open sea. Unlike other sea turtles, leatherbacks lack boney shells and don't have claws on their flippers. The shell-like covering consists of thin, irregular plates of bone in the leathery skin. Seven ridges that run the length of their leathery bodies provide structural support.

～

Leatherbacks have great strength and are quite formidable if attacked or captured. In one account, a leatherback chased a shark that tried to attack it; after driving off the shark it then turned on the boat of observers. I recall as a teenager one summer seeing an article in a Ft. Lauderdale newspaper about a man who harpooned an adult leatherback off the south Florida coast. According to the man, the turtle defended itself quite vigorously, including attempting to climb into the boat several times to get at the man, nearly capsizing the small skiff. Other than rooting for the turtle, the part that I most remember was that the leatherback was reported to have been very vocal. A number of unsuccessful studies attempted to learn if turtles can even hear, so the idea of a "screaming, crying" turtle sent me straight to the library to see what I could learn about leatherbacks. It turned out that indeed this was true. Leatherbacks are the most vocal and noisiest of all turtles. When captured or attacked, they emit whistles, moans, groans, and roars. No other reptile can match such a range of sounds, yet there is no larynx (voice box) as in mammals, and no bird-like syrinx. The only conclusion is that they can regulate sound by modification of the opening to the trachea (windpipe). The trachea of leatherbacks is far more elaborate than in other reptiles; it contains jointed bones that can move independently from three different directions. What is the point of airborne sounds for an underwater turtle? A leatherback's hearing is probably no different from other turtles in that its ear lacks a normal eardrum and is filled with massive fat deposits. How do they use these sounds? In Indonesia the leatherback hunters chant to them prior to the hunt, but why should grown Indonesian men chant to turtles unable to hear?

For an animal so large, leatherbacks are relatively weak-jawed and eat mostly soft-bodied prey. Their upper digestive tract is quite different from most other animals. I first learned this peering into the mouth of the dead leatherback that I found near the Virginia line on Corolla Beach. It was in an early stage of decay and a very advanced state of rigor mortis, but I somehow managed to pry open the mouth with a tire iron. I was looking to see if the cause of the turtle's death was from swallowing plastic, a common form of mortality among sea turtles. Clear plastic looks like a large jellyfish, and once swallowed the undigested plastic results in intestinal blockage, or in some cases, suffocation, when the turtles try to disgorge the aberrant food item. I was surprised to see that the mouth and throat was lined with long white spines, some were up to two inches long. They were thick and pointed back toward the esophagus. I later learned that these spines continue down much of the length of the turtle's digestive track. A leatherback's upper digestive track is simple—a long, spine-filled cylinder that makes more than a full loop on the left side of the turtle's body cavity. This odd digestive apparatus is six or seven feet long, and certainly longer in really big individuals. The spines are linked to its habit of feeding largely on jellyfish. The turtles suck in the jellyfish, and with them large amounts of seawater. The downward-pointing spines are believed to hold the jellyfish and jellyfish-like scraps in place when the turtles expel the water back up their digestive system. The long esophagus may also be a food storage area allowing leatherbacks with full stomachs to continue to feed. While these turtles are also reported to eat sea urchins, crustaceans, mollusks, squid, fish, tunicates, and algae, their primary food is jellyfish, and probably the Portuguese man-of-war.

On their deep dives researchers suspect they are seeking out bioluminescent abyssal jellyfish and glowing tunicates. Of the entire world's 300 or so species of turtles, this one is the most highly specialized feeder. How an animal this large makes a living digesting the little amount of protein that is in the watery tissue of a jellyfish is a mystery to me. But we have also seen that ocean sunfish, another large pelagic species, also specializes in jellyfish.

⌒

Because of their tropical nesting it was long assumed that leatherbacks, like our other marine turtles, were tropical and that records from northern seas were of misplaced vagrants. Even as recently as October 2011 the press reported on a large dead male that drifted onto an Irish beach. The local people were amazed that such a beast actually lived in the Irish Sea. Still it is now clear that these turtles regularly follow drifting schools of jellyfish northward to high-latitude seas on a regular basis. Females don't nest in consecutive years, so they actually spend a significant portion of their life in cold and temperate waters stalking large jellyfish. From the point of view of economics, this makes sense because cool water holds more oxygen and thereby supports more life than the warm tropical seas. Furthermore, the long days of summer produce vast quantities of phytoplankton that in turn generate massive blooms of jellyfish. With decreasing day length the turtles retreat to temperate and subtropical seas.

But how does a cold-blooded "tropical" reptile manage to stay functional in northern seas? They should not be able to—leaving the little untidy problem that healthy leatherbacks are persistently found in waters off New England and the eastern Canadian provinces. In the early 1970s researchers found that in 45° F waters off Nova Scotia, leatherbacks maintain body temperatures of about 80° F. This in itself is quite remarkable and the findings were promptly reported in *Science*, a journal reserved for prestigious research of obvious importance. How is this possible? Are these turtles actually warm-blooded? They already fail to match many of the other characteristics of cold-blooded reptiles. What is going on here?

In 1972, researchers seeking the answer descended on a leatherback that had died at the New England Aquarium. They found that to some degree, the heat is controlled metabolically as it is in birds and mammals, but leatherbacks also contribute to temperature regulation by a totally different process. The constant swimming activity of the creatures, the same behavior that makes it impossible to maintain them in captivity, keeps them warm. So muscular activity generates the heat. Humans already understand this—we take a short jog on a cool winter day and we start to overheat. Swimming, however, is another story. Even in relatively warm water it is possible to become hypothermic. Even water somewhat cooler than 98.6° F will eventually draw the heat from our bodies faster than we can produce it. On leatherbacks, however, the large size compared to their body surface area allows for a more efficient storage of heat. The leathery shell insulates the bulk of the animal from the cool water and the oils in their body act as heat reservoirs. They also have insulating blubber like that found in marine mammals and a brown heat-producing fat.

This leaves one small, but important, obstacle to overcome. Blood circulating out into the long flipper-shaped limbs is quickly cooled by sub-Arctic waters and the cooled blood returning directly to the body should numb and eventually kill any leatherbacks making even short visits to frigid seas. The flippers are large and have a huge surface area compared to the turtle's size, so the blood cools rapidly. Muscle activity alone would not generate enough heat to keep the blood from cooling. The careful dissection of the New England Aquarium specimen showed that leatherbacks have solved this problem much the same way as tuna, by having the incoming veins (cool blood) packed adjacent to the outgoing arteries (hot blood). The system is simple and functional. Heat is rapidly lost by the flippers, but it is not critical to have the blood in the flippers at 80° F; it is only necessary to have the blood carry oxygen. The blood cools as it reaches the capillaries, but on return the veins running alongside the arteries are warmed. The closer the blood gets to the turtle's body the warmer it becomes, so by the time it reaches the heart and lungs it is back up to 80° F.

In addition, lipids in the flippers act as antifreeze and cool much slower than similar ones found elsewhere in the turtle. The system is beautiful. The veins and arteries are wrapped in insulating fibrous bundles designed for all purposes, like telephone cables. Instead of the outgoing blood losing all its heat to the water, it transfers most of it to the returning blood as it moves out. And it's all surrounded by antifreeze. Leatherbacks are believed to have a similar system in their nasal passages, enabling them to breathe cold air. Mammals and birds have also made use of this system. Blood in a beaver's tail and a duck's feet share the same problems that it faces in the turtle's flippers—a relatively large unprotected surface area and a small amount of tissue exposed to water and heat loss. Examination of the circulatory system of these animals shows that in the exposed parts of their bodies their veins and arteries are arranged in parallel heat-transfer systems similar to those of leatherbacks. And as we have seen, tuna too have developed a similar heat-exchange system that likewise allows them to maintain body temperatures above that of the surrounding water.

So how does the leatherback's specialized heating system work in the tropics, where the seas are warm? It's not a real problem. The turtles normally hunt at depths where the water is less than 80° F, and, of course, they can cut back on muscle activity, as they don't need to swim just to keep warm. Their large size not only stores heat, it also prevents a rapid buildup of heat. Leatherbacks only visit warm surface waters briefly, to breath, and the females crawl ashore to lay their eggs at night when air temperatures are less stressful.

In the mid-1970s, when I was first starting seabird surveys in the Gulf Stream off Cape Hatteras, we were finding all sorts of interesting birds. Yet, what excited me the most were the first leatherbacks we encountered. They were creatures I had read about since childhood and I felt honored to be able to see them wild in the open sea. Surprisingly, they did not bob on the surface like typical sea turtles. On calm days it was not unusual to spot loggerheads basking on the surface, but the leatherbacks were always several feet below it. Their dark heads and shells, sprinkled with white specks, were hard to see, and often we would be nearly on top of them before we knew they were there. They had no need to surface-bask since they maintained a constant body temperature with their odd arterial plumbing. I became interested in their seasonal distribution.

Accumulated newspaper accounts, scientific literature, museum records, and other reports of leatherbacks provided much information. I scoured all sources for reports between New Jersey and South Carolina. Even a few Bermuda records were obtained. The total of 67 records that I tracked down ranged from 1835 to 1980. The cumulative information showed that these turtles were present off the Atlantic coast throughout the year. The highest concentrations occurred between May and October and the most individuals were recorded from midsummer. I now think this showed little more than the time of year most people are boating. I was surprised to see that Bermuda had only a few records, and that most of my North Carolina sightings were from shallow shelf waters—the majority of my effort was beyond the outer continental shelf, in deeper waters. Perhaps this turtle is not necessarily as pelagic as existing literature indicates. Thought of as a species that nests in the tropics, there have been increasing numbers of leatherbacks nesting on beaches along the southeastern Atlantic coast, and they now nest regularly on central Florida beaches. Since 1966, when the first one was reported as nesting in North Carolina, and since 1998 when the presence of viable nests were confirmed, there has been a steady growing number of reports for the state. The Outer Banks presently represents the northernmost nesting station for this species.

～

Despite all their bizarre differences, most of today's biologists do not believe that the marine adaptations of leatherbacks were independently derived from those of other marine turtles. The leatherback just took on a far greater degree of specialization than any other of our living, more lethargic, turtles. Animals held together mostly by oily leather and cartilage do not contribute much to fossil history. The story of leatherbacks is far from complete, and the parts that are involved in the fossilization process do not have much to tell. However, it is apparent from the fossil record that even though only one extant species exists today, in the past, several different leatherback lineages existed at one time or another, and several occurred concurrently. Over the past 50 million years, these various lineages of leatherbacks became extinct, leaving only *Dermochelys* (our living leatherback), a genus that appears nowhere in the fossil record. Did all these various lineages share a similar anatomy and physiology? For the anatomy, the answer is clearly yes, for it is the anatomy that allows paleontologists to recognize they are all leatherbacks. As for physiology? Well, who knows, but leatherback-like fossil fragments from New Zealand and Antarctica suggest that the hot-blooded physiology is not something unique to *Dermochelys*. And if this is so, where did these hot-blooded leatherbacks of the late Cretaceous (100 million YBP) come from? There was nothing else like them then, just as there is nothing like them now. As one learns more about things, patterns should emerge, and eventually an understanding of how all these sundry leatherback facts fit together should become apparent. But a lot of things about leatherbacks just don't seem to jell. The questions are not so extreme that I want to declare that I have become a creationist, but spontaneous creation would clearly be the easiest explanation for this reptilian oddity. This turtle may be our best evidence yet for the existence of aliens. Perhaps leatherbacks are ancestors of unwanted pets dumped off on Earth eons ago by space visitors who grew tired of the turtle's constant moaning and whistling.

One thing we do know about leatherbacks is that they are highly endangered. A 1980 global survey of the number of turtles found on nesting beaches suggested a world population of 115,000 adult nesting females. A similar survey in 1995 calculated about 34,500—less than one-third of the amount just 15 years before. Some of the difference may be in better survey methods, or natural fluctuations in nesting activity, but for a number of regions, at least, the decline is very real. Of the 28 known major nesting beaches, the number of females coming ashore has noticeably declined on 10 of them. These figures do not include major nesting areas such as India, where the turtles have been wiped out since early in the previous century. A beach in Malaysia that had over 3,000 nesting females in the late 1960s had but two by 1994. As highly specialized as these turtles are, it is of little help when it comes to near complete harvesting of eggs by subsistence hunters, a high mortality from fishing trawls and nets, entanglement in lines of lobster and crab pots, injuries from ship props, choking on plastic left to float in the sea, and the development of prime nesting beaches by the tourist industry. One saving feature is that after feeding on certain species of jellyfish, leatherbacks actually store the stinging nematocyst toxins and can in some cases be poisonous if eaten. There is a report from the Philippines of the deaths of 17 out of 33 people who became ill after eating a leatherback.

It is not just the eggs that are exploited. In May 2007, 5,000 rare and endangered animals were discovered on an abandoned, broken-down, drifting ship near China's coast. Found on board were crates of live animals including pangolins, monitor lizards, rare freshwater turtles from Brazil, and numerous bear claws wrapped in newspaper. Also included in the illegal cargo were 44 leatherbacks. The ship was found on one of the world's most lucrative smuggling routes, bringing internationally protected species to the restaurants of southern China. The populations of leatherbacks in the Pacific are doing far worse than those in the Atlantic. The problems in the Pacific are due to by-catch in fishing gear, the general lack of protection of nesting beaches, and direct exploitation of the turtles themselves.

Population models show that now even incidental mortality from commercial fisheries will result in the loss of various breeding stocks if the activity continues. As with other marine turtles, the cumulative factors of high loss of eggs from harvesting and unnatural mortality of adults causes a rapid reduction of populations. Off the coast of the United States where the turtles are completely protected by law, except for natural loss, all mortality is incidental. Over 100 leatherbacks float ashore each year with fatal wounds from ropes, nets, and ship props. It is estimated that at least that many again are killed that do not wash ashore. Programs are now in place to protect some nesting beaches, and hopefully through education much of the incidental mortality can be curtailed. At this time the western Atlantic population is the largest in the world, and here conservation efforts are the most enforced. The protection of nesting sites is the key to the survival of these turtles. Insurance of a high hatching rate combined with the rapid maturity will have a dramatic effect on populations in a relatively short period. Protecting the hatchlings on their first day as they emerge from nests and head to sea doubles their chances of survival to adulthood. One of the advantages to being big is that these turtles can produce large and multiple clutches. In some populations clutch size averages 100 eggs, and a few individual females have been shown to produce as many as 11 clutches in a single season. In French Guiana, where the activity of researchers has deterred poaching of eggs by local people, the number of nesting females increased about fivefold in just a 10-year period.

※

It's exciting to think of the sea as the biologically unexplored world that it is. To some this means mysteries of Vernian depths, to others man-eating sharks or sea monsters and other real, or mythical, beasts. For me, just knowing of the existence of jellyfish-stalking, gigantic, oily turtles, with their warm-blood-pumping hearts, makes the sea seem a little wider and a little wilder. A huge, fast-growing, fast-swimming, warm-blooded, vocal turtle lacking scales is a paradox that shatters nearly all our simplistic, generalized concepts of reptiles. Leatherbacks are a living reptilian counterculture, and they give cause to pause, wonder, and smile. In breaking all the rules, these guys have bypassed reptilian stereotypes, and for eons they have been highly successful while doing so.

CHAPTER 18 FATHOMING THE DARK WATERS

I attempted to read the "In Case of Emergency" instructions as the submersible swayed back and forth. Twelve feet below me was the aft deck, in the rear of the research vessel *Steward Johnson*. The sub swung clear of the ship's railing and was lowered into the sea. As the sub was disconnected from the cables, I continued skimming the instructions and came to the part about the life-support system being good for five days, so I put the instruction card aside. I would have enough time to memorize it if the need arose. I turned my attention to the instrument panels that filled every available space inside the viewing bubble. It was as impressive as the starship *Enterprise*, just a little more cramped. It took some time to sort through the array of digitalized displays and to locate all the buttons, dials, and gauges that were of interest to me—thermometers, depth gauges, and the undersea camera triggers. The system check seemed to go on forever, it was like a countdown for a space shuttle launch, every little detail was checked, rechecked, and confirmed back on the ship. I wondered what percent of this was just to increase the anxiety levels of people who had never in their lives been more than 15 or 20 feet below the surface.

This particular August, I was 32 miles east-northeast of Cape Hatteras aboard a research vessel commissioned by the Undersea Research Center at the University of North Carolina in Wilmington, preparing for a 2,200-foot underwater decent. Our destination was the edge of the outer continental shelf, the geologic feature that delineates the continent of North America from the bottom of the Atlantic. The four-man submersible, *Johnson Sea Link II*, was carefully lowered into the Gulf Stream, where we bobbed on the surface until the cables were released. I was wedged into the passenger seat. Somewhere under my knees was my backpack, containing my field notebook, a camera, a well-worn denim jacket, and a small number of odds and ends that I thought might be of use. Through the clear bubble window I could see the stern of the ship in both of its elements. Below the surface the bubble and the water magnified the hull. The props spun holding the ship in posi-

Lanternfish are named for their ability to produce light generated by tiny organs known as photophores. A chemical process within the photophores produces the bright glow.

tion. Within minutes we received permission from the bridge to descend. The world became a quiet blue. The surface glistened.

Then the little submersible did what subs do; we were descending into the blue sea. In the darker and colder waters we were about to visit I realized that time, temperature, and distance to the surface would be my only points of reference. I was surprised how rapidly we descended. I could tell from the faint glow above that the surface was up there somewhere, but it was getting farther away by the minute. This was a first for me and I *was* feeling some anxiety.

10 August 1991; 07:58 leave the surface, water temperature 27.2 C. light level 2,380 foot-candles. 08:00 200 feet down, outside temperature 23 C. Visible light from the surface all but disappeared by 230 feet. By 8:05 we were 420 feet below the surface. We were descending at a rate of about 90 feet per minute. It was dark (2 foot-candles), cold (57° F), and the turbulence from the Gulf Stream held us in a cloud of suspended silt. The sub's pilot turned on the floodlights. Visibility was less than two feet. The instruments told us that we had overshot our planned landing site on the upper edge of the continental slope by a considerable distance. The current of the Stream was carrying us north and west at about eight-tenths of a knot.

The geology and biology of the outer continental shelf in the area of The Point was being considered for gas and oil exploration. Camera sleds recording video, observations from submersibles, and samples trawled from the bottom were piecing together a story of very diverse geological features and a patchy but extremely diverse and often dense bottom fauna. The studies would eventually reveal that the site exhibits an unusual combination of geography, hydrography, and biology, largely as a result of this being the region of convergence for the Western Deep Boundary Current, the slope of the outer continental shelf, the Gulf Stream, and some lesser known currents. From assemblages of phytoplankton and zooplankton in the mid-water to the composition of the bottom fish communities, everything was quite different from what the researchers originally expected. In many respects what other researchers were finding here rather closely paralleled what I had been reporting about the marine birds flying above this same site. For example, the fishes found on the slope of the shelf were present in densities four to seven times greater than similar shelf studies conducted to the north and south of the Hatteras area. Not only were the various fish populations abnormally dense, but also a number of the species present here were ones living at the extreme southern periphery of their range, where normally one would expect only a few random individuals. Furthermore, the dominant species were totally different groups of fish than those reported from adjacent study areas.

I was about to learn that the life here, both in mid-water depths and on the bottom, was not exactly the stagnant, food-deprived community I pictured from reading marine ecology texts. Still, most of the concepts dictating the ecology of deep-water communities were in play. Comparative submersible dives to areas north and south of this study site would later demonstrate how alive The Point's benthic, or bottom-dwelling, community was, and how this was all governed by the variation in nutrient-mixing currents of the Stream as it ran across or above different configurations of the bottom. Here along the steep contours of the shelf, our study site was a distinctive, one-of-a-kind, deep-sea wilderness; one that in many aspects, if I could compare it to a land area, rivaled Yellowstone National Park.

Here at The Point, the slope of the outer edge of the shelf descends down from 600 feet to depths exceeding 6,000 feet. The construction of the submersible is such that its working limits, the pressures it can withstand without looking like it had been placed into some gigantic can crusher, only go down to 3,000 feet, but this was irrelevant in that the mission was to video document life along the middle slope at a mere depth of 2,200 feet.

Unfortunately, it turned out that the factors contributing to the interesting assemblages of marine life at this spot are not always conducive to underwater filming. Overnight, the Gulf Stream had moved inshore just enough that its western wall was brushing against the slope. The process kicked up clouds of silt, and, between our limited visibility and the current, our itinerary needed adjustment. After considerable discussion with the crew and the scientists above, it was decided that we should try to do a few video transections near the top of the slope. After an hour or so of trial-and-error touchdowns we managed to find a few spots where the undersea weather, while still patchy, allowed us to complete a number of our re-assigned filming runs.

Because we still had some dive time, though, the sub's crew took me on a slight detour. Instead of going directly back to the ship, we made a quick visit to some deeper sites within the water column out past the shelf slope. The slope itself would require another trip.

The Gulf Stream extends downward for nearly a thousand feet. As we discovered, visibility is often poor where the Stream washes against the edge of the shelf. On this dive we first hit silt at only about 200 feet into the water column. Nevertheless, when the sub was able to find marine canyons, and on the backsides of ridges, a mere 10 feet or more of visibility allowed fair views and acceptable conditions for photography. Since the cameras were positioned outside the bubble, and well forward of where we sat inside, we often got a better idea of what was around the sub by watching the monitor. Reviewing the tapes after the dive provided footage of many biological treasures I had overlooked.

The sub's floodlights reflected off every particle of silt and gave the illusion of an undersea Vermont snowstorm. It was lost snow, not going anywhere in particular, and certainly not falling. It was moving, but at the same time it seemed suspended. I pushed my face as close as possible to the inside of the viewing bubble, looking for miniature life forms—planktonic invertebrates, fish larvae, anything. At first I concluded that the blizzard was lifeless. I was wrong. When we turned off the floodlights to get an ambient-light reading (now so much lower than one foot-candle that I was not even sure I had the decimal point in the right place), and my eyes readjusted to the dark, I could see thousands of starry glows. The snow was full of pulsating transparent marine creatures, comb jellies, larval crustaceans, and other wondrous invertebrates carrying their own lights. Perhaps they were looking at us.

Once out of the silt blizzards, the swarming plankton was much easier to see. Minute photophores, tiny organs that generate light, outlined the bizarre shapes of sea creatures I had been forced to read about in invertebrate zoology courses. We flashed the lights back on, hoping to catch our quarry by surprise, but they weren't to be seen. Many were translucent—it was like trying to spot a lost contact lens under water. At times our spotlights seemed to attract the creatures, like moths around a back porch light on a warm summer evening.

I was using my camera primarily to obtain readings on the light level. With a 200 ASA film setting I could calculate ambient-light readings from the lens opening and f-stops as we descended. I later converted the readings to foot-candles—the amount of light a candle gives off at the distance of one foot. This little tidbit of knowledge of how to accurately measure light with a single-lens reflex camera was a leftover piece of trivia from back when I taught nature photography. It was one of the few times that it actually proved useful. In looking back at a number of the photographs I took that day, I can see little detail; in the reflection of our incandescent lights the living snow appears as over exposed yellow flakes against a sea of black. Still I can make out different shapes and sizes of various animals that compose this plankton swarm. It's difficult to make out the actual size because of underwater magnification, the distortion resulting from the curved Plexiglas, and the blurry images resulting from the extremely slow shutter speeds, but there is easily a whole magnitude of difference in size between the biggest and smallest creatures. Scattered in the wall of yellow are several sizes of bright, shining red dots coming from enlarged pigmented eyes.

Eventually I was able to determine that among the darting, swimming, drifting, and zigzagging swarms were thousands of small colorless shrimp sporting very black eyes, the red glows I had captured on film. On earlier occasions I had seen them in nets brought up from mid-water plankton tows. They looked incandescent white in our lights, but I knew they were transparent. When brought to the surface and exposed to natural light they turn a pale pink. Their black eyes are what really stood out. While their transparent nature provided some degree of invisibility to the lanternfish and other predators, in order for eyes to function, they must have pigment cells and in this dim light they needed a lot of pigment. The eyes are not for seeing, but for perceiving light.

I knew from reading that about half the creatures down here have eyes, while the other half are totally blind. The jellyfish we are accustomed to seeing are mostly transparent and are difficult to spot even in surface waters. Many of the jellyfish living in the deeper zones would be difficult to see as well, except for the fact that of number of species forage on bioluminescent plankton and glow from within. To counter this, the jellyfish have dark outer coverings to shield them from detection in the black waters. It can be a confusing world.

The sub's movements were deliberate and slow, like the creatures around us we were predators too, capturing unsuspecting marine life of various forms on videotape, or sucking them up with vacuum hoses attached to collecting chambers. Like the other predators, we were suspended in the water column, floating and waiting, while the prey eluded us with flips of their tails, darting away in reverse gear. The sub's thin hull and large Plexiglas window seemed to provide little insulation, and I understood why we were asked to bring jackets. The water at the surface was a pleasant 81° F. But one of the dives the previous day went down to 2,200 feet and recorded water temperatures of 48° F. Even in the excitement of everything being new, I was sensing the invading chill would not be something I could just ignore. (Only later did I learn that the sub is well insulated; the chill was from the air conditioning system.)

At 500–600 feet it becomes impossible to detect the surface. There was a faint glow of light, but it was not really clear where it was coming from. Out of the haze darted small lanternfish, deep-sea fish with their own running lights, and within moments they swarmed like moths around the sub's lights. They are a common enough fish; of the thousand or so species of fish that live in the twilight zones of the world's seas, about one-third of them represent some species of lanternfish. Yet, despite both their diversity and abundance, because of where they live, these are fish that are seldom encountered. If I had seen nothing else but the flickering of their lights, my brief undersea adventure would have been worthwhile.

Lanternfish have rather large eyes in proportion to their three-inch lengths, in this zone of perpetual twilight the large eyes are a necessity. Compared to some of the really bizarre-looking types of fishes that live down here, the lanternfish superficially resemble standard-issue minnows, minnows with flashlights. In addition to their lighting systems, one of the outstanding peculiarities of lanternfish is the delicate attachment of their scales. In the process of catching them in nets many of their scales are quickly lost. Those that are trawled from the depths, with a host of other wiggling and flapping creatures, when dumped onto the decks of research vessels end up virtually void of all their scales. It's a protective strategy used by all of the world's species of lanternfish; not unlike a lizard losing its tail when grabbed from the wrong end. One of the primary predators of lanternfish are squid; when they dart out and grasp the fish with their suckered arms, like a snake that finds it has hold on only a wiggly lizard tail, the squid discovers that all they have captured is an armful of fish scales. The fish swims off and over time grows new scales.

Other types of fish live in the twilight zone; many of them appear as monsters in miniature. With odd shapes, enlarged pointed sets of teeth, and hinged jaws, they drift through the dim waters with lights and lures, snatching up lanternfish and pretty much anything else they can grab. For the deep-sea hatchetfish and the others, meals can be infrequent, so they have perfected the concept of predation to an art form. Many can overpower and swallow species three times their size. They passively lurk, waiting, carefully timing their strike. They seldom miss.

There are also a number of planktonic jelly-type animals in these water columns. Some of the most biologically significant species are salps. The fact that most people have never heard of them, a group often skipped over in invertebrate zoology courses, does not make them any less important. Salps are transparent pelagic tunicates, which is to say a subphylum of efficient marine herbivores that blindly siphon up bacteria and phytoplankton. Looking like open-ended barrels, they feast on plankton blooms and their reproduction accelerates. Salps can go into a state of drifting torpor when currents and other features carry them into unproductive areas of the sea. Beating cilia move the transparent creatures forward and direct the siphoned water across mucus, which strains out the small particulate food and delivers everything to a primitive but efficient digestive system. The mucus is later recycled and the feeding process is for all purposes continuous. Bands of muscles surround the creatures, and by contracting them, they assist the cilia in weakly propelling the salps through the water. Salps are but one of many marine invertebrates that have alternating generations—switching back and forth between colonial and solitary animals. The solitary generation reproduces asexually through a budding process that produces a colonial whorl that eventually breaks free of its non-gendered parent, becoming a chain of female salps. Individuals grow to one and a half to three inches in length, and the rope-like chains can reach lengths of up to five feet. Each link in the chain produces one egg that is fertilized by drifting sperm released by the older male salps. The egg results in the next generation of solitary salps, while the females' chain ages and becomes all male.

Strange as these creatures are, their abundance makes them key contributors to the natural communities of the deep abyss, because they serve as a major link in the undersea food chain. Salps consume one-celled planktonic creatures, and the larger marine animals such as comb jellies, jellyfish, marine mollusks, flying fish, and a few marine birds then feed on the salps. Some of the largest of marine species, including tunas—even the giant bluefin—are known to eat them. Accounts consistently state that leatherback sea turtles and ocean sunfish feed on jellyfish, but it's likely that they too rely heavily on other jelly-type creatures such as salps.

I continue to be amazed that large marine creatures can live off of jelly-like bags of water. Salps are 95 percent water, and about 3.5 percent salt so that they can remain in osmotic balance with the sea. This leaves only approximately 1 percent protein. Creatures that feed on salps and other jelly-like marine animals get only about one-twentieth the protein value that is available in more conventional prey. But for predators the solution is simple—just eat more. On occasion there are opportunities where people can appreciate how abundant salps can become within the marine environment. When winds and tides are right, and eddies that break free from the Stream drift close to shore, the waters adjacent to Atlantic beaches become a soup of Jell-O, as waves deposit piles of the gooey jell along the tide line. Many a beach goer's weekend vacation has been dampened by "invasions" of the gelatinous salps. In that context, blooms of salps that might bother human travelers on the beach are a godsend for pelagic predators. Foraging must consist of little more than swimming about with their mouths open.

What makes these creatures so abundant is their efficient respiratory rate. While most animals of similar size all have similar respiratory rates, salps, because of their watery tissues, respire at rates of creatures one-thirtieth of their size. They are not disadvantaged by low temperatures and reduced oxygen levels like many of the other deep-water creatures, and under the right feeding conditions their numbers can increase thousandfold in a single year.

For the deep-sea community, what may be more important than what the salps eat and who eats them is what comes out of the other end of their transparent barrels. Salps feed constantly and are constantly producing fecal pellets. These droppings, ones about the size produced by your average neighborhood bat, are rich in ammonium, so rich that they meet the nitrogen needs of the surrounding phytoplankton. These pellets also sink more rapidly than the by-products of other species, descending downward thousands of feet per day. They provide needed nutrients to the benthic community below. Yes, poop is important; only in our world of flush toilets and septic systems is it actually dismissed as simply waste.

Many types of salps migrate vertically on a daily basis, sometimes as much as a mile and a half. They move toward the surface at night, and back down into the depths during the day. This allows the salps to exploit more of the sea and to broadcast their droppings more effectively. The migration also brings them into contact with a wider array of predators.

⤚

One of the stranger aspects of the deep-water areas over the continental shelf is this upward nocturnal migration of plankton and the deep-sea creatures that follow their food source as it drifts toward the surface. We tend to think of migrations as north to south, resulting from decreased food resources brought on by seasonal drought or declining temperatures. The vertical movements in the sea are daily ones and have nothing in common with geese or southward-bound interstate travelers in Airstreams trying to escape the cold. For years, researchers believed that the supposed nightly migration was actually an artifact of sampling; it was thought that more creatures were captured at night because they were unable to detect the sampling nets. But as it turns out, there is a major circadian movement of marine life in the open sea. This movement is of such magnitude that it can even be tracked with sonar. The nocturnal vertical migration of zooplankton is based on the need to move into the food-rich waters that are closer to the surface to feed. They descend back into the depths during the daylight hours to avoid predators that hunt by sight.

For the various animals that live in the twilight zone, salps and lanternfish among them, the distance of the vertical migrations—500 feet or more in a matter of hours—seems beyond belief in light of the temperature and pressure changes the creatures must endure. Considering that most of these life forms are tiny (1–3 inches long, many much smaller), these daily migrations are as impressive as any in nature. Just think of it: these planktonic creatures are not particularly strong swimmers, yet they propel themselves upward with tiny cilia, adjust gas levels in swim bladders, and wiggle upward on translucent fins.

Marine biologists refer to the bands of concentrated organisms that drift below in the twilight zone as deep scattering layers, or DSL. (For some reason scientists love their shorthand acronyms, using them for any agency, organization, or term that they find they must use more than once or twice a day. The system works great for saving time as they communicate with each other, but unfortunately, many of them seem to prefer using that time to think up new acronyms instead of remembering how to communicate with a wider public.) During the day the DSL is composed of a number of sub-layers of different species assemblages that occupy different levels in and below the twilight zone. Each may migrate toward the surface at slightly different rates as the sun begins to set. By the middle of the night, however, most have converged near the surface. Not all the members of the scattering layer make the commute every night. Some lanternfish and hatchetfish that feasted well the previous night remain behind. This not only lessens their exposure to predators but also helps them conserve precious energy.

The driving force behind these vertical migrations is the phytoplankton. By its very nature it grows and blooms in the upper surface waters where the photosynthetic process is at its best. Under the cover of darkness the zooplankton moves upward to dine on the minute plants, as do the small invertebrates such as scalps. In turn, larval crustaceans and fish join in on the growing feast, soon followed by larger, and yet larger, predatory squid and fish. And just think, this can all be summed and conveyed by simply saying "DSL."

I have spent a number of nights on the decks of ships shining spotlights into the night waters. Early on I was trying to get glimpses of seabirds, to see which ones fed nocturnally, but I soon discovered that on nights with calm seas not only could I see the hordes of creatures coming to the surface but also it was apparent that my light was attracting them. Yes, flying fish even fly at night, and one pair conducted their courtship rituals under my light. Once when a small squid made a move toward a flying fish, it took to the air and smacked nose-first, square into the hull of the ship. Another nearby squid darted up and grabbed the stunned fish. I netted up all sorts of marine life, everything from ghostly surface-swimming worms to miniature sailfish less than 2 inches long. Even at that size, they already had their full complement of rigging.

Lanternfish came to my light as well. They looked silvery in the light, and now and then they flashed little red lights. I first assumed these were displays of photophores, but they were their eyes. The enlarged eyes, with reflecting pigment-filled cells, caught and reflected back the light, just as eyes of possums, skunks, and other nocturnal animals shine red when caught in our car headlights. I remember catching several of the fish with my long-handled dip net, hoping to be able to examine their detachable scales. But the lanternfish were naked; their scales must have slipped through the mesh before I could get them on deck. Larger fish, or at least their shadows, appeared and disappeared from the light, but for the most part they remained deeper down. A number of types of squid hung, seemingly suspended, perhaps dazed by the light. I have seldom seen the sea so alive.

Like the DSL, we were migrating upward too, not that it was becoming night but because our dive time was up. Coming up into the light was comforting, but everything seemed a little overexposed. It was not unlike a Woody Allen movie where one of the characters is depicted as he is about to enter heaven. In the white light it took my eyes a minute or so to adjust to the surface glare. The submersible had to be tethered to cables and hoisted back onto the deck of the mother ship. Our pilot had a long checklist to run through before we could disembark. All this took time. Without all the distractions of the undersea life I began to realize how cozy the sub's interior was. Space not occupied by knees and elbows was filled with instrument panels. A research program from the *Sea Link* would be an unfortunate career decision for people who incessantly worry about things that might go wrong or for claustrophobic marine biologists.

CHAPTER 19 BATTERIES NOT INCLUDED— UNCANNY LIGHTS IN THE DEEP

The otherwise dark water was aglow with night-lights, one of the strangest of all natural phenomena. As we descended downward, the sub's crew had killed the spotlights. Depth perception was lost in a wall of near black as I watched the instrument panel: 250 meters, 275, 300. The trip down was faster than I had suspected. Out somewhere past the Plexiglas bubble that served as our viewing window I could see lights—small dots, some flickering on and off, others appearing as slow-motion tracers. As my eyes became adjusted to the blackness, the lights began to show patterns and motion. They were in different intensities; many had seemingly purposeful movement, and there were subtly different colors. Here and there the lights appeared to be blinking Morse code messages to each other. Was I seeing some strange underwater chorus? I knew that these lights were ones embedded in lanternfish, deep-sea squid, and probably a host of other creatures that dwelled here unseen in the darkness.

But perhaps to understand all this, a primer on bioluminescent lighting is in order. As diurnal surface-dwelling creatures, we are not intuitively programmed to appreciate the dark. With torches, candles, oil lamps, lightbulbs, and flashlights, we have through time done our best to keep the dark at bay.

For thousands of years, and long before the appearance of monthly utility bills, people had pondered in disbelief the nature of sparkling and shining seas, glowing heads of old dead fish, and marine worms that light up when they are poked. Sailors far from home watched swirls of light as their oars dipped into the night seas, while Druids were enchanted by logs glowing deep in the woods. These various lights seemed unrelated to sunlight or moonlight, fire, stars or comets, the reflective glow of the eyes of wolves surrounding campfires, or lightning flashes. The strange lights were haunting; they gave off no heat and worked equally well in cold, wet conditions that would normally quench fire. When superstition was the science of the time, these lights defied logical explanations. It was a time when even lightning

Bioluminescence achieves its greatest development in squid, but jellyfish and many other species are also bioluminescent.

bugs were suspected of being messengers from the dead. Aristotle, our foremost naturalist of antiquity, was fascinated by the nocturnal glow of certain wood, unaware that the light actually came from a fungus growing within the trees in ancient Greece. Some things, he noted, seem to produce light though they are not by their nature composed of fire itself, or indeed of any kind of fire. Of course the oxidization process that is responsible for fueling the light remained a mystery, and in fact oxygen itself, as an element, was unknown. The lights lacked a flame and sparks and gave off no heat.

This eeriness was not limited to the trunks of olive trees. In the eastern Mediterranean Sea, near Aristotle's home, there were also luminescent squid and cuttlefish. So the mysterious lights remained in a world best explained by the supernatural and magic. Druids, wizards, alchemists, and children alike carried their thoughts as to the origins and meaning of the living lights through the times of the Dark Ages and well beyond. Indeed, the foxfire seen by those living in Appalachia retained its mysterious nature even into modern times. The light reflected during the day was obviously different than what the same organisms produced after dark; yet the thought of dissecting problems through careful study and experiments was unheard of.

Our understanding of bioluminescence slowly began to change in the mid-1600s. Bio of course stems from biological, lumin is Latin for "light," and escent means "beginning." Robert Boyle (1627–91), one of the founders of the Royal Society of London, was a chemist and a leader in the use of experiments to get to the bottom of things. "Experiment was the interrogation of Nature." By today's standards his experiments seem rather simplistic, but this was 1667. Boyle put a section of luminescent wood under a bell jar and pumped out all the air. The light went out, but when air was allowed back in the wood again glowed. Those inclined toward biology might have assumed the glow was alive and needed oxygen. But Boyle was a chemist and his assumption was, as it turns out, the right one. The light was the result of a chemical reaction. Later, he tested a glowing piece of red-hot iron; when the air was removed the glow continued. Basically these simple demonstrations illustrate the major differences between bioluminescent and incandescent light. Other experiments continued the quest to understand the strange light, from a French scientist in the late 1800s, to ones at Johns Hopkins University in the mid-1900s.

It would be irresponsible to discuss biological luminescence without mentioning Dr. Raphael Dubois. Dubois, a professor of physiology at the University of Lyons, France, led us into the modern era of understanding bioluminescence. His work with luminescent click beetles from the West Indies and a luminescent clam demonstrated that three basic structures were necessary to obtain cold light: an organic compound that can combine with oxygen, the proper enzyme that will allow this to happen, and, of course, oxygen itself.

Now here comes the good part, Dr. Dubois was also apparently into showmanship. At the Paris International Exposition of 1900 he illuminated an entire room with bacteria light; the reviews reported a vast chamber wherein the evening lighting was as soft and mellow as moonlight yet bright enough that people could recognize each other and even make out the headlines of newspapers. The lighting source was six-gallon glass containers filled with a mixture of bioluminescent bacteria and nutrients. (Boy would this have been a popular hit on YouTube.) He later suggested that his cold light source would be a good safe one for lighting up warehouses where ammunition was stored; after all it was approaching wartime in Europe, and perhaps there were practical uses for his work. The French populace was even more creative, putting together gourmet platters of seafood that glowed in the dark, displaying the fish and other items illuminated with only their glowing bioluminescent bacteria.

I recall as a grade school student collecting bounties on fireflies; my mother would drive me to the Johns Hopkins campus so I could collect my penny per insect. I, of course, had no idea that the university professors I was giving them to, Drs. McElroy and Seiger, were at the time the leading investigators in molecular biochemistry and the bioluminescent process. And knowing what I know now, it seems that even a child could reason out that the lights were chemical. Kids in my neighborhood were forever pulling the tail end off of fireflies to discover that they continued to glow even when disconnected from the living insects.

Though we've learned a great deal from science, the intrigue with bioluminescence continues. Hollywood still loves to show off ghosts and related spirits, friendly and unfriendly space aliens, and other hard-to-explain phenomena. These and other surreal subjects that are hard to depict almost always appear as some form of luminescent object.

While for many of us the most frequently seen example of bioluminescence is the flickering of fireflies, lots of organisms carry their own self-contained light source, everything from toadstools to fishes. Of the 25 major phyla of animals, at least 11 have representatives that are luminescent, and if this were broken down to smaller divisions of the animal kingdom, about one-third of the 64 classes of animals have at least one member that can light up. This ability is particularly common among many of the lower invertebrates and the more primitive plants. Since many of these groups are not particularly well known perhaps it would be more efficient to first discuss which animals lack the ability to produce light. It is totally lacking in mammals, birds, reptiles and amphibians, and all vascular plants. Vascular plants, and for the most part other photosynthesizing plants, are unable to produce cold light.

The study of nature would be far less interesting if glittering generalities did not have important exceptions, particularly ones that at first seem to make little sense. While photosynthesis captures light to make energy, bioluminescence uses up substances within the organism to produce light. And while photosynthesis gives off oxygen as a by-product of its energy production, the biotic lights need to take in oxygen in order to function. Thus, logic would dictate that the two opposing processes would not occur in the same life forms. And this is basically true. In marine flagellates, however, both chemical reactions occur in the same creatures. Flagellates are a group of protozoa; the most primitive of animals, they live as free single-celled organisms. They give off a faint glow at night and during the day produce energy from sunlight. And don't underrate them because of their small size. They make up for this in numbers. Only 10–15 percent of the earth's photosynthesis takes place in the green leaves and stalks of the terrestrial plants more well known to us; the remaining 85–90 percent is accomplished in the sea, much of it from single-celled marine flagellates.

So what types of organisms can produce cold light? Among the plants, it is limited to certain woodland fungi and some types of bacteria. In the animal kingdom the list is much longer: protozoa, sponges, corals, jellyfish, comb jellies and their relatives, marine ribbon worms, snails, clams and squid, marine and sand worms, earthworms, sea spiders, copepods and their kin, shrimp, crabs, lobsters, millipedes, centipedes, insects, brittle stars, tunicates, hagfish, sharks and rays, and true bony fish. Of course, in most cases only a few individual species from any of these groups have bioluminescent powers, but this varies widely. In ctenophores, the comb jellies, every known species is luminescent. So, while bioluminescence is lacking in most plants and occurs irregularly in animals, it is not unusual. Nearly all animals with luminescence are lower invertebrates that are basically nocturnal, obligate cave dwellers, or live at depths in the sea where little light filters down from above.

Most creatures that produce light do it through a chemical process similar to that used by fireflies. A substance called luciferin (a devilish word derived from Lucifer—the light bearer), when combined with oxygen and a catalyst (an enzyme named luciferase), produces light. The chemical process is complex and there are numerous variations in the way different organisms actually produce the light. It is generally believed that our earliest life forms used bioluminescence as a way to burn off oxygen, and the energy released is in the form of light. Oxygen was a rare commodity in the days when life began and was toxic to bacteria and the one-celled animals that were trying to adapt to our Earth's harsh environment. Chemically burning off the oxygen to get it out of their systems was a good solution, the earliest of creatures did not need to be concerned with attracting the attention of predators as eyes were still a thing of the future. Luminescence in many modern-day organisms may not form any function at all; it may simply be a holdover from earlier times. Over time various animals that retained the ability to glow modified their lights and put them to use, while others simply made use of luminescent bacteria for their lighting systems.

Bioluminescence achieves its greatest development in squid, so they are perhaps my best choice to explain the diversity of the lighting mechanisms.

Of the 400 or so species of squid, over 120 of them are luminescent; mostly they are the smaller species and ones that dwell in dark oceanic depths. When you think about it, this is not particularly surprising, as even the deep-sea squid have extremely well-developed eyes that would benefit from having something to see. Squid use three totally different methods for their lighting. For some, photophores, special structures within the cells, produce light from within the squid's tissues. Each of the species with photophores has a specific distribution of lights, and they can range in number from just a few to over a hundred. Each photophore is covered with dark pigmented cells that prevent the light from shining through the skin. When the squid draws the structures with the pigment cells away from the photophores, the light shines through.

In other types of squid the water around the squid lights up when the creature ejects secretions into the sea and the oxygen in the water triggers a chemical reaction. In lighted environments, startled squid and octopi eject inky liquids into the sea that act as smoke screens to confuse predators as they dart backward and escape. This is a good trick, but it is totally useless in the dark waters of the deep sea. So in its place the squid discharge a luminous blast that achieves the same purpose. Again it is the chemical reaction of the discharged liquid and the oxygen in the seawater that produces the instantaneous light. The cloud of luminous material also contains a small amount of a deadening chemical that further disorients predators who fail to notice the squid has turned off its own lights and darted away.

In yet other types, the squid's skin supports colonies of luminescent bacteria. The bacteria living in pockets of the skin produce the light. The bacteria glow constantly, but the squid has ways of screening the light with an inky film that allows them to partly or completely mask the light. In addition, reflecting cells are in place below the pockets of bacteria and lenses are above them that direct and focus the lights when they are in the "on" position.

Biological lighting is not confined to the depths; it also occurs near the surface and in shallow bays in the Bahamas, Bermuda, and Jamaica. I recall one winter in the mid-1960s when my parents took me to see the show of lights in Luminous Lagoon, near Jamaica's Montego Bay. A local guide rowed us out in his skiff, and soon after dark, the waters were aglow. It was a tourist thing; we were given some folklore explanation, and it was years later before I had any idea what it was I had witnessed. These were certainly dinoflagellates, a single-celled plankton, but any number of luminescent invertebrates can rise from the depths and swarm near the surface on dark nights. They swarm for mating rituals that are often tied to tides and phases of the moon. The best-known light shows are produced by segmented marine worms known as syllids, representing various species of the genus *Odontosyllis*. These worms are suspected to be what Columbus saw when he reported a moving candle in the sea just prior to his 1492 landing in the New World. In the Bahamas, where the fireworms have been studied, the worm swarms take place soon after sunset and are triggered by the last quarter of the moon. The females swim toward the surface and will suddenly switch on their lights. The on-off switch is flicked a few times as the female worms scatter eggs and eject luminescent fluids into the sea. The smaller males swim up from below and release sperm into the glowing waters. Once the ritual is complete the lights are turned off and the worms drift back to the dark bottom.

The animated lights are put to different uses. In addition to romance and defense they can serve in species recognition, as lures, as headlights, and as deep-sea camouflage. So let's look at some examples.

Twilight-zone pelagic shrimp emit light-burst secretions similar to those of squid as they slip away with a powerful flip of their stiff tails. Some comb jellies emit both light and squirts of ink when they are disturbed, but many of the predators of these and other lighted marine animals are eyeless, so the use of light burst in defense is not as clear-cut as it would first seem. Of course this can also work against the light-bearers as their flashing attracts predators with vision that quickly learn which signals represented a free meal. Conversely, the lights could attract prey, at least prey species with some levels of light perception.

Species recognition is clearly an important component of biological lighting. It can enable individuals to locate mates in dark waters and allow schooling species to remain in groups. The arrangement of lights, or peculiar flashing patterns, announces who is who, and for some species even identifies the flasher's gender.

The deep-sea anglerfish have carried this concept to a new level. They use lighted lures to attract prey. The modified first ray of their dorsal fin supports the lure. The fish patiently wait on the bottom, mouths open, hinged teeth positioned and ready, tongues extended, while they wiggle their flashing lure. When prey approaches to examine the light they pull in their tongue creating a vacuum, sucking the unsuspecting animal into their large tooth-filled mouth. Still other species have clusters of photophores at the tips of long tentacles or streamer-like growths. Often these are longer than the fish itself. They are used in ways similar to the way fishermen use lures at the end of lines.

The lights can also be used for countershading. Many flying and swimming animals are countershaded, a form of camouflage that makes white-bellied, dark-backed creatures less conspicuous when viewed from below or above. In the darker zones of the sea, however, this is not effective, as even species that are light ventrally would stand out as dark silhouettes against any faint light coming from the surface. They would be easy prey. To adjust for this, deep-dwelling and mid-water fishes have photophores distributed all over their bellies. They control the bioluminescent light level based on the amount of light coming from above. One species of mid-water fish has reflectors to intensify the light and enlarged moveable scales that adjust the light's distribution so it evenly blends with the ambient light from above.

And, of course, some animals actually use their luminescence as spotlights. The viper fish, a deep-sea creature, sports large lights behind and under each eye that shoot out headlight-like beams. The lights can be turned on or off, but the lights can also be covered with a black layer of skin. There are also smaller lights that point directly into the fish's eye. They are turned on just prior to firing up the headlights, and the fish adjust their eyes so as not to be blinded by their built-in high beams.

So the lights are versatile, and the various organisms put them to use in all sorts of strange ways. Now add to the mix the fact that for some species the lights are on timers. There are marine protozoa that are photosynthetic by day and luminescent by night. The night-lights apparently burn off the excess oxygen produced during the process of photosynthesis. The lights are dimmed during daylight hours and shine brightly after dark.

Needless to say the glowing, blinking, and shining lights I was seeing from the submersible had my attention and interest. I wished I knew more; while I understood the process of bioluminescence and the potential benefits that it gave to the deep-sea creatures, it would have been great to know who was flashing whom. I was glued to the bubble window, but not entirely understanding what I was witnessing.

The twilight zone ends about 600 feet down—below that, light from above is nonexistent. While we tend to think that at the really great depths deep-sea fishes make their way about the ocean floor with lights, in truth most light-bearing creatures occur within three miles of the surface; below that depth few free-swimming species are to be found. At the greater depths eyes tend to become rudimentary, and light organs serve little purpose to their owners. The lights that are present are greatly reduced in size. Because of this, most of the really luminescent species are mid-water forms and the bottom-dwellers distributed along continental slopes and submerged plateaus.

I could not have been in a better spot to witness the show. Off North Carolina, much of the continental slope is below the twilight zone and well above the three-mile depth. Accordingly, the dark waters are alive with various luminescent creatures. Bottom creatures, as well as ones living in the water column above the seafloor, have lights or headlamps or they simply glow. Even organisms lacking lights set off minor displays of fireworks as they swim through clouds of flickering plankton. Sponges and other growths anchored to the bottom that may lack the ability to produce light themselves glow from bacteria and marine worms that live on them. Other lower invertebrates have self-contained lights—horned corals, sea pens, jellyfish, and luminescent hydroides. Famed naturalist and the original undersea explorer, William Beebe, reported that about two-thirds of the deep-sea species he studied were luminescent, and this likely holds true for the deep-water creatures off North Carolina as well.

Matching the lights to the creatures remained almost impossible. When the sub turned on the outside lights, everything would scuttle and dart about and nothing seemed to remain in the same place where the lights had glowed moments before. When our lights were turned off, everything had long changed position before my eyes could re-adjust to the dark. It was fascinating and frustrating all at the same time. No matter; I probably would not know most of what I was seeing anyway. Worldwide, about two thousand species of fishes live in the ocean's dark waters; most of these are primitive soft-rayed types of our typical boney fish. The lanternfish and hatchetfish represent nearly two-thirds of these species. In that I did not know any of these fish well enough to identify specific species, I realized how inadequately I had prepared myself for this dive. So for the remainder of my deep-sea experience I just watched and enjoyed the lights, both our incandescent spot lights and the flickering bioluminescent ones.

There is considerable variation in the amount of biological light with changes in depth. In general, an imperceptible glow becomes progressively less intense as one moves down in the water column, and as the light-producing organisms become less abundant. Yet, at the right depths we are not talking about flickering of lights here and there. While the light level is neither steady nor uniform, considering the source, it can be surprisingly bright. Undersea recording equipment has shown as many as 100 light pulses per minute, nearly one every half second. Even at depths of two miles, sometimes the light levels can be equivalent to moonlight in your backyard on a clear night. Nonetheless, all this remains a topic difficult to study; the lights are undetectable when undersea camera lights are on, and the deep-sea species are difficult to maintain in captivity because of the need to duplicate the intense pressures under which they normally live.

Nevertheless, I trust my account of my trip to the floor of the outer continental shelf has shed some light on the topic. In our modern world, we light up the night with fireworks, and armies light enemy camps with smart bombs. Large lighted billboards and signs with flashing LEDs tell us what to buy and where to find it. Red lights over Mexican bars suggest that more than *cerveza* is being offered. Streetlights and stoplights show us where we are and tell us what to do, and the bulbs in our refrigerators turn on as we search for late-night snacks. Back-lit clocks in belfries and beams from lighthouses guide us. Internal lighting on our computer screens direct us to social networks, TV screens send us information on a minute-by-minute basis, and Christmas lights decorate our homes and relay our joyous moods.

Creatures living deep beneath the sea are doing much the same thing with their self-contained lighting systems, but without all the wires and cords. Our wires and cords are just now starting to become obsolete—of the two co-evolved wireless societies, though, ours is somewhat behind our friends in the deep waters beneath the Gulf Stream.

CHAPTER 20 LIFE ON THE BOTTOM
Weird, Ancient, and Abundant

Prior to the mid-19th century, everyone assumed that the bottom of the deep sea was virtually lifeless. The intense cold, high pressure, and utter darkness did not seem conducive to life. However, a few bottom hauls had produced some tantalizing creatures, many similar to species previously known only from fossils. Scientists, eager to expand on Darwin's work, were hell-bent on obtaining more and better specimens of these prehistoric-like creatures. The research was motivated by the proposed idea of undersea telegraph cables to enable better communication between the continents. Little was known about the sea floor where the cables would be laid, so at the peak of her imperial power, Britain undertook what was to become one of the top ten exploratory voyages of all time. The flagship commissioned for the voyage was the HMS *Challenger*.

By this time the world's continents and seas had been rather well explored, so logically the ocean floor was the next frontier. The Challenger Expedition's (1872–76) three-and-a-half-year voyage represents the birth of oceanography, becoming the world's first major scientific undertaking. The ship was refitted with state-of-the-art laboratories, heavy-duty winches, and 249 miles of rope. It was the first scientific expedition to make use of photography as a means of documentation. All together the *Challenger* sailed 68,890 nautical miles, covering major portions of the seven seas. The crew conducted 25 successful dredgings at depths in excess of 14,700 feet, with the deepest one being 18,701 feet. While the primary goal was bottom surveys, researchers on board conducted many other studies, including a large number of deep mid-water trawls for plankton and other marine life. The first tangible result was a large 50-volume publication of the *Challenger*'s scientific findings; these volumes totaled over 29,550 pages. But perhaps more important was the public's interest generated by the voyage. Even today marine biologists are examining the biological and geological treasures collected by the expedition, and the effort was responsible for the subsequent sharing of oceanographic information between nations.

Hagfish, one of the most disgusting-looking bottom-dwellers, live in the substrate of the cold deep water along the sloping edge of the outer continental shelf.

My dive experience on the *Johnson Sea Link II* was just one minute piece of an effort that had been ongoing for over 100 years, one that had its birth on the decks of the *Challenger*.

Our dive site was at the epicenter of my seabird study site, an area local fishermen refer to as The Point. Here bottom contours come together to form a hump on the charts, and in less than a mile the edge of the continental shelf drops from a depth of 250 feet down to 3,000 feet. Within three miles it goes down to 9,800 feet. Elsewhere along the Carolina coast the drop-off is less extreme and the slope begins much farther from shore.

We had intended to start from the upper rim of the shelf and work our way downslope. We hovered, then the thrusters moved us upward; bearings from the ship redirected us inshore several hundred yards. We identified a steep ledge with our sonar and moving up it, at a depth of 230 feet, we came into clear water and the top edge of the continental shelf.

The submersible's floodlights lit up the sandy ooze of the ocean floor. There were small ridges and areas packed with mud, and behind the ridges and in places where the current was less strong the visibility improved. By now even a 10-foot visibility seemed good. It was a quiet and seemingly slow-motion world. The first creature I saw, well at least the first one I could identify, was a large female horseshoe crab. She slowly worked her way, tank like, through the silty substrate. A horseshoe crab? We were 30 some miles at sea and here was a creature that typically lives in estuaries and annually forms large breeding aggregations on coastal beaches. I watched her for some time, and could even make out the tracks she left in the soft bottom. There were the two grooves from its shell plowing along the floor, and between there was a faint irregular line from the tail drag, identical to the trails I had seen horseshoe crabs make in the spring on beaches and coastal mud flats. This seemed an unbelievable migration for such a creature.

Limulus, or horseshoe crabs, are often referred to as living fossils, a fitting label for a life form that has inhabited coastal waters since before the time tectonic plate movement set in place the current positioning of our continents. These are creatures that would regard pterodactyls, saber-toothed tigers, and incandescent lightbulbs as passing fads; in their larval stage, horseshoe crabs resemble the ancient trilobites of the Cambrian seas. For people who think I Love Lucy reruns are something out of the Dark Ages, the lineage of horseshoe crabs must be beyond comprehensible.

Some weeks later, when back onshore, a little library work showed that while most horseshoe crabs live at shallower depths and mostly within three miles of shore, they can occur far out to sea. They have been captured in trawls at depths of up to 950 feet along the edge of the continental shelf of Virginia and North Carolina, and one was photographed from a submersible off Charleston at a depth of 3,600 feet. Another was found off Ocean City Maryland, 100 miles offshore. So while my sighting was not that unusual, it poses a question as to how they can survive under the pressure at these depths. The volumes of research studies addressing how horseshoe crabs cope with changing osmotic conditions when salinity shifts as they move about in estuaries discuss ion transport through the creatures' gills, intercellular adjustments, dealing with limited oxygen supplies and exposure to air, and their response to temperature change. But I could not find a single sentence as to how they manage to survive the great pressures of the deep. It's not just the crushing aspects of the pressure; its effects on the creature's blood alone would be enough to kill most animals that normally live in shallower water.

Horseshoe crabs are bizarre, so much so that it's hard to know where to begin to describe them. They are not crabs at all; their closest living relatives are spiders and mites. Our North Atlantic species ranges from Maine to Mexico and can take the cold to the point that they sometimes literally freeze into ice in New England waters, but they also do well in the tropical waters of

Florida and Yucatan. While growing, they molt their way through 18 stages over a 10-year period, and they can live for more than 20 years. Their blood is blue; while this is a result of copper in their blood, perhaps it also attests to their ancient and noble lineage. I should also mention that these "crabs" eat through their brains and chew with their legs. Horseshoe crabs have 13 pairs of appendages—legs with both hooks and pincher-like and paddle-like tips. The legs are multipurpose. They are used for burrowing, locomotion, food gathering, and chewing. The first seven pairs are for feeding, the next five pairs are the walking legs, and the last ones are used like our molars for crushing shells of small clams and other food items. The food is actually masticated as it moves forward toward its mouth.

I would be neglectful discussing horseshoe crabs if I failed to mention their eyes. They have more than their share, and if you think you understand vision, just forget everything you know and start anew when looking at a horseshoe crab. The two large compound eyes, probably the only ones you would immediately recognize as having something to do with vision, have lenses and the receptors are so large that you can see them without a magnifying glass. These individual ommatidia number about 1,000 per eye and are 100 times the size of the rods and cones in our eyes. In addition to the primary lateral eyes, Limulus has eight additional ones. Nine of the eyes transmit signals to optic nerves that go to the brain. At night signals from the ultraviolet sensitive median eyes, the only other eyes that have lenses, enhance the sensitivity of the compound eyes. The remaining six eyes are just primitive photosensitive organs. Two of these are located near the mouth and indicate light levels beneath the animal and inform it when it is upside down. At night a built-in clock transmits signals to the optic nerves to increase the light sensitivity of the two large compound eyes and to a pair of median eyes located near the front center of the carapace. Photoreceptors that occur along the top ridge of the "tail" synchronize to clock the brain with the daily cycles of light and dark. The overall sensitivity of the composite visual system may be without equal. Imagine an animal that can respond to starlight in 30 feet of murky estuarine water. It took some doing to figure out the purposes of the various "eyes" as horseshoe crabs in research labs responded to the artificial lighting and the eyes' sensitivity was reduced. And what about the horseshoe crab I saw from the submersible in 230 feet of water? It was living in near total darkness, there really is nothing it could actually see except perhaps bioluminescent creatures. Yet, its internal clock lets it know when it's time for the 30-plus-mile pilgrimage to shore for spring spawning.

Almost as interesting as the "crab" itself is the host of creatures that make use of its exoskeleton as a home. With a long list of associated marine wild-life that takes advantage of the hard shell as a substrate for attachment they can become walking invertebrate zoological gardens. The free ride allows hitchhikers constant access to new food sources and wider dispersal of their eggs, while providing some degree of protection. The carapace of the adult horseshoe crabs can be simultaneously encrusted with barnacles, blue mus-sels, slipper limpets, bryozoans, anemones, tube worms, oyster drills, sea strawberries, sponges, sea stars, oysters, scale worms, castle worms, and marine algae. The underparts, particularly the gills, support bloodworms, scuds, skeleton shrimp, and Limulus leaches. In addition there are para-sitic flatworms. Occasionally clams attach to the legs, which can hobble the horseshoe crabs. Collectively, all these guests can slow movement and often cover eyes and other key sites, inhibiting the creatures' ability to function. Adult horseshoe crabs molt their exoskeletons once a year; the process dis-lodges its guests, and the host crawls away. During the molting process, horseshoe crabs also secrete mucus on the new carapace, which serves as an antifouling agent.

Of all the new creatures I was seeing on my trip to the bottom, however, I was the most impressed with the hagfish. I had known about them ever since college zoology classes, but these were the first I had ever seen. They were everywhere, mostly half buried in the bottom sediments. Despite their small size (most were less than a foot long), their pink bodies made them quite conspicuous. They are disgustingly ugly fish! Technically they aren't true fish, though some texts continue to classify them as such, but everyone will agree that they are disgusting and ugly. And I should mention slimy.

Hagfish have two main attributes: their slime glands and their ability to tie themselves into knots. There are 60 or so species worldwide; the com-mon one found off North Carolina, *Myxine glutinosa*, has 90 slime-oozing pores. It's not mere worm slime. In minutes, captured hagfish can ooze out enough slime to fill a bucket and displace all its water. The function of the slime is to discourage predators; it is full of little cords of protein that choke predatory fishes by clogging up their gills. Meanwhile, the knotting behavior of hagfish gives them leverage to crawl into and out of dead fish and other large food items that sink to the sea's floor, and to neatly slip out of their self-made slime balls.

In our area, hagfish occur only in cold deep waters along the edge and slope of the outer continental shelf. The species I was seeing was pale pink in color, its skin loose and wrinkly, with a few whiskers growing around its obscene looking mouth. They can live at depths of 1,600 feet and more, so there is little light, and while they are eyeless, they do have skin receptors that can sense faint amounts of light. Like many deep-sea animals, they have luminescent photophores that glow. But their ugliness is only skin deep; inside they are plain Janes. Structurally, hagfish are simple tubes. They have a mouth and a single nostril at one end for water intake, and a hole near mid-body to let it out. The mouth is situated inside a groove on the underside of the head. Four short tentacle-like processes stick out from either side. There is no indication of even vestigial eyes, their gills are pouches, their heart is a series of separate chambers, and their "blood," close to seawater in composition, is three times saltier than that of any other vertebrate. A hagfish's digestive track, nervous system, and respiratory system are simply long tubes. Every hagfish has both male and female parts, but for most individuals, only the female parts are functional. These sea hags are scale-less, finless, toothless, and brainless (they have a bump for a brain box). They are also jawless so they are forced to feed like vacuum cleaners, and they have a rasping tongue. Because of this, they are primarily scavengers, but they also prey on marine worms and other slurpable bottom-dwelling things. The far end of the wiggly pink sucking tube is flattened and somewhat paddle-like. They use the paddle to swim, but spend most of their time burrowed into the organic ooze of the sea floor.

Fossil records show that hagfish have been around for 220 million years, and hagfish-like creatures go back from that another 500 million years. Calling these animals fish is misleading. By the dictionary definition they are fish, but from an evolutionary point of view hagfish are not even distantly related to goldfish, trout, and other familiar fishes. Most textbooks place them in the same group as lampreys, but lampreys are much more advanced, and the only shared similarities are their lack of jaws and their eel-like shapes. This taxonomic relationship is mostly one of convenience. In some ways hagfish are more closely related to sea squirts and other primitive chordates than they are to modern, living vertebrates, or even to the many makes and models of jawless fishes that once roamed Silurian and Devonian seas. Lampreys and hagfish each have different feeding methods, different forms of reproduction, and totally different life cycles. The nervous systems are also on quite different plans. Major anatomical features that are used to show relationships of animal groups are mostly lacking in hagfish. While it is obvious that hagfish are not directly related to true modern-day bony fishes, it is also unlikely that they are kin to lampreys.

I wanted to collect some in the worst way, and our submersible was set up to gather samples and even individual specimens. Like a hagfish, we had some powerful vacuums attached to mechanical arms outside the sub. The sub's crew was reluctant; in the past they had some nasty experiences with hagfish slime fowling up their collecting gear. Several years back they tried to catch some hags for visiting researchers. They set a trap baited with fish heads and instantly attracted hundreds of them. But their activity created such quantities of slime that the crew feared the thrusters of the sub would become inoperable. When the sub was finally hauled onto the deck of the support ship, the entire exterior had to be de-slimed with high-pressure hoses before the crew could get out of the sub. But my begging was persistent enough that the crew gave in and we effortlessly sucked up two or three.

Horseshoe crabs and hagfish notwithstanding, not everything living down there on the bottom was of pre–Jurassic Park vintage. There were modern-day squid, wolf and short-finned eelpouts, witch flounder, longfin hakes, and rattails. In some places, the eelpouts were present in incredible numbers. The presence of these fishes and the other bottom-dwelling fauna around The Point was documented from a composite of 81 middle-slope transects recorded on eight and a half hours of videotape on this and other submersible dives. Thirty-three species of fish were identified and several others were present, but their identifications were inconclusive. The density averages 183 individuals per 10-minute video transect. The eelpouts, witch flounder, and hagfish made up over 82 percent of the total fish fauna. Not exactly your everyday seafood-market species, but two at least were modern-day bony fishes nonetheless. The researchers, when comparing the results of these studies to those conducted elsewhere but at similar depths along the slope of Atlantic's outer continental shelf, found the individuals of most species to be considerably smaller than those encountered elsewhere, a Lilliputian bottom community.

Deeper still are creatures even less familiar. Deep-sea bottom trawlers have haphazardly snatched eyeless fishes that support themselves on fins that serve as tripods and rolled-up marine pill bugs the size of volleyballs. It's hard to imagine a more bizarre world than the one I had just visited, but there is one that is darker, deeper, and colder, and it's only a few thousand feet farther down.

⤙

Finding the edge of the shelf hadn't been easy. We were quite lost and were forced to maneuver for nearly an hour in the Gulf's current and a layer of dense suspended silt prior to coming into the clear water. Although we still had dive time to spare we did not have the time to go back through the silt cloud and find a new area of the bottom to explore. We got permission to ascend and slowly worked out way farther offshore and then back down and then up through the dark water, observing the various organisms living in the water column. From the undersea videos made on other dives, the literature describing the biology of the sea stars and benthic fishes, geological interpretation of the bottom ooze, specimens collected, and hundreds of still photographs of the bottom, I have pieced together a biological cross section of the slope. It is a vicarious tour that still has many missing pieces—strange animals on video that cannot be identified, areas clouded by perpetual suspension of sediments, failed cameras, and areas passed over because of current forces greater than the sub's thrusters. Previous dives to the shelf's slope returned with specimens, video, and still photographs of beds of brittle stars. Thousands of individuals grouped in patches and spread like latticework across the bottom. The specimens retrieved by the sub's vacuums were all of a single species, *Ophiura sarsi*, and here they were sometimes present in densities of 31 individuals per square meter. This same species occurs at similar depths off New England, England, and Japan. The ones collected had growth rings that suggested they were all 15 years of age. From the videotapes I could see that the tips of all their arms were touching, suggesting some form of communication within the group. There was little movement, as with the other creatures that shared their world, energy conservation was the way of life. Close examination of the brittle stars showed they were heavily preyed upon by the local fish community. Many were missing arms, or portions of them, and others were in the process of regenerating new ones. Even individual brittle stars picked over by predators so badly that the damage appeared almost lethal continued to regenerate new appendages.

Other invertebrates living on the slope included deep-water species of sea pens, anemones, and polychaete tube-dwelling worms. There are also a large protozoan, *Bathysiphon filiformis*, that made white tubes that protruded from the bottom sediments, as well as Jonah, spider, and red crabs. The densities of creatures are high, with some species showing a wide variation in depth ranges, while others are quite restricted to narrow zones, and others preferred specific bottom types.

What I had seen did not exactly match the description that the marine biologists working for Mobil had come up with when they were trying to persuade the Bureau of Land Management to lease rights to explore for fossil fuels on the floor of the slope. In a 1989 summary of their drill plan they state:

The sea bottom at the proposed well site is not "live bottom," defined as 1) naturally occurring hard substrate with attached epifauna (e.g., sea fans and whips, anemones, hydroids, ascidians, corals, sponges, bryozoans), or 2) areas "which favor the accumulation of turtles, fishes, or other fauna."

The report, in drawing attention to a live, hard-bottom habitat, suggested that other bottom habitats, like the soft-bottom ones on the slope, are unimportant, unproductive, and uninteresting. From my brief and partly aborted visit, this was clearly untrue. Bottom sampling done earlier, studies that they themselves contracted, showed the density of life to be phenomenal, average counts from a little more than a square yard of bottom sediments ranged from 37,282 to 46,255 individuals. The variation was a result of depth and even the small number of bottom samples taken from 6,500 feet had densities consistently higher than 8,500 individuals. I guess the authors of the bureau's report had overlooked the significance of their own studies.

Meanwhile, back on deck we unloaded all the sundry equipment we had packed into the submersible and retrieved the hagfish and a few other specimens we had vacuumed from the sea floor. One of the crew members showed me a Styrofoam cup he had placed in the starboard collection basket outside the sub. What had been a medium-sized slightly used coffee cup had been reduced to one half the size of a shot glass. The pressure during the dive had compressed the Styrofoam, but the cup still retained its original shape. Our specimens too had suffered; the change in water pressure during our ascent had resulted in exploding internal organs and chemical changes in the blood. But my prized hagfish arrived at the surface in good condition and seemed to be alive. The good news was that they didn't slime up the collection boxes. Maybe the sub's crew will invite me to tag along again.

POSTSCRIPT

. . . and thou wilt cast all their sins into the depths of the sea.—Micah 7:19

The *Country Girl* pulled away from Pirates Cove Marina at 5:05 AM and by
5:35 passed under the Bonner Bridge. Courtesy of Big Al, the captain, I was
along on a chartered fishing trip. Along for the ride was Al's first mate and
son, Charles, who had worked on the *Country Girl* for the last six years, and
six fishermen rounding out the group. By 7:00 AM we were in the Stream; as
we crossed a modest line of *Sargassum*, the water temperature jumped from
69° to 75° F. Within minutes Charles had nine lines over, each baited with ballyhoo. Two additional lines ran behind the boat. These were dragging teas-
ers, florescent pink and blue plastic squid that jumped through our wake. It
was their job to lure tuna up from the 10–12 fathom depths where they were
hanging out. This had the promise of being a good day. The yellowfins had
shown up the previous week, and with only a 7-mph wind, the Atlantic was
about as calm as one could hope for.

The *Country Girl* was Al's third boat. The first one, the *Gal-O-Mine*, was
built in 1971 when diesel fuel was 17 cents a gallon. Then came the first *Country Girl*, replaced years later by a newer version of the same name. This lat-
est one, a bit bigger and faster, was supported by $17,000 of new electrical
equipment that could simultaneously track our surface position, fish on the
bottom at over 100 fathoms, the water temperature, and the inner edge of
the Gulf Stream from satellite images. In the early days, we used compasses
and degree lines to determine distance and direction from the inlet. This
advanced to Loran A and, later, Loran B positioning. We now had pinpoint
satellite-based latitude and longitude in decimals—nailing down our position to the nearest 10 yards. In addition to the onboard microwave and small
refrigerator, new features for the convenience of his fishing parties, I noted
two signs that had been added to the boat since my last offshore excursion.
The small one requesting no smoking on the bridge was long overdue, but
it was the large red one on the lower deck that got my attention. Its message
was straightforward: "$100 Fine for Throwing up in the Cabin."

Al's stories were continuous. It had been some years since I'd been off-shore with him; we did have to catch up. Still, much of our conversation involved reminiscing about earlier trips. My favorite new one was from just the previous week when one of the other charter captains radioed Al and told him he had just seen a tropicbird. May 20 is a little early in the season for summering tropicbirds, but still five days later than my earliest recorded report. Another captain got on the radio and announced to the entire Oregon Inlet fishing fleet "that means it's summer and it's 'bout time for Al to stop wearing his long johns."

As the hours wore on, the topic of discussion shifted to our mutual concerns. South Carolina was allowing companies to harvest *Sargassum* out of the Gulf Stream, the same *Sargassum* that should flow past Hatteras a day or two later. Al was told they were selling it to supplement cattle feed. This clearly could affect the fishing, as *Sargassum* mats attracted game fish. And this would have an impact on some of the seabirds as well. The fishing regulations were becoming stricter too. While the new rules at first seemed reasonable, as Al explained it, there were some confounding issues. Commercial fishermen did not have the same restrictions as recreational fishing boats. The numbers of dolphins and tuna allowed per person had been lowered, and were expected soon to be lowered even more. Seasonal and size regulations were also taking their toll on the sport fishermen. And hanging over all this was the resurrected threat of offshore development, exploration for gas and oil that was to take place in the exact epicenter of what, based on the marine diversity, I am now beginning to refer to as the Yellowstone of the North Atlantic.

At 8:05 we were still inside the 100-fathom contour when we hooked our first fish—a small blackfin tuna. The other charter boats were starting to catch fish too, but for much of the morning everyone's catch was mostly dolphin. Good-sized ones, all in the 20–35-pound range. The captains were referring to the dolphins they were catching simply as "gaffers." The term relates to the size of the fish; all were of a size that they could not be simply flipped into the boat's fish-box, because the line would break. The fish needed to be brought aboard with the long-handled gaff. The smaller 2–7 pounders, "bailers," could be pulled up just by grabbing the leader.

The yellowfins started to hit later in the day. Several times we had fish on four lines simultaneously. Big Al and Charles had their work cut out for them. With so many lines running behind the boat, the fish were constantly crossing under and over lines, some of which extended out 100 yards or more. Rods were passed in a dizzying basket weave as the fishermen worked on landing the tuna, and the fish attempted to swim off in different directions. The larger tuna, a couple of which weighed perhaps as much as 75 pounds, took up to 30 minutes to land. They were impressive-sized fish but dwarfed by the one my wife Mary caught years before.

I spent the better part of the day on the bridge, talking to Al in between his caring for his paying customers, tallying the birds we encountered, enjoying the calm seas, and listening to familiar voices of the various Oregon Inlet charter-boat captains as they shared information on what fish were being caught where. After the other captains heard I was on board with Al, the VHF channels buzzed with bird reports from a number of charter boats. The Stream was even more enchanting than I remembered.

⤙

The positive effects of the Gulf Stream are immeasurable in terms of dollars. Of course its economic value to the fishing industry is significant. But it also plays an important role in our modern culture, weather, and, of course, on marine ecosystems. There are other important currents off Japan and Chile, but on a global scale they pale in comparison to the overall influence of the Stream. While it is impossible to state for certain that the Gulf Stream is solely responsible for the relativity mild climate of western Europe, think of the northern tip of Ireland. It has the same latitude as Moscow and is well north of all the major cities of the United States and Canada. On good Irish winters, roses bloom at Christmas.

The Stream assisted the travels of explorers, conquistadors, pirates, and ships of war. Today it continues to provide an important route of international transport between two continents, supports vital recreational and commercial fisheries, and quickly melts troublesome icebergs that drift southward into major shipping lanes. Some have credited this giant marine river as being responsible in significant measure for the cultural history of Europe, the plantation system of the old South, the cod and herring fisheries on the Grand Banks, sport fishing off Hatteras, refueling landward-bound hurricanes, and not to be forgotten, the appearance of unexpected seabirds off the North Carolina coast. The principles of physics that drive the current, and for that matter the whole North Atlantic gyre, are beyond complex and in many ways still not completely understood. Studies are no longer based on thermometers lowered on strings, but through the proxy of satellite images sent back to us from space and elaborate computer programs run from research vessels.

The birds represent more than just interesting ornithological records;

they are the tell-tale indicator of the surprising diversity focused in a relatively small area of the Atlantic—an area that was once assumed to be a "biological desert." The seabirds are attracted by dependable food sources, prey that concentrated here as a result of a combination of oceanic currents and contours of the outer continental shelf. Off the Carolina coast the Gulf Stream intersects with currents coming from Virginia coastal waters and the cooler Western Boundary Undercurrent. The blending of these currents and their nutrient- and oxygen-enriched waters creates a basis for a food chain that feeds not just the surface-foraging marine birds, but a host of animals living in the water column and the floor of the sea.

At the surface this site is dynamic, and the position of the current edges shifts about not just seasonally but often daily. The marine birds, as well as the charter boats, are constantly moving and regrouping as the surface conditions change. They are responding to minor shifts in the oceanic flows of considerable force, mixing water masses, stirring up bottom sediments, and causing predictable eddies, upwelling, and frontal boundaries that in combination make the inner edge of the Gulf Stream off Cape Hatteras one of the major biological hot spots in the Atlantic. The outer continental shelf east of Hatteras is a key nursery, feeding station, migration stopover, home, and/or breeding ground for a diverse assemblage of pelagic birds, marine mammals and turtles, larval and adult fishes, and pelagic, deep-water, and benthic invertebrates. This is an area of global importance, one worthy of appreciation and protection.

We have been casting our sins into the sea for millennia. Trash, pollutants, and other waste, if they are not dumped directly into the sea, go into rivers that feed into it. Today, the effects of these age-old habits are amplified by the threat of climate change. With luck most of the sins will biodegrade quickly; it's the intangible stuff that worries me. While the increased media coverage regarding the general health of our oceans would make the problems seem as ones of recent origin, the results of our greedy exploitation date back to at least the colonial period. Prior to European contact the western North Atlantic had a population of gray whales. They disappeared before anyone was keeping records of such things. Hard evidence of their former existence in North Carolina waters first surfaced when various bones of gray whales became exposed through beach erosion on the Outer Banks. Carbon dating showed them to be of recent origins. Atlantic gray whales would appear to have the honor of being the first New World species driven to extinction by European man. By the mid-1600s the Carolina coast was recognized as promising whaling grounds. Whale fishing was even mentioned in the 1669 Fundamental Constitutions of the Carolinas. The whales that were processed originally came from sick and dying ones that washed ashore. The coastal inhabitants began to rely on them and soon the whales became hunted, harpooned from boats set out from coastal fishing villages and later from commercial whaling ships deployed from northern ports. Both the oil and the baleen were of value, and right and gray whales were the whales of choice. Their size and habit of migrating close to shore made them the perfect targets for men seeking their commercially valuable baleen and oil. The local coastal whaling had gone on for several generations prior to September 1667, when the first commercial whaling ship set out from South-ampton to hunt whales along the Carolina coast. The Atlantic gray whales were probably already extinct by this time as the written records in British customs ledgers of whale oil and baleen imported from Maryland, Virginia, and Carolina show no records of gray whales between 1696 and 1733.

It was only in the latter part of the 20th century that technologies were developed to establish baselines and track whale stocks, acidification, over-fishing, chemical pollutants, changes in primary productivity, declines in the standing crop of *Sargassum* in the North Atlantic, and climate change. It was not until recently that we came to grips with concerns like endangered species or began to understand and document the lasting effects of major oil spills.

The same rivers and streams that allow eels and shad to migrate far inland and bring drift seeds from tropical jungles are also corridors that transport chemicals and other pollutants out to the sea. It's not simply that the world's oceans have become dumping grounds; our river basins are storm drains that run to the sea. The entire continent of North America east of the Rockies drains into the Atlantic and Gulf of Mexico, and while there are all sorts of regulations in place to protect our rivers and estuaries, technologies always remain decades behind solutions to control runoff from agricultural and industrial chemicals and the other creations of our modern world. Further-more, the acid rain that has seriously degraded northern freshwater ponds and lakes to the point that we are seeing high mortality in loons, is now affecting our seas. The air, polluted from emissions of factories and coal-burning energy plants, also drifts out over the North Atlantic, where the accumulation of acid rain is actually resulting in the acidification of the sea. In many ways these problems, because of how rivers and oceanic currents work, are all continually transported through the biologically rich area off the Outer Banks.

As the *Country Girl* was docking, a small crowd gathered to look over our catch. It was just a little after five. Once the mate tossed the single blackfin tuna, 6 large yellowfins, and 13 "gaffers" onto the dock, we disembarked. Our one 45-pound sailfish had been photographed and released. For me it had been a good day; while I did not see anything that unusual for this time of year, all in all I tallied up over 275 marine birds offshore representing 17 species. In addition to the always-present bottlenose dolphins and the standard-issue flying fish, there were several nice schools of spotted dolphins, and we encountered hundreds of 300–400-pound migrating hammerheads and 4 or 5 manta rays. Based on photos, I now suspect the sharks were all smooth hammerheads, a species known to reach lengths of 13 feet and weights of up to 900 pounds. Positive identification is best confirmed by the smooth edges of their teeth. Al and I tried to persuade Charles to jump overboard for a quick dental exam, but he declined. I did manage to get a good look at an arctic tern, a rarely encountered species I first documented from the waters off North Carolina in the spring of 1979. Perhaps most interesting, the charter boat that docked two slips down from the *Country Girl* called in to report that they had seen several beaked whales and two sperm whales that afternoon. They were only about five miles distant at the time, and normally we would have run over to take a look. But this had been a fishing party, we were in a hot fishing area, and it was almost time to start back toward shore.

The 30-plus-mile run back to the inlet was uneventful and, as is always the case, devoid of birds. Until you get within about 12 miles of the beach, the inner continental shelf is rather unproductive. On the way in we did spot two large loggerheads basking on the surface; with their flippers pulled back on top of their barnacle-encrusted shells they were enjoying the late afternoon sun. I thanked Big Al, both for inviting me to tag along and for a new *Country Girl* t-shirt he wanted me to give to my wife, and I started home.

On the drive back I reflected on the day—from just casual observation not much had changed out there over the last 35 years, yet during this period our knowledge of the outer continental shelf off the Outer Banks has been greatly enhanced. Not just through my seabird research, but researchers from numerous agencies and universities had studied the area from top to bottom. Research conducted in late 1980s and early 1990s showed this area to be one of the biological hot spots of the North Atlantic—one of such global significance that it would be in our best interest to not develop it. One of my bookshelves has about five to six running feet of environmental reports and other documents generated by these studies, all saying, from different perspectives, that this area should remain unspoiled. And now, just into our second decade of the 21st century, some are again suggesting the untapped energy sources off the Outer Banks need to be developed. To say Al and the other charter-boat fishermen, as well as almost everyone involved in Outer Banks tourism, are frustrated is an understatement.

In the final analysis, all the problems presently facing the world's oceans may actually date back to the period when our modern-day religious beliefs were first evolving. With a one-God system there are now way too many of us, and only one of Him; how can we expect Him to look after everything? And He is stuck with this task for eternity. The Romans and ancient Greeks may have had it right—many different Gods, each with a specifically assigned task. There were individual Gods and Goddesses who looked after war and love and everything in between; let's not forget adventure heroes that interacted with them. Real heroes, ones who by comparison would make Charles Bronson and Sylvester Stallone look like cub scouts. The Greeks had Poseidon, and the Romans their rip-off version—Neptune—to look after the world's seas. In our modern world we pass this all off as mythology. In the ancient world the lure of singing sirens and the River Styx were real, the Gods all took their tasks seriously, and our oceans were in much better shape. Sure we now have saints that oversee this and that, but I know of none assigned to the seas, or even to just the western North Atlantic. Our federal agencies have yet to achieve God-like powers and simply monitor our sundry activities of pollution and exploitation as we continue to "*cast our sins into the sea.*"

And so it appears that it's up to us mere mortals to make changes that sustain healthy oceans and all that is connected to them. Are you ready?

APPENDIX

In this section, common and scientific names are given for the primary species discussed in *Gulf Stream Chronicles: A Naturalist Explores Life in an Ocean River* as well as lists of some species that may be found in the waters discussed in the book. These are provided to pique the reader's interest and encourage further exploration. Additionally, these lists are a partial indication of the richness of the inshore and offshore waters of North Carolina. Both the currently accepted common and scientific names are provided. With the exception of chapter 11, a chapter about plant seeds, these lists are arranged in phylogenetic order.

CHAPTER 1 A Community of Castaways

Floating reefs of pelagic brown algae of the genus *Sargassum* are an extremely important biological feature in tropical and subtropical marine environments. Two species, *Sargassum natana* and *S. fluitans*, support diverse and abundant fish and invertebrate faunas in the western North Atlantic. The invertebrate fauna associated with *Sargassum* includes both sessile (attached in place) and motile (free swimming) species. The epizoans that cling to the algae include 21 genera and 54 species of colonial hydrozoans. The conspicuous motile fauna include various marine worms and 18 species of decapod crustaceans. There are also at least 16 species of mollusks of various classes and orders including numerous nudibranchs and various species of polychaetes, flatworms, isopods, and amphipods. Eight orders, 23 families, 30 genera, and 54 species of fishes have been documented from *Sargassum* off the southeastern states. Some occur seasonally, as larval forms, or as predators that follow the algae as it drifts northward in the Gulf Stream. Other fishes use the *Sargassum* for spawning, early larval stages, or as a food resource. *Sargassum* is also important to a number of marine turtles and seabirds. The hatchlings of all the Atlantic sea turtles except leatherbacks find food and shelter in the floating algae, and over 20 species of pelagic birds forage on the fishes and invertebrates living within the mats. Some of the invertebrate and vertebrate fauna associated with *Sargassum* mats off the Carolina coast are listed here.

Sargassum anemone, *Anemonia sargassensis*

Sargassum swimming crab, *Portunus sayi*

Blotched swimming crab, *Portunus spinimanus*

Sargassum shrimp, *Latreutes fucorum* and *Leander tenuicornis*

Sargassum snail, *Litiopa melanostoma*

Dusky pipefish, *Syngnathus floridae*

Sargassum pipefish, *Syngnathus pelagicus*

Atlantic Tripletail, *Lobotes surinamensis*

Yellow jack, *Carangoides bartholomaei*

Blue runner, *Caranx cryos*

Bar jack, *Caranx ruber*

Greater amberjack, *Seriola dumerili*
Bigeye scad, *Selar crumenophthalmus*
Round scad, *Decapterus punctatus*
Dolphin, *Coryphaena hippurus*
Bermuda chub, *Kyphosus sectatrix*
Sergeant major, *Abudefduf saxatilis*
Freckled driftfish, *Psenes cyanophrys*

Scrawled filefish, *Aluterus scriptus*
Fringed filefish, *Monacanthus ciliatus*
Planehead filefish, *Stephanolepis hispidus*
Pygmy filefish, *Stephanolepis setifer*
Orangespotted filefish, *Cantherhines pullus*
Grey triggerfish, *Balistes capriscus*
Sargassum fish, *Histrio histrio*

CHAPTER 2 *Physalia* | Iridescent Bubbles with a Zap

Commonly known as the Portuguese man-of-war, *Physalia* is a floating marine animal composed of colonies of different cell types. Despite its ability to sting beach visitors, these simple creatures support a number of pelagic animals that use the floating colonies for protection as well as a primary food source.

Portuguese man-of-war, *Physalia pelagica* (Atlantic) (some consider the one in the Indo-Pacific a separate species, *Physalia utriculus*)
Moon jellyfish, *Aurelia aurita*
Violet snail, *Janthina janthina* (There are six other species of snails in the genus

Janthina, but they are not known to eat *Physalia*.)
Pelagic sea slug, *Glaucus atlanticus*
Violet blanket octopus, *Tremoctopus violaceus* (small ones use *Physalia* tentacles for defense)
Man-of-war fish, *Nomeus gronovii*

CHAPTER 3 Fish That Fly

There are 23 U.S. species of flying fish in North American waters; 17 of these are found in the North Atlantic, including two occurring in both the Atlantic and Pacific oceans. The family Exocoetidae also contains halfbeaks and ballyhoos. Flying fish known from North Carolina's waters are listed here:

Margined flyingfish, *Cheilopogon cyanopterus*
Bandwing flyingfish, *Cheilopogon exsiliens*
Spotfin flyingfish, *Cheilopogon furcatus*
Atlantic flyingfish, *Cheilopogon melanurus*
Flying halfbeak, *Euleptorhamphus velox*
Oceanic two-winged flyingfish, *Exocoetus obtusirostris*
Tropical two-winged flyingfish, *Exocoetus volitans*
Balao halfbeak, *Hemiramphus balao*

Ballyhoo, *Hemiramphus brasiliensis*
Fourwing flyingfish, *Hirundichthys affinis*
Blackwing flyingfish, *Hirundichthys rondeleti*
Halfbeak, *Hyporhamphus unifasciatus*
Smallwing flyingfish, *Oxyporhamphus micropterus*
Sailfin flyingsfish, *Parexocoetus brachypterus*
Blunt-nosed flyingfish, *Prognichthys gibbifrons*

CHAPTER 4 Fish That Sunbathe

There are three species of ocean sunfish in the family Molidae. All three occur in the Atlantic, while the ocean sunfish and slender mola also occur in the Pacific. These species represent some of the largest and most evolutionarily advanced boney fish. All Molidae skin lacks scales and their skeletons are largely cartilaginous.

Sharptailed mola, *Mola lanceolata*
Ocean sunfish, *Mola mola*
Slender mola, *Ranzania laevis*

CHAPTER 5 Mary's Tuna

Tuna and mackerel are important food and game fish that occur in all temperate and tropical seas. They swim in schools at high speeds, often near the surface. While they are mostly pelagic, a few species, such as Spanish mackerel, feed in shallow sounds and bays and are often caught by those fishing from bridges and piers. There are 16 species of tuna and mackerels (family Scombridae) occurring in the western North Atlantic.

Wahoo, *Acanthocybium solandri*
Frigate mackerel, *Auxis thazard*
Little tunny, *Euthynnus alletteratus*
Skipjack tuna, *Katsuwonus pelamis*
Striped bonito, *Sarda orientalis*
Atlantic bonito, *Sarda sarda*
Atlantic chub mackerel, *Scomber colias*
Atlantic mackerel, *Scomber scombrus*
King mackerel, *Scomberomorus cavalla*

Spanish mackerel, *Scomberomorus maculatus*
Cero, *Scomberomorus regalis*
Albacore, *Thunnus alalunga*
Yellowfin tuna, *Thunnus albacares*
Blackfin tuna, *Thunnus atlanticus*
Bigeye tuna, *Thunnus obesus*
Atlantic bluefin tuna, *Thunnus thynnus*

CHAPTER 6 Feathered Nomads of the Open Sea

There are 89 species of marine birds that have been documented from North Carolina waters. The majority of these seabirds are migrants or species that spend their adolescence and non-breeding season far at sea. Those that are known to nest in the state are identified with an asterisk (*). The species within the four orders that comprise this assemblage breed in the Arctic, Antarctic, the Bahamas and West Indies, and the Mediterranean, as well as various islands in the South Atlantic.

Red-throated loon, *Gavia stellata*
Pacific loon, *Gavia pacifica*
Common loon, *Gavia immer*
Yellow-nosed albatross, *Thalassarche chlororhychos*
Black-browed albatross, *Thalassarche melanophris*
Northern fulmar, *Fulmarus glacialis*
Herald petrel, *Pterodroma arminjoniana*
Bermuda petrel (cahow), *Pterodroma cahow*
Black-capped petrel, *Pterodroma hasitata*
Fea's petrel, *Pterodroma feae*
Bulwer's petrel, *Bulweria bulwerii*
Cory's shearwater, *Calonectris diomedea*

Cape Verde shearwater, *Calonectris edwardsii*
Great shearwater, *Puffinus gravis*
Sooty shearwater, *Puffinus griseus*
Manx shearwater, *Puffinus puffinus*
Audubon's shearwater, *Puffinus lherminieri*
Wilson's storm-petrel, *Oceanodroma oceanicus*
White-faced storm-petrel, *Pelagodroma marina*
European storm-petrel, *Hydrobaties pelagicus*
Black-bellied storm-petrel, *Fregetta tropica*
Swinhoe's storm-petrel, *Oceanodroma monorhis*

Leach's storm-petrel, *Oceanodroma leucorhoa*

Band-rumped storm-petrel, *Oceanodroma castro*

White-tailed tropicbird, *Phaethon lepturus*

Red-billed tropicbird, *Phaethon aethereus*

Magnificent frigatebird, *Fregata magnificens*

Masked booby, *Sula dactylatra*

Brown booby, *Sula leucogaster*

Northern gannet, *Morus bassanus*

Double-crested cormorant, *Phalacrocorax auritus**

Great cormorant, *Phalacrocorax carbo*

American white pelican, *Pelecanus eryhrorhynchos*

Brown pelican, *Pelecanus occidentalis**

Red-necked phalarope, *Phalaropus lobatus*

Red phalarope, *Phalaropus fulicarius*

Great skua, *Stercorarius skua*

South polar skua, *Stercorarius maccormicki*

Pomarine jaeger, *Stercorarius pomarinus*

Parasitic jaeger, *Stercorarius parasiticus*

Long-tailed jaeger, *Stercorarius longicaudus*

Dovekie, *Alle alle*

Common murre, *Uria aalge*

Thick-billed murre, *Uria lomvia*

Razorbill, *Alca torda*

Black guillemot, *Cepphus grille*

Long-billed murrelet, *Brachyramphus perdix*

Atlantic puffin, *Fratercula arctia*

Black-legged kittiwake, *Rissa tridactyla*

Sabine's gull, *Xema sabini*

Bonaparte's gull, *Chroicocephalus philadelphia*

Black-headed gull, *Chroicocephalus ridibundus*

Little gull, *Hydrocoloeus minutus*

Laughing gull, *Leucophaeus atricilla**

Franklin's gull, *Leucophaeus pipixcan*

Black-tailed gull, *Larus crassirostris*

Mew gull, *Larus canus*

Ring-billed gull, *Larus delawarensis*

Herring gull, *Larus argentatus**

California gull, *Larus californicus*

Thayer's gull, *Larus thayeri*

Iceland gull, *Larus glaucoides*

Lesser black-backed gull, *Larus fuscus*

Slaty-backed gull, *Larus schistisagus*

Glaucous gull, *Larus hyperboreus*

Great Black-backed gull, *Larus marinus**

Brown noddy, *Anous stolidus*

Sooty tern, *Onychoprion fuscatus**

Bridled tern, *Onychoprion anaethetus*

Least tern, *Sternula antillarum**

Gull-billed tern, *Sterna nilotica**

Caspian tern, *Hydroprogne caspia*

Black tern, *Chlidonias niger*

White-winged tern, *Chlidonias leucopterus*

Roseate tern, *Sterna dougallii**

Common tern, *Sterna hirundo**

Arctic tern, *Sterna paradisaea*

Forster's tern, *Sterna forsteri**

Royal tern, *Sterna maximus**

Sandwich tern, *Thalasseus sandvicensis**

CHAPTER 7 Sea Devils | An Epic Tale of Amazing Survivors

The cahow, or sea devil to some, was thought to be extinct for 330 years. In 1951 the species was rediscovered in Bermuda when 18 nesting pairs were located by a team searching for remnant populations. The discovery led to decades of conservation efforts that included the elimination of animals (including owls) that prey on three species of ground-nesting birds in Bermuda.

Snowy Owl, *Bubo scandiacus*

Bermuda petrel (Cahow), *Pterodroma cahow*

Audubon's shearwater, *Puffinus lherminieri*

White-tailed tropicbird, *Phaethon lepturus*

CHAPTER 8 The Loon Craze

Three species of loons have been documented from North Carolina, but two are not seen regularly in North Carolina waters. The loon that is most often observed is the common loon; one that was an important food source when the species was more abundant in Harkers Island waters.

Red-throated loon, *Gavia stellata*
Pacific loon, *Gavia pacifica*
Common loon, *Gavia immer*

CHAPTER 9 Chickens, Sailor Gulls, Witches, and Devils

Common names for some seabirds, like "chickens" and "devils" come from behaviors that were observed but not well understood. All of these birds are members of a distinct order of highly pelagic marine birds that differ from gulls, terns, and other familiar species most notably by having tube-like nostrils. Members of this group include:

Bermuda petrel, *Pterodroma cahow*
Black-capped petrel, *Pterodroma hasitata*
Great shearwater, *Puffinus gravis*
Audubon's shearwater, *Puffinus lherminieri*
Wilson's storm-petrel, *Oceanites oceanicus*
Band-rumped storm-petrel, *Hydrobates castro*

CHAPTER 10 Getting to Know a Gallery of Gulls

Seagulls, or gulls, are associated with the sea, but can also be found on island lakes, at golf courses, and around landfills inland. They present special challenges to the bird watchers, having different plumages at different stages of their lives and sometimes seasonally depending on the species. The list below includes most of the gulls seen in or near North Carolina waters. Those that are known to nest in the state are identified with an asterisk (*).

Black-legged kittiwake, *Rissa tridactyla*
Sabine's gull, *Xema sabini*
Bonaparte's gull, *Chroicocephalus philadelphia*
Black-headed gull, *Chroicocephalus ridibundus*
Little gull, *Hydrocoloeus minutus*
Laughing gull, *Leucophaeus atricilla**
Franklin's gull, *Leucophaeus pipixcan*
Black-tailed gull, *Larus crassirostris*
Mew gull, *Larus canus*
Ring-billed gull, *Larus delawarensis*
Herring gull, *Larus argentatus**
California gull, *Larus californicus*
Thayer's gull, *Larus thayeri*
Iceland gull, *Larus glaucoides*
Lesser black-backed gull, *Larus fuscus*
Slaty-backed gull, *Larus schistisagus*
Glaucous gull, *Larus hyperboreus*
Great black-backed gull, *Larus marinus**

There are over 100 species of plants that produce floating seeds and fruits (sea beans) that drift onto the beaches of the south Atlantic states. The following list includes some of the ones most commonly encountered. The 10 most regularly found sea beans are identified with an asterisk (*). These plant species are arranged alphabetically by common name.

Anchovy pear, *Grias cauliflora*
Antidote vine, *Fevillia cordifolia*
Bay-bean, *Canavalia rosea**
Blister pod, *Sacoglottis amazonica*
Bloodwood, *Pterocarpus officinalis*
Box fruit, *Barringtonia asiatica*
Cabbagebark, *Andira inermis*
Calatola, *Calatola costaricensis*
Candlenut, *Aleurites moluccana*
Coconut palm, *Cocos nucifera*
Coin vine, *Dalbergia ecastaphyllum*
Crabwood, *Carapa guianensis*
Gray nickernut, *Caesalpinia bonduc*
Hamburger bean, *Mucuna* (multiple species)*
Hog plum, *Spondias mombin**
Jamaican naval-spurge, *Omphalea diandra*

Laurelwood, *Calophyllum calaba*
Little marble, *Oxyrhynchus trinervius*
Manchineel, *Hippomane mancinella*
Mary's bean, *Merremia discoidesperma*
Moonflower, *Ipomoea pes-caprae**
Nutmeg, *Myristica fragrans*
Pond apple, *Annona glabra*
Prickly palm, *Acrocomia aculeata*
Red mangrove, *Rhizophora mangle**
Sandbox tree, *Hura crepitans*
Sea coconut, *Manicaria saccifera**
Sea grape, *Coccoloba uvifera*
Sea heart, *Entada gigas**
Sea purse, *Dioclea reflexa*
Starnut palm, *Astrocaryum* spp.*
Tropical almond, *Terminalia catappa**
Water hickory, *Carya aquatic*
White inkberry, *Scaevola taccada*

CHAPTER 12 Up from the Sea

American shad are related to sardines, anchovies, herring, alewives, and to other species of shad. There are 28 species of shad-like fish (family Clupeiformes) in North America, only five of which are confined to the Pacific. Ten species live at least portions of their life in both freshwater and marine habitats; the remainder are confined to saltwater. Anadromous species spend most of their lives at sea but return to freshwater to spawn.

Anadromous species

Alabama shad, *Alosa alabamae*
Alewife, *Alosa pseudoharengus*
American shad, *Alosa sapidissima*
Blueback herring, *Pomolobus aestivalis*

Marine species

Bay anchovy, *Anchoa mitchilli*
Finescale menhaden, *Brevoortia gunteri*
Gulf menhaden, *Brevoortia patronus*
Yellowfin menhaden, *Brevoortia smithi*
Atlantic menhaden, *Brevoortia tyrannus*

Atlantic herring, *Clupea harengus*
Round herring, *Etrumeus teres*
False pilchard, *Harengula clupeola*
Redear sardine, *Harengula humeralis*
Scaled sardine, *Harengula jaguana*

Dwarf herring, *Jenkinsia lamprotaenia*
Little-eye herring, *Jenkinsia majua*
Shortband herring, *Jenkinsia stolifera*

Atlantic thread herring, *Opisthonema oglinum*
Spanish sardine, *Sardinella aurita*
Orangespot sardine, *Sardinella janeiro*

Freshwater species
Hickory shad, *Alosa mediocris*
Gizzard shad, *Dorosoma cepedianum*
Threadfin shad, *Dorosoma petenens*
Skipjack herring, *Pomolobus chrysochloris*

CHAPTER 13 **Slithery, Slimy, and Elegant—Eels**

The numerous families of eels (Order Anguilliformes) are primarily tropical, however, there are quite a few temperate species. One family of freshwater eels (family Anguillidae) is comprised of 16 species, all in one genus—*Anguilla*. These species occur in all temperate and tropical regions except for the eastern Pacific. The *Anguilla* species all develop as larvae in marine environments, but as adults they live in freshwater. Two species occur in the North Atlantic basin.

American eel, *Anguilla rostrata*
European eel, *Anguilla anguilla*

CHAPTER 14 **Cold War, Warm Waters**

The Russian fishery that worked the offshore Atlantic waters of North America was well organized and efficient. Having different-size classes of ships and the ability to interchange gear among them allowed the fleet to work throughout the year, exploiting various depths and most of the commercially available species. North Carolina fish commercially harvested by the Russian fleet included:

Sharks, species in the orders Lamniformes and Squaliformes
Skates, various species in the family Rajidae
Sturgeons, *Acipenser oxyrhinchus* and possibly *A. brevirostrum*
American eel, *Anguilla rostrata*
Alewife, *Alosa pseudoharengus*
American shad, *Alosa sapidissima*
Atlantic menhaden, *Brevoortia tyrannus*
Atlantic herring, *Clupea harengus*
Atlantic thread herring, *Opisthonema oglinum*
Atlantic cod, *Gadus morhua*
Hakes, species in the family Gadidae
Blackfin goosefish, *Lophius gastrophysus*
Atlantic needlefish, *Strongylura marina*
Northern searobin, *Prionotus carolinus*
Bank sea bass, *Centropristis ocyurus*
Black sea bass, *Centropristis striata*
Jacks, species in the family Carangidae
Snappers, species in the family Lutjanidae
Pigfish, *Orthopristis chrysoptera*
Sheepshead, *Archosargus probatocephalus*
Porgys, *Calamus* (multiple species)
Pinfish, *Lagodon rhomboides*
Scup, *Stenotomus chrysops*
Silver perch, *Bairdiella chrysoura*
Atlantic cutlassfish, *Trichiurus lepturus*
Mackerels, various species in the family Scombridae

Tuna, various members in the family
 Scombridae
Swordfish, *Xiphias gladius*
Sailfish, *Istiophorus platypterus*
Blue marlin, *Makaira nigricans*

White marlin, *Kajikia albidus*
Longbill spearfish, *Tetrapturus pfluegeri*
Butterfish, *Peprilus triacanthus*
Flounders, various species in the order
 Pleuronectiformes

CHAPTER 15 Migrant Clouds and Radar Dots

Each fall vast numbers of birds fly far out over the Atlantic and across the Gulf of Mexico, shortcutting to their South American wintering grounds. The fact that millions of birds use this route can be confirmed with radar. The high-flying birds appear simply as tiny dots moving across the radar screen, and while the species composition of the clouds of dots can't be determined, some clues as to which species are migrating can be pieced together from tired and exhausted individuals that fall out and try to land on ships at sea. Land-based birds observed at sea off the Carolina coast include:

Northern pintail, *Anas acuta*
Blue-winged teal, *Anas discors*
Lesser scaup, *Aythya affinis*
White-winged scoter, *Melanitta fusca*
Red-breasted merganser, *Mergus serrator*
Pied-billed grebe, *Podilymbus podiceps*
Double-crested cormorant, *Phalacrocorax
 auritus*
Brown pelican, *Pelecanus occidentalis*
Great blue heron, *Ardea herodias*
Snowy egret, *Egretta thula*
Little blue heron, *Egretta caerulea*
Cattle egret, *Bubulcus ibis*
Osprey, *Pandion haliaetus*
Northern harrier, *Cirus cyaneus*
Sharp-shinned hawk, *Accipiter striatus*
Clapper rail, *Rallus crepitans*
King rail, *Rallus elegans*
Purple gallinule, *Porphyrio marinicus*
American coot, *Fulica americana*
Black-bellied plover, *Pluvialis squatarola*
American golden plover, *Pluvialis dominica*
Spotted sandpiper, *Actitis macularis*
Solitary sandpiper, *Tringa solitaria*
Semipalmated plover, *Charadrius
 semiplmatus*
Greater yellowlegs, *Tringa melanoleuca*
Willet, *Tringa semipalmata*
Whimbrel, *Numenius phaeopus*
Ruddy turnstone, *Arenaria interpres*

Red knot, *Calidris canutus*
Sanderling, *Calidris alba*
Least sandpiper, *Calidris minutilla*
Semipalmated sandpiper, *Calidris pusilla*
Short-billed dowitcher, *Limnodromus
 griseus*
Mourning dove, *Zenaida macroura*
Chimney swift, *Chaetura pelagica*
Belted kingfisher, *Megaceryle alcyon*
Red-headed woodpecker, *Melanerpes
 erythrocephalus*
Downey woodpecker, *Picoides pubescens*
Northern flicker, *Colaptes auratus*
American kestrel, *Falco sparverius*
Merlin, *Falco columbarius*
Peregrine falcon, *Falco peregrinus*
Acadian flycatcher, *Empidonax virescens*
Least flycatcher, *Empidonax minimus*
Tropical kingbird, *Tyrannus melancholicus*
Tree swallow, *Tachycineta bicolor*
Bank swallow, *Riparia raparia*
Cliff swallow, *Petochelidon pyrrhonota*
Barn swallow, *Hirundo rustica*
American crow, *Corvus brachyrhynchos*
Red-breasted nuthatch, *Sitta canadensis*
Brown creeper, *Certhia americana*
House wren, *Troglodytes aedon*
Golden-crowned kinglet, *Regulus satrapa*
Ruby-crowned kinglet, *Regulus calendula*
Gray catbird, *Dumetella carolinensis*

European starling, *Sturnus vulgaris*
Cedar waxwing, *Bombycilla cedrorum*
Lapland longspur, *Calcarius lapponicus*
Northern waterthrush, *Pakesia noveboracensis*
Black-and-white warbler, *Mniontila varia*
Prothonotary warbler, *Protonotaria citrea*
Orange-crowned warbler, *Oreothlypis celata*
Nashville warbler, *Oreothlypis rufcapilla*
Mourning warbler, *Geothlypis philadelphia*
Kentucky warbler, *Geothlypis formosa*
Common yellowthroat, *Geothlypis trichas*
American redstart, *Setophaga ruticilla*
Cape May warbler, *Setophaga tigrina*
Bay-breasted warbler, *Setophaga castanea*
Yellow warbler, *Setophaga petechia*
Blackpoll warbler, *Setophaga striata*
Palm warbler, *Setophaga palmarum*
Black-throated blue warbler, *Setophaga caerulescens*
Yellow-rumped warbler, *Setophaga coronata*
Yellow-throated warbler, *Setophaga dominica*

Prairie warbler, *Setophaga discolor*
Black-throated green warbler. *Setophaga virens*
Yellow-breasted chat, *Icteria virens*
Eastern towhee, *Pipilo erythropthalmus*
American tree sparrow, *Spizella arborea*
Chipping sparrow, *Spizella passerina*
Field sparrow, *Spizella pusilla*
Savannah sparrow, *Passerculus sandwichensis*
Song sparrow, *Melospiza melodia*
Swamp sparrow, *Melospiza georgiana*
White-throated sparrow, *Zonotrichia albicollis*
White-crowned sparrow, *Zonotrichia leucophrys*
Dark-eyed junco, *Junco hyemalis*
Indigo bunting, *Passerina cyanea*
Dickcissel, *Spiza americana*
Bobolink, *Dolichonyx oryzivorus*
Eastern meadowlark, *Sturnella magna*
Boat-tailed grackle, *Quiscalus major*
Orchard oriole, *Icterus spurius*
Baltimore oriole, *Icterus galbula*

CHAPTER 16   Pods of Potheads

The diversity of marine mammals occurring in North Carolina's waters is largely a result of the state's latitude; both boreal and subtropical species overlap. This factor influences the distribution of many groups of plants and animals. For this reason the Cape Hatteras area is referred to as a biological Mason-Dixon line. In addition to all the temperate and subtropical species there are a number of others that seasonally migrate through the state's waters. Furthermore, the Hatteras barrier islands project well out to sea, catching carcasses and thus providing biologists the opportunity to document and study the marine mammal fauna. Marine mammals known from North Carolina are listed here.

Cetacea: Whales and Porpoises

Minke whale, *Balaenoptera acutorostrata*
Sei whale, *Balaenoptera borealis*
Fin whale, *Balaenoptera physalus*
Gray whale, *Eschrichtius robustus* (extinct in North Atlantic since colonial times)
Right whale, *Eubalaena glacialis*

Humpback whale, *Megaptera novaeangliae*
Saddleback dolphin, *Delphinus delphis*
Short-finned pilot whale, *Globicephala macrorhynchus*
Atlantic pilot whale, *Globicephala melas*
Grampus, *Grampus griseus*

Northern bottlenose whale, *Hyperoodon ampullatus*
Pygmy sperm whale, *Kogia breviceps*
Dwarf sperm whale, *Kogia simus*
Dense-beaked whale, *Mesoplodon densirostris*
Antillean beaked whale, *Mesoplodon europaeus*
True's beaked whale, *Mesoplodon mirus*
Killer whale, *Orcinus orca*
Harbor porpoise, *Phocoena phocoena*

Sperm whale, *Physeter macrocephalus*
False killer whale, *Pseudorca crassidens*
Striped dolphin, *Stenella coeruleoalba*
Bridled dolphin, *Stenella frontalis*
Spinner dolphin, *Stenella longirostris*
Atlantic spotted dolphin, *Stenella frontalis*
Rough-toothed dolphin, *Steno bredanensis*
Atlantic bottlenose dolphin, *Tursiops truncatus* (inshore and pelagic—forms differ)
Goosebeaked whale, *Ziphius cavirostris*

Pinnipedia: Seals

Harbor seal, *Phoca vitulina*
Hooded seal, *Cystophora cristata*

Sirenia: Sea Cows

Florida manatee, *Trichechus manatus*

CHAPTER 17 **A Hide of Leather and a Warm Heart**

All of the sea turtles found in the Atlantic can occur in North Carolina's waters. While loggerheads are the only species that nest regularly on the state's beaches, except for hawksbills, the others nest here on occasion. Marine turtles occurring off North Carolina and the southeast United States include:

Green sea turtle, *Chelonia mydas*
Hawksbill sea turtle, *Eretmochelys imbricata*
Loggerhead sea turtle, *Caretta caretta*

Kemp's ridley sea turtle, *Lepidochelys kempii*
Leatherback sea turtle, *Dermochelys coriacea*

CHAPTER 18 **Fathoming the Dark Waters**

Life exists throughout the water column, from the surface of the water all the way down to the bottom (the benthic community), and even within the silt and substrate on the bottom. What appears to be silt dispersed in some places in the water column are actually tiny plants and animals (phytoplankton and zooplankton). At the mid-water depths and below where light becomes scarce and even non-existent, organisms have developed interesting and bizarre adaptations. Many organisms at this depth make their own light. Shrimp, jellyfish, and squid can be found at all levels in the water column, with different species occupying different heights of the column. Some of the inhabitants of the different water depths offshore are listed below.

Pelagic tunicates or Salps, *Salpa* (various species)
Slender snipe eel, *Nemichthys scolopaceus*
Stareye lightfish, *Pollichthys mauli*
Sloan's viperfish, *Chauliodus sloani*
Boa dragonfish, *Stomias boa*

Bristlemouth, *Cyclothone* (six species)
Atlantic pearlside, *Maurolicus weitzmani*
Slope hatchetfish, *Polyipnus clarus*
Atlantic silver hatchetfish, *Argyropelecus aculeatus*

Hatchetfish, *Sternoptyx* species, including *Sternoptyx diaphana*
Oceanic lightfish, *Vinciguerria nimbaria*
Power's deep-water bristlemouth, *Vinciguerria poweriae*

Atlantic barracudina, *Lestidium atlanticum*
Elongated bristlemouth, *Gonostoma elongatum*
Duckbilled eel in families Derichthyidae and Nettastomatidae

CHAPTER 19 Batteries Not Included—Uncanny Lights in the Deep

There is light in deep water where sunlight doesn't penetrate. Many organisms produce their own light through a chemical process known as bioluminescence. It occurs widely in marine vertebrates and invertebrates, even those that live higher in the water column where sunlight is produced. The bay luminescence is triggered by dinoflagellates, oceanic plankton that produce a glow when disturbed.

Glacier lanternfish, *Benthosema glaciale*
Horned lampfish, *Ceratoscopelus maderensis*
Atlantic headlightfish, *Diaphus dumerillii*
Soft lanternfish, *Diaphus mollis*

Metallic lanternfish, *Myctophum affine*
Wisner's lanternfish, *Myctophum selenops*
Patchwork lampfish, *Notoscopelus resplendens*

CHAPTER 20 Life on the Bottom | Weird, Ancient, and Abundant

One would expect the bottom of the open ocean, where little or no light penetrates, to have little to offer plants or animals. Life can be rich there and varies according to whether there is hard substrate or a soft bottom. Sea pens, anemones, annelid worms, polychaete tube-dwelling worms, spider crabs, and benthic fish are among the many inhabitants of cold deep dark waters. In some places densities of creatures are high, others are virtual deserts. A few of the bottom-dwelling species occurring offshore North Carolina are listed below.

Invertebrates

Benthic diatoms, *Nitzschia* and *Navicula*
Forminiferian, *Bathysiphon filiformis*
Deep-water anemone, *Actinauge verrilli*
Burrowing anemone, *Cerianthus borealis*
Stimpson's liomesus (welk), *Liomesus stimpsoni*
Parasitic aegid isopod, *Syscenus infelix*
Polychaete tube-dwelling worms, *Cossura longocirrata*, *Levesenia gracilis*, *Nicolea* spp., and *Scalibregma inflatum*
Quillworm, *Hyalinoecia tubicola*
Horseshoe crab, *Limulus polyphemus*
Red crab, *Geryon quinquedens*
Jonah crab, *Cancer borealis*

Spider crab, *Libinia emarginata*
Anemone crabs, *Parapagurus* species
Squat lobster, *Munida valida*
Sea stars, *Asterias forbesi*, *Astropecten americanus*, *A. articulatus*, and *Laidia clathrata*
Brittlestar, *Ophiomusium lymani*
Sea pens, *Distichoptilum gracile* and *Kophobelemnon stelliferum*
Oligochaetes, *Limnodriloides medioporus* and *Tubificoides intermedius*
Polychates, *Aricidea quadrilobata* and *Tharyx kirkegaardi*

Demersal fish (fish that live and feed on or near the bottom, in the demersal zone)

Atlantic hagfish, *Myxine glutinosa*

Chain dogfish, *Scyliorhinus retifer*

Black dogfish, *Centroscyllium fabricii*

Atlantic torpedo, *Torpedo nobiliana*

Skate, *Raja* (multiple species)

Snubnosed eel, *Simenchelys parasitica*

Northern cutthroat eel, *Synaphobranchus kaupii*

Margined snake eel, *Ophichthus cruentifer*

Duckbilled eel, *Venefica procera*

Argentines (herring smelts), in the family Argentinidae

Shortnose greeneye, *Chlorophthalmus agassizi*

Tripod fishes, in the family Bathypteroidae

Cusk, *Brosme brosme*

Offshore hake, *Merluccius albidus*

Longfin hake, *Phycis chesteri*

Red hake, *Urophycis chuss*

Spotted hake, *Urophycis regia*

Rattails and grenadiers, species in the family Macrouridae

Longnose grenadier, *Coelorhynchus carminatus*

Marlin-spike, *Nezumia bairdii*

Digitate cusk eel, *Dicrolene introniger*

Goosefish, *Lophius americanus*

Redeye gaper, *Chaunax stigmaeus*

Atlantic batfish, *Dibranchus atlanticus*

Beardfish, *Polymixia lowei*

Scaley hedgehogfish, *Ectreposebastes imus*

Blackbelly rosefish, *Helicolenus dactylopterus*

Rimspine searobin, *Peristedion thompsoni*

Longfin snailfish, *Careproctus longipinnis*

Lowfin snailfish, *Paraliparis calidus*

Great northern tilefish, *Lopholatilus chamaeleonticeps*

Scup, *Stenotomus chrysops*

Common wolf eel, *Lycenchelys paxillus*

Wolf eelpout, *Lycenchelys verrillii*

Atlantic eelpout, *Lycodes terraenovae*

Atlantic soft pout, *Melanostigma atlanticum*

Wrymouth, *Cryptacanthodes maculatus*

Silver-rag, *Ariomma bondi*

Gulf Stream flounder, *Citharichthys arctifr*

Fourspot flounder, *Paralichthys oblongus*

Witch flounder, *Glyptocephalus cynoglossus*

Agassiz's smoothhead, *Leptochilichthys agassizi*

Halosaur, *Aldrovandia* (multiple species)

Shortbeard codling, *Laemonema barbatulum*

SELECTED LITERATURE FOR FURTHER READING

For each chapter in *Gulf Stream Chronicles: A Naturalist Explores Life in an Ocean River* the curious are invited to explore further the captivating topics narrated by the author, David S. Lee. This supplemental reading was provided so as to furnish complementary books, reports, and journal articles that (1) match whenever possible the key points raised by the author, (2) amplify the depth or breadth of the topic with pertinent overviews and syntheses, and (3) offer perspectives that are unique to North Carolina's portion of the western Atlantic Ocean generally and the Gulf Stream in particular. By visiting most of these sources, the reader can also access their reference sections in order to trek even further into the fascinating journey weaved by *Gulf Stream Chronicles*. Prepared by J. Christopher Haney

CHAPTER 1 A Community of Castaways

Carr, A., and A. B. Meylan. 1980. Evidence of passive migration of green turtle hatchlings in *Sargassum*. *Copeia* 1980: 366–68.

Casazza, T. L, and S. W. Ross. 2008. Fishes associated with pelagic *Sargassum* and open water lacking *Sargassum* in the Gulf Stream off North Carolina. *Fishery Bulletin* 106: 348–63.

Gower, J. F. R., and S. A. King. 2011. Distribution of floating *Sargassum* in the Gulf of Mexico and the Atlantic Ocean mapped using MERIS. *International Journal of Remote Sensing* 32: 1917–29.

Moser, M. L., and D. S. Lee. 2012. Foraging over *Sargassum* by western North Atlantic seabirds. *Wilson Journal of Ornithology* 124: 66–72.

Settle, L. R. 1997. Commercial harvest of pelagic *Sargassum*: A summary of landings since June 1995. In South Atlantic Fishery Management Council. Essential Fish Habitat Workshop 9: October 7–8, 1997 Pelagic Habitat *Sargassum* and Water Column. South Atlantic Fishery Management Council. Charleston, SC. May 1997. 66 pp.

Stoner, A. W. 1983. Pelagic *Sargassum*: evidence for a major decrease in biomass. *Deep-Sea Research* 30: 469–74.

Stoner, A. W., and H. S. Greening. 1984. Geographic variation in the macro faunal associates of pelagic *Sargassum* and some biogeographic implications. *Marine Ecology Progress Series* 20: 185–92.

Tracey, K. L., and D. R. Watts. 2012. On Gulf Stream meander characteristics near Cape Hatteras. *Journal of Geophysical Research: Oceans* (1978–2012) 91: 7587–602.

CHAPTER 2 *Physalia* | Iridescent Bubbles with a Zap

Bayer, F. M. 1963. Observations on pelagic mollusks associated with the Siphonophores *Velella* and *Physalia*. *Bulletin of Marine Science* 13: 454–66.

Jenkins, R. L. 1983. Observations on the commensal relationship of *Nomeus gronovii* with *Physalia physalis*. *Copeia* 1983: 250–52.

Karplus, I. 2014. The associations between fish and siphonophores. Pp. 202–211. In Symbioses in fishes: The biology of interspecific partnerships. John Wiley & Sons. 449 pp.

Lane, C. E., and E. Dodge. 1958. The toxicity of *Physalia* nematocysts. *Biological Bulletin* 115: 219–26.

Purcell, J. E., and M. N. Arai. 2001. Interactions of pelagic cnidarians and ctenophores with fish: a review. *Hydrobiologia* 451: 27–44.

Russell, F. E. 1965. Marine toxins and venomous and poisonous marine animals. *Advances in Marine Biology* 3: 255–384.

Wittenberg, J. B. 1960. The source of carbon monoxide in the float of the Portuguese man-of-war, *Physalia physalia* L. *Journal of Experimental Biology* 37: 698–705.

CHAPTER 3 Fish That Fly

Davenport, J. 1994. How and why do flying fish fly? *Reviews in Fish Biology and Fisheries* 4: 184–214.

Fish, F. E. 1990. Wing design and scaling of flying fish with regard to flight performance. *Journal of Zoology* 221: 391–403.

Kappes, M. A., H. Weimerskirch, D. Pinaud, and M. Le Corre. 2011. Evidence of resource partitioning in sympatric tropical boobies. *Marine Ecology Progress Series* 441: 281–94.

Kawachi, K., I. Yoshinobu, and A. Azuma. 1993. Optimal flight path of flying fish. *Journal of Theoretical Biology* 163: 145–59.

Lewis, J. B., J. K. Brundritt, and A. G. Fish. 1962. The biology of the flying fish *Hirundichthys affinis* (Günther). *Bulletin of Marine Science* 12: 73–94.

Richard, K. R., and M. A. Barbeau. 1994. Observations of spotted dolphins feeding nocturnally on flying fish. *Marine Mammal Science* 10: 473–77.

Weimerskirch H., M. Le Corre, and C. A. Bost. 2008. Foraging strategy of masked boobies from the largest colony in the world: Relationship to environmental conditions and fisheries. *Marine Ecology Progress Series* 362: 291–302.

Zainuddin, M. 2011. Preliminary findings on distribution and abundance of flying fish in relation to oceanographic conditions of Flores Sea observed from multi-spectrum satellite images. *Asian Fisheries Science* 24: 20–30.

CHAPTER 4 Fish That Sunbathe

Cartamil, D., and C. G. Lowe. 2004. Diel movement patterns of ocean sunfish *Mola mola* off southern California. *Marine Ecology Progress Series* 266: 245–53.

Lee, D. S. 1986. Seasonal, thermal, and zonal distribution of the ocean sunfish, *Mola mola*, off the North Carolina coast. *Brimleyana* 12: 75–83.

Pope, E. C., G. C. Hays, T. M. Thys, T. K. Doyle, D. W. Sims, N. Queiroz, V. J. Hobson,

L. Kubicek, and J. D. R. Houghton. 2009. The biology and ecology of the ocean sunfish *Mola mola*: a review of current knowledge and future perspectives. *Reviews in Fish Biology and Fisheries*. DOI 10.1007/s11160–009–9155–9

Santini, F., and J. C. Tyler. 2002. Phylogeny of the ocean sunfishes (Molidae, Tetraodontiformes), a highly derived group of teleost fish. *Italian Journal of Zoology* 69: 37–43.

Schwartz, F. J., and D. G. Lindquist. 1987. Observations on *Mola* basking behavior, parasites, echeneidid associations, and body-organ weight relationships. *Journal of the Elisha Mitchell Scientific Society* 103: 14–20.

Sims, D. W., and E. J. Southall. 2002. Occurrence of ocean sunfish *Mola mola* near fronts in the western English Channel. *Journal of the Marine Biological Association of the United Kingdom* 82: 927–28.

Sims, D. W., N. Queiroz, N. E. Humphries, F. P. Lima, and G. C. Hays. 2009. Long-term GPS tracking of ocean sunfish *Mola mola* offers a new direction in fish monitoring. *PLoS ONE* 4: e7351.

CHAPTER 5 Mary's Tuna

Block, B. A., and E. D. Stevens. 2001. Tuna: physiology, ecology, and evolution. Academic Press, San Diego, CA. 468 pp.

Block, B. A., H. Dewar, S. B. Blackwell, T. D. Williams, E. D. Prince, C. J. Farwell, A. Boustany, S. L. H. Teo, A. Seitz, A. Walli, and D. Fudge. 2001. Migratory movements, depth preferences, and thermal biology of Atlantic bluefin tuna. *Science* 293: 1310–14.

Bohnsack, B. L., R. B. Ditton, J. R. Stoll, R. J. Chen, R. Novak, and L. S. Smutko. 2002. The economic impacts of the recreational bluefin tuna fishery in Hatteras, North Carolina. *North American Journal of Fisheries Management* 22: 165–76.

Katz, S. L., D. A. Syme, and R. E. Shadwick. 2001. High-speed swimming: enhanced power in yellowfin tuna. *Nature* 410: 770–71.

Korsmeyer, K. E., H. Dewar, N. C. Lai, and J. B. Graham. 1996. The aerobic capacity of tunas: adaptation for multiple metabolic demands. *Comparative Biochemistry and Physiology Part A: Physiology* 113: 17–24.

Maury, O., D. Gascuel, F. Marsac, A. Fonteneau, and A.-L. De Rosa. 2001. Hierarchical interpretation of nonlinear relationships linking yellowfin tuna (*Thunnus albacares*) distribution to the environment in the Atlantic Ocean. *Canadian Journal of Fisheries and Aquatic Sciences* 58: 458–69.

Rudershausen, P. J., J. A. Buckel, J. Edwards, D. P. Gannon, C. M. Butler, and T. W. Averett. 2010. Feeding ecology of blue marlins, dolphinfish, yellowfin tuna, and wahoos from the North Atlantic Ocean and comparisons with other oceans. *Transactions of the American Fisheries Society* 139: 1335–59.

CHAPTER 6 Feathered Nomads of the Open Sea

Lee, D. S. 1986. Seasonal distribution of marine birds in North Carolina waters, 1975–1986. *American Birds* 40: 409–12.

Lee, D. S. 1995. Marine birds off the coast of North Carolina. *The Chat* 59: 113–71.

Lee, D. S. 1999. Pelagic seabirds and the proposed exploration for fossil fuels off North Carolina: A test for conservation efforts of a vulnerable international resource. *Journal of the Elisha Mitchell Scientific Society* 115: 294–315.

McGinnis, T. W., and S. D. Emslie. 2001. The foraging ecology of royal and sandwich terns in North Carolina, USA. *Waterbirds* 24: 361–70.

Moser, M. L., and D. S. Lee. 1992. A fourteen-year survey of plastic ingestion by western North Atlantic seabirds. *Colonial Waterbirds* 15: 83–94.

Parnell, J. F., W. W. Golder, M. A. Shields, T. L. Quay, and T. M. Henson. 1997. Changes in nesting populations of colonial waterbirds in coastal North Carolina, 1900–1995. *Colonial Waterbirds* 20: 458–69.

Haney, J. C., K. M. Fristrup, and D. S. Lee. 1992. Geometry of visual recruitment by seabirds to ephemeral foraging flocks. *Ornis Scandinavica* 23: 49–62.

CHAPTER 7 Sea Devils | An Epic Tale of Amazing Survivors

Carlile, N., D. Priddel, F. Zino, C. Natividad, and D. B. Wingate. 2003. A review of four successful recovery programmes for threatened sub-tropical petrels. *Marine Ornithology* 31: 185–92.

Carlile, N., D. Priddel, and J. Madeiros. 2012. Establishment of a new, secure colony of endangered Bermuda petrel *Pterodroma cahow* by translocation of near-fledged nestlings. *Bird Conservation International* 22: 46–58.

Gehrman, E. 2012. Rare birds: the extraordinary tale of the Bermuda petrel and the man who brought it back from extinction. Beacon Press, Boston. 256 pp.

Lee, D. S. 1987. December records of seabirds off North Carolina. *The Wilson Bulletin* 99: 116–21.

Madeiros, J., N. Carlile, and D. Priddel. 2012. Breeding biology and population increase of the endangered Bermuda petrel *Pterodroma cahow*. *Bird Conservation International* 22: 35–45.

Wingate, D. B. 1972. First successful hand-rearing of an abandoned Bermuda petrel chick. *Ibis* 114: 97–101.

Wingate, D. B. 1990. Living museum of Bermuda's precolonial terrestrial biome. Pp. 133–150. In The earth in transition: patterns and processes of biotic impoverishment (Woodwell, G. M., ed.). Cambridge University Press, Cambridge. 548 pp.

Wurster, C. F., and D. B. Wingate. 1968. DDT residues and declining reproduction in the Bermuda petrel. *Science* 159: 979–81.

CHAPTER 8 The Loon Craze

Evers, D. C., J. D. Kaplan, M. W. Meyer, P. S. Reaman, W. E. Braselton, A. Major, N. Burgess, and A. M. Scheuhammer. 1998. Geographic trend in mercury measured in common loon feathers and blood. *Environmental Toxicology and Chemistry* 17: 173–83.

Haney, J. C. 1990. Winter habitat of common loons on the continental shelf of the southeastern United States. *Wilson Bulletin* 102: 253–63.

Kenow, K. P., M. W. Meyer, D. C. Evers, D. C. Douglas, and J. Hines. 2002. Use of satellite telemetry to identify common loon migration routes, staging areas and wintering range. *Waterbirds* 25: 449–58.

Lee, D. S. 1987. Common loons wintering in offshore waters. *The Chat* 51: 40–42.

Olson, S. L., H. Loftin, and S. Goodwin. 2010. Biological, geographical, and cultural origins of the loon hunting tradition in Carteret County, North Carolina. *The Wilson Journal of Ornithology* 122: 716–24.

Paruk, J. D., D. Long, IV, C. Perkins, A. East, B. J. Sigel, and D. C. Evers. 2014. Polycyclic aromatic hydrocarbons detected in common loons (*Gavia immer*) wintering off coastal Louisiana. *Waterbirds* 37: 85–93.

Spitzer, P. R. 1995. Common loon mortality in marine habitats. *Environmental Review* 3: 223–29.

CHAPTER 9 Chickens, Sailor Gulls, Witches, and Devils

Lee, D. S. 1984. Petrels and storm-petrels in North Carolina's offshore waters: including species previously unrecorded for North America. *American Birds* 38: 151–63.

Lee, D. S. 2009. Mass die-offs of greater shearwaters in the western North Atlantic: effects of weather patterns on mortality of a trans-equatorial migrant. *The Chat* 73: 37–47.

Lee, D. S. 2011. Searching for "devils" and "witches" at sea. *Caribbean Compass* 194: 36–37.

Lee, D. S., and N. Viña. 1993. A re-evaluation of the status of *Pterodroma hasitata* in Cuba. *Ornithologica Neotropical* 4: 99–101.

Manly, B., B. S. Arbogast, D. S. Lee, and M. Van Tuinen. 2013. Mitochondrial DNA analysis reveals substantial population structure within the endangered black-capped petrel (*Pterodroma hasitata*). *Waterbirds* 36: 228–33.

Haman, K. H., T. M. Norton, R. A. Ronconi, N. M. Nemeth, A. C. Thomas, S. J. Courchesne, A. Segars, and M. K. Keel. 2013. Great shearwater (*Puffinus gravis*) mortality events along the eastern coast of the United States. *Journal of Wildlife Diseases* 49: 235–45.

Simons, T. R., D. S. Lee, and J. C. Haney. 2013. Diablotin *Pterodroma hasitata*: A biography of the endangered black-capped petrel. *Marine Ornithology* 41: S3–S43.

CHAPTER 10 Getting to Know a Gallery of Gulls

Fussell, J. O., III, M. H. Tove, and H. E. LeGrand, Jr. 1982. Report on six recent sightings of the Iceland gull in North Carolina with comments on problems of field identification. *The Chat* 46: 57–71.

Grant, P. J. 1986. Gulls: A guide to identification. T. & A. D. Poyser, London. 352 pp.

Haney, J. C., and D. S. Lee. 1994. Air-sea heat flux, ocean wind fields, and offshore dispersal of gulls. *The Auk* 111: 427–40.

Howell, S. N. G., and J. Dunn. 2007. Gulls of the Americas. Houghton Mifflin Harcourt, New York. 528 pp.

Marshall, H. 1947. Longevity of the American herring gull. *The Auk* 64: 188–98.

Olsen, K. M. 2003. Gulls of Europe, Asia and North America. Christopher Helm, London. 608 pp.

Parnell, J. F., and R. F. Soots. 1975. Herring and great black-backed gulls nesting in North Carolina. *The Auk* 92: 154–57.

CHAPTER 11 Donkey's Eyes, Sea Purses, and Fairy Eggs

Gunn, B. F., L. Baudouin, and K. M. Olsen. 2011. Independent origins of cultivated coconut (*Cocos nucifera* L.) in the Old World tropics. *PLoS ONE* 6: e21143.

Gunn, C. R., and J. V. Dennis. 1972. Stranded tropical seeds and fruits collected from Carolina beaches. *Castanea* 37: 195–200.

Harries, H. 1981. Germination and taxonomy of the coconut. *Annals of Botany* 48: 873–83.

Maloney, B. K. 1993. Palaeoecology and the origin of the coconut. *GeoJournal* 31: 355–62.

Nelson, E. C. 1978. Tropical drift fruits and seeds on coasts in the British Isles and western Europe, 1. Irish beaches. *Watsonia* 12: 103–12.

Perry, E. L., IV, and J. V. Dennis. 2003. Sea-beans from the tropics: A collector's guide to sea-beans and other tropical drift on Atlantic shores. Krieger, Malabar, FL. 232 pp.

Vander Velde, N., and B. Vander Velde. 2006. Mary's bean and other small drift materials of plant origin found on Bikini Atoll. *Plant Species Biology* 21: 41–48.

CHAPTER 12 Up from the Sea

Dadswell, M. J., G. D. Melvin, P. J. Williams, and D. E. Themelis. 1987. Influences of origin, life histories, and chance on the Atlantic coast migration of American shad. *American Fisheries Society Symposium* 1: 313–30.

Devries, D. R., and R. A. Stein. 1990. Manipulating shad to enhance sport fisheries in North America: an assessment. *North American Journal of Fisheries Management* 10: 209–23.

Gerstell, R. 1998. American shad in the Susquehanna River Basin: a three-hundred-year history. Penn State University Press, University Park. 220 pp.

Hightower, J. E., and K. L. Sparks. 2003. Migration and spawning habitat of American shad in the Roanoke River, North Carolina. *American Fisheries Society Symposium* 35: 193–99.

Hightower, J. E., A. M. Wicker, and K. M. Endres. 1996. Historical trends in abundance of American shad and river herring in Albemarle Sound, North Carolina. *North American Journal of Fisheries Management* 16: 257–71.

Limburg, K. E., and J. R. Waldman. 2009. Dramatic declines in North Atlantic diadromous fishes. *BioScience* 59: 955–65.

Parker, J. A. 1992. Migratory patterns and exploitation of American shad in the near shore ocean waters of southeastern North Carolina. *North American Journal of Fisheries Management* 12: 752–59.

CHAPTER 13 Slithery, Slimy, and Elegant—Eels

van Ginneken, V., E. Antonissen, U. K. Müller, R. Booms, E. Eding, J. Verreth, and G. van den Thillart. 2005. Eel migration to the Sargasso: remarkably high swimming efficiency and low energy costs. *The Journal of Experimental Biology* 208: 1329–35.

Haro, A., W. Richkus, K. Whalen, A. Hoar, W.-D. Busch, S. Lary, T. Brush, and D. Dixon. 2000. Population decline of the American eel: implications for research and management. *Fisheries* 25: 7–16.

Kleckner, R. C., J. D. McCleave, and G. S. Wippelhauser. 1983. Spawning of American eel, Anguilla rostrata, relative to thermal fronts in the Sargasso Sea. *Environmental Biology of Fishes* 9: 289–93.

Moser, M. L., W. S. Patrick, and J. U. Crutchfield, Jr. 2001. Infection of American eels, Anguilla rostrata, by an introduced nematode parasite, Anguillicola crassus, in North Carolina. *Copeia* 3: 848–53.

Powles, P. M., and S. M. Warlen. 2002. Recruitment season, size, and age of young American eels (Anguilla rostrata) entering an estuary near Beaufort, North Carolina. *Fisheries Bulletin* 100: 299–306.

Vélez-Espino, L. A., and M. A. Koops. 2010. A synthesis of the ecological processes influencing variation in life history and movement patterns of American eel: towards a global assessment. *Reviews in Fish Biology and Fisheries* 20: 163–86.

Wirth, T., and L. Bernatchez. 2003. Decline of North Atlantic eels: a fatal synergy? *Proceedings of the Royal Society of London B: Biological Sciences* 270: 681–88.

CHAPTER 14 Cold War, Warm Waters

Juda, L. 1991. World marine fish catch in the age of exclusive economic zones and exclusive fishery zones. *Ocean Development & International Law* 22: 1–32.

Lear, W. H. 1998. History of fisheries in the Northwest Atlantic: the 500-year perspective. *Journal of Northwest Atlantic Fishery Science* 23: 41–54.

Pauly, D., and J. Maclean. 2003. In a perfect ocean: the state of fisheries and ecosystems in the North Atlantic Ocean. Island Press, Washington, D.C. 208 pp.

Sealy, T. S. 1974. Soviet fisheries. *Marine Fisheries Review* 36: 5–22.

Srinivasan, U. T., R. Watson, and U. R. Sumaila. 2012. Global fisheries losses at the exclusive economic zone level, 1950 to present. *Marine Policy* 36: 544–49.

Tuck, G. N., R. A. Phillips, C. Small, R. B. Thomson, N. L. Klaer, F. Taylor, R. M. Wanless, and H. Arrizabalaga. 2011. An assessment of seabird-fishery interactions in the Atlantic Ocean. *ICES Journal of Marine Science: Journal du Conseil* 68: 1628–37.

Watson, R., A. Gelchu, and D. Pauly. 2001. Mapping fisheries landings with emphasis on the North Atlantic. Fisheries impact on North Atlantic marine ecosystems (Zeller, D., R. Watson, and D. Pauly, eds.). *Fisheries Centre Research Reports* 9: 1–11. University of British Columbia.

CHAPTER 15 Migrant Clouds and Radar Dots

Butler, R. W. 2000. Stormy seas for some North American songbirds: are declines related to severe storms during migration? *The Auk* 117: 518–22.

Cherry, J. D., D. H. Doherty, and K. D. Powers. 1985. An offshore nocturnal observation of migrating blackpoll warblers. *The Condor* 87: 548–49.

Larkin, R. P. 1991. Flight speeds observed with radar, a correction: slow "birds" are insects. *Behavioral Ecology and Sociobiology* 29: 221–24.

Larkin, R. P., D. R. Griffin, J. R. Torre-Bueno, and J. Teal. 1979. Radar observations of bird migration over the western Atlantic Ocean. *Behavioral Ecology and Sociobiology* 4: 225–64.

Lowery, G. H. 1946. Evidence of trans-Gulf migration. *The Auk* 63: 175–211.

Moore, F., and P. Kerlinger. 1987. Stopover and fat deposition by North American wood-warblers (Parulinae) following spring migration over the Gulf of Mexico. *Oecologia* 74: 47–54.

Nisbet, I. C. T., D. B. McNair, W. Post, and T. C. Williams. 1995. Transoceanic migration of the blackpoll warbler: summary of scientific evidence and response to criticisms by Murray. *Journal of Field Ornithology* 66: 612–22.

Yong, W., and F. R. Moore. 1994. Flight morphology, energetic condition, and the stopover biology of migrating thrushes. *The Auk* 111: 683–92.

CHAPTER 16 Pods and Potheads

Fire, S. E., Z. Wang, T. A. Leighfield, S. L. Morton, W. E. McFee, W. A. McLellan, R. W. Litaker, P. A. Tester, A. A. Hohn, G. Lovewell, C. Harms, D. S. Rotstein, S. G. Barco, A. Costidis, B. Sheppard, G. D. Bossart, M. Stolen, W. Noke Durden, and F. M. Van Dolah. 2008. Domoic acid exposure in pygmy and dwarf sperm whales (*Kogia* spp.) from southeastern and mid-Atlantic U.S. waters. *Harmful Algae* 8: 658–64.

Hamazaki, T. 2002. Spatiotemporal prediction models of cetacean habitats in the mid-western North Atlantic Ocean (from Cape Hatteras, North Carolina, USA to Nova Scotia, Canada). *Marine Mammal Science* 18: 920–39.

Mintzer, V. J., D. P. Gannon, N. B. Barros, and A. J. Read. 2008. Stomach contents of mass-stranded short-finned pilot whales (*Globicephala macrorhynchus*) from North Carolina. *Marine Mammal Science* 24: 290–302.

Reeves, R. R., and E. Mitchell. 1988. History of whaling in and near North Carolina. National Oceanic and Atmospheric Administration Technical Report NMFS 65. http://spo.nwr.noaa.gov/tr65°pt.pdf.

Simpson, M. B., Jr., and S. W. Simpson. 1988. The pursuit of leviathan: a history of whaling on the North Carolina coast. *The North Carolina Historical Review* 65: 1–51.

Waring, G. T., C. P. Fairfield, C. M. Ruhsam, and M. Sano. 2007. Sperm whales associated with Gulf Stream features off the north-eastern USA shelf. *Fisheries Oceanography* 2: 101–5.

Watwood, S. L., P. J. O. Miller, M. Johnson, P. T. Madsen, and P. L. Tyack. 2006. Deep-diving foraging behavior of sperm whales (*Physeter macrocephalus*). *Journal of Animal Ecology* 75: 814–25.

CHAPTER 17 **A Hide of Leather and a Warm Heart**

Davenport, J., D. L. Holland, and J. East. 1990. Thermal and biochemical characteristics of the lipids of the leatherback turtle Dermochelys coriacea: evidence of endothermy. Journal of the Marine Biological Association of the United Kingdom 70: 33–41.

Eckert, S. A. 2006. High-use oceanic areas for Atlantic leatherback sea turtles (Dermochelys coriacea) as identified using satellite telemetered location and dive information. Marine Biology 149: 1257–67.

Hays, G. C., J. D. R. Houghton, C. Isaacs, R. S. King, C. Lloyd, and P. Lovell. 2004. First records of oceanic dive profiles for leatherback turtles Dermochelys coriacea, indicate behavioral plasticity associated with long-distance migration. Animal Behaviour 67: 733–43.

Heaslip, S. G., S. J. Iverson, W. D. Bowen, and M. C. James. 2012. Jellyfish support high energy intake of leatherback sea turtles (Dermochelys coriacea): video evidence from animal-borne cameras. PLoS ONE 7: e33259.

Houghton, J. D. R., T. K. Doyle, J. Davenport, R. P. Wilson, and G. C. Hays. 2008. The role of infrequent and extraordinary deep dives in leatherback turtles (Dermochelys coriacea). The Journal of Experimental Biology 211: 2566–75.

Lee, D. S., and W. M. Palmer. 1981. Records of leatherback turtles, Dermochelys coriacea (Linnaeus), and other marine turtles in North Carolina waters. Brimleyana 5: 95–106.

Lutcavage, M., and P. L. Lutz. 1986. Metabolic rate and food energy requirements of the leatherback sea turtle, Dermochelys coriacea. Copeia 1986: 796–98.

CHAPTER 18 **Fathoming the Dark Waters**

Blake, J. A., and B. Hilbig. 1994. Dense infaunal assemblages on the continental slope off Cape Hatteras, North Carolina. Deep Sea Research Part II: Topical Studies in Oceanography 41: 875–99.

Bunn, A. R., and B. A. McGregor. 1980. Morphology of the North Carolina continental slope, western North Atlantic, shaped by deltaic sedimentation and slumping. Marine Geology 37: 253–66.

Gartner, J. V., Jr., K. J. Sulak, S. W. Ross, and A. M. Necaise. 2008. Persistent near-bottom aggregations of mesopelagic animals along the North Carolina and Virginia continental slopes. Marine Biology 153: 825–41.

Hecker, B. 1994. Unusual megafaunal assemblages on the continental slope off Cape Hatteras. Deep Sea Research Part II: Topical Studies in Oceanography 41: 809–34.

Rhoads, D. C., and B. Hecker. 1994. Processes on the continental slope off North Carolina with special reference to the Cape Hatteras region. Deep Sea Research Part II: Topical Studies in Oceanography 41: 965–80.

Rowe, G. T., and R. J. Menzies. 1969. Zonation of large benthic invertebrates in the deep-sea off the Carolinas. Deep Sea Research and Oceanographic Abstracts 16: 531–37.

Tietjen, J. H. 1971. Ecology and distribution of deep-sea meiobenthos off North Carolina. Deep Sea Research and Oceanographic Abstracts 18: 941–57.

CHAPTER 19 Batteries Not Included—Uncanny Lights in the Deep

Bush, S. L., B. H. Robison, and R. L. Caldwell. 2009. Behaving in the dark: Locomotor, chromatic, postural, and bioluminescent behaviors of the deep-sea squid *Octopoteuthis deletron* Young 1972. *Biological Bulletin* 216: 7–22.

Gaston, G. R., and J. Hall. 2000. Lunar periodicity and bioluminescence of swarming *Odontosyllis luminosa* (Polychaeta: Syllidae) in Belize. *Gulf and Caribbean Research* 12: 47–51.

Haddock, S. H. D., and J. F. Case. 1999. Bioluminescence spectra of shallow and deep-sea gelatinous zooplankton: ctenophores, medusae and siphonophores. *Marine Biology* 133: 571–82.

Haddock, S. H. D., M. A. Moline, and J. F. Case. 2010. Bioluminescence in the sea. *Annual Review of Marine Science* 2: 443–93.

Haygood, M. G., and D. L. Distel. 1993. Bioluminescent symbionts of flashlight fishes and deep-sea anglerfishes form unique lineages related to the genus *Vibrio. Nature* 363: 154–56.

Herring, P. J. 1977. Bioluminescence of marine organisms. *Nature* 267: 788–93.

Tett, P. B., and M. G. Kelly. 1973. Marine bioluminescence. *Oceanography and Marine Biology: An Annual Review* 11: 89–173.

CHAPTER 20 Life on the Bottom | Weird, Ancient, and Abundant

Cerame-Vivas, M. J., and I. E. Gray. 1966. The distributional pattern of benthic invertebrates of the continental shelf off North Carolina. *Ecology* 47: 260–70.

Murray, J. 1895. A summary of the scientific results obtained at the sounding, dredging and trawling stations of HMS *Challenger*. Volume 1, Neill and Company.

Quattrini, A. M., and S. W. Ross. 2006. Fishes associated with North Carolina shelf-edge hardbottoms and initial assessment of a proposed marine protected area. *Bulletin of Marine Science* 79: 137–63.

Ross, S. W. 2007. Unique deep-water ecosystems off the southeastern United States. *Oceanography* 20: 130–39.

Ross, S. W., E. F. Aschenbach, III, and J. Ott. 2001. Literature and data inventory related to the Hatteras middle slope ("The Point") area off North Carolina. *Occasional Papers of the NC State Museum of Natural Sciences and the NC Biological Survey* No. 13. Raleigh, NC. 360 pp.

Schwartz, F. J. 1989. Zoogeography and ecology of fishes inhabiting North Carolina's marine waters to depths of 600 meters. Pp. 333–372. In Carolina coastal oceanography (George, R. Y., and A. W. Hulbert, eds.). National Oceanic and Atmospheric Administration-NURP Research Report 89-2.

Zintzen, V., C. D. Roberts, M. J. Anderson, A. L. Stewart, C. D. Struthers, and E. S. Harvey. 2011. Hagfish predatory behaviour and slime defence mechanism. *Scientific Reports* 1: 131. DOI:10.1038/srep00131

ACKNOWLEDGMENTS

Deepest gratitude is expressed to our talented friend, Leo Schleicher, for preparing the lovely pen and ink illustrations for each chapter. Special thanks to Chris Haney, friend and long-time pelagic bird research colleague, for writing the foreword and providing the supplemental reading lists for each chapter. His support in all ways, and his prompt response to many requests, big and small, made challenges to finishing the book much less daunting.

So many people were generous with their time, sharing concerns and interests, helping to satisfy Dave's insatiable curiosity and supporting his work. I am so grateful for the countless hours that Rudolph Inman, Jean Beasley, and David Wingate spent with Dave. All inspired stories and provided valuable information and insight into conservation issues, ecosystem components, and species that are discussed in *Gulf Stream Chronicles*.

This book is the result of several decades of work and observation onshore and in near and offshore waters of the mid-eastern and Gulf coasts. The boat captains, especially Allan Foreman and Harry Baum, their mates, and others involved in sea trips became valued partners and contributed much more than the labor and services expected on the trips. Those who collected big buckets of stinking chum (myself included) to disperse at sea to attract seabirds and the assistants who collected, recorded, and processed specimens and data all contributed to the content of this book.

MARY KAY CLARK
(wife of the author, David S. Lee)

INDEX

Note: Illustrations and photographs are indicated with *italic* page numbers.